Helidon Revealed

A Practical Guide to Oracle's Microservices Framework

Michael P. Redlich

apress®

Helidon Revealed: A Practical Guide to Oracle's Microservices Framework

Michael P. Redlich
Flemington, NJ, USA

ISBN-13 (pbk): 979-8-8688-0293-5 ISBN-13 (electronic): 979-8-8688-0294-2
https://doi.org/10.1007/979-8-8688-0294-2

Copyright © 2024 by Michael P. Redlich

This work is subject to copyright. All rights are reserved by the Publisher, whether the whole or part of the material is concerned, specifically the rights of translation, reprinting, reuse of illustrations, recitation, broadcasting, reproduction on microfilms or in any other physical way, and transmission or information storage and retrieval, electronic adaptation, computer software, or by similar or dissimilar methodology now known or hereafter developed.

Trademarked names, logos, and images may appear in this book. Rather than use a trademark symbol with every occurrence of a trademarked name, logo, or image we use the names, logos, and images only in an editorial fashion and to the benefit of the trademark owner, with no intention of infringement of the trademark.

The use in this publication of trade names, trademarks, service marks, and similar terms, even if they are not identified as such, is not to be taken as an expression of opinion as to whether or not they are subject to proprietary rights.

While the advice and information in this book are believed to be true and accurate at the date of publication, neither the authors nor the editors nor the publisher can accept any legal responsibility for any errors or omissions that may be made. The publisher makes no warranty, express or implied, with respect to the material contained herein.

Managing Director, Apress Media LLC: Welmoed Spahr
Acquisitions Editor: Shaul Elson
Desk Editor: Laura Berendson
Editorial Project Manager: Gryffin Winkler

Cover designed by eStudioCalamar

Cover image designed by Freepik (www.freepik.com)

Distributed to the book trade worldwide by Springer Science+Business Media New York, 1 New York Plaza, Suite 4600, New York, NY 10004-1562, USA. Phone 1-800-SPRINGER, fax (201) 348-4505, e-mail orders-ny@springer-sbm.com, or visit www.springeronline.com. Apress Media, LLC is a California LLC and the sole member (owner) is Springer Science + Business Media Finance Inc (SSBM Finance Inc). SSBM Finance Inc is a **Delaware** corporation.

For information on translations, please e-mail booktranslations@springernature.com; for reprint, paperback, or audio rights, please e-mail bookpermissions@springernature.com.

Apress titles may be purchased in bulk for academic, corporate, or promotional use. eBook versions and licenses are also available for most titles. For more information, reference our Print and eBook Bulk Sales web page at http://www.apress.com/bulk-sales.

Any source code or other supplementary material referenced by the author in this book is available to readers on GitHub. For more detailed information, please visit https://www.apress.com/gp/services/source-code.

If disposing of this product, please recycle the paper

First and foremost, to my wonderful wife, best friend, and soulmate, Rowena Redlich, *for her never-ending support while I was writing this book and for keeping me focused when I needed it. I will* forever *appreciate everything you've done to make this very first book come to fruition.*

To Barry Burd, *one of the co-directors at the Garden State Java User Group, who, through our many writing collaborations, demonstrated that computer books don't have to be boring. He has an awesome writing style. I also appreciate his expert advice on many things related to the publishing process.*

To Dmitry Kornilov, *Helidon Project Lead and Senior Software Development Manager at Oracle, who took the time to attend my Helidon presentation at CodeOne 2019 despite it being the last session of the day. I also appreciate his support even when he was writing his own Helidon book.*

Table of Contents

About the Author xv

About the Technical Reviewer xvii

Part I: Getting Started 1

Chapter 1: Introduction to Project Helidon 3

Helidon SE... 3

    Functional Style 4

Helidon MP.. 5

    Declarative Style (Helidon MP) 6

Helidon Architecture.. 7

Helidon Landscape.. 8

Getting Started 9

    Helidon Quickstarts 9

    Helidon CLI 9

    Helidon Project Starter 10

Helidon and the Java Community 10

    Helidon and GraalVM 10

    Helidon and Jakarta Persistence Specification 10

    Helidon and Micronaut Data 11

    Helidon and Kotlin 11

    Helidon and MicroStream 11

    Helidon and Log4j2 11

    Improved Helidon Support in IntelliJ IDEA 11

Release History 12

    Helidon 0.10.0 12

    Helidon 1.0.0 12

TABLE OF CONTENTS

    Helidon 2.0.0 13

    Helidon 3.0.0 13

    H elidon 4.0.0 14

Summary 14

Chapter 2: The MicroProfile Specifications 15

MicroProfile Joins the Eclipse Foundation 16

    Eclipse Working Groups 17

    MicroProfile Working Group 17

Compatible Implementations 18

MicroProfile Release History 19

    MicroProfile 7.0 19

Meet the MicroProfile Specifications 21

    Jakarta Contexts and Dependency Injection (CDI) 21

    Jakarta JSON Processing (JSON-P) 22

    Jakarta RESTful Web Services (JAX-RS) 22

    Config 23

    Fault Tolerance 24

    Metrics 24

    JWT Propagation 25

    Health 26

    Open Tracing 26

    Open API 26

    Rest Client 27

    Jakarta JSON Binding (JSON-B) 29

    Jakarta Annotations 29

    Reactive Messaging 30

    Reactive Streams Operators 30

    Context Propagation 31

    GraphQL 31

    Long-Running Actions (LRA) 31

    Telemetry 31

MicroProfile Starter 32

Summary 33

Chapter 3: The Jakarta EE Specifications 35

Evolution of Java EE/Jakarta EE 36

    Eclipse Working Groups 36

    Jakarta EE Working Group 37

Compatible Implementations 37

Jakarta EE Profiles 38

    Platform 38

    Web Profile 38

    Core Profile 39

Jakarta EE Release History 40

    Jakarta EE 8 40

    Jakarta EE 9 41

    Jakarta EE 9.1 41

    Jakarta EE 10 41

    Jakarta EE 11 42

Meet the Updated Jakarta EE Specifications 42

    Jakarta Annotations 42

    Jakarta Authentication 42

    Jakarta Authorization 43

    Jakarta Concurrency 43

    Jakarta Contexts and Dependency Injection 43

    Jakarta Data 43

    Jakarta Expression Language 44

    Jakarta Faces 44

    Jakarta Interceptors 44

    Jakarta Pages 44

    Jakarta Persistence 45

    Jakarta RESTful Web Services 45

    Jakarta Security 45

Jakarta Servlet	45
Jakarta Validation	46
Jakarta WebSocket	46
Summary	46

Part II: Helidon SE 47

Chapter 4: Creating a Small Working Project with Helidon SE 49

Prerequisites	49
Quickstarts	50
Generate the Application	51
Build the Application	53
Initiate the Application	54
The Client URL and JSON Pretty Printer Utilities	54
Exercise the Application via the Command Line	55
Exercise the Application via the Browser	56
Server Shutdown	57
Command-Line Interface	57
Installation	57
Project Starter	63
Summary	68

Chapter 5: Helidon WebServer 69

WebServer Component	69
Signature	69
Create Method	70
Builder Pattern	71
Configuration	71
Direct Configuration	71
External Configuration	72
Routing and HttpRouting	73
Signature	73
Builder Pattern	74

Putting It All Together	75
Dependencies	75
Build and Execute the Application	80
Exercising the Application	81
Summary	83

Chapter 6: Helidon WebClient 85

WebClient Component	85
Signature	85
Create Method	86
Builder Pattern	87
Configuration	87
Direct Configuration	87
External Configuration	88
Putting It All Together	89
Dependencies	90
ServerApplication Class	90
ClientApplication Class	92
Build and Execute the Application	96
Exercising the Application	97
Summary	98

Chapter 7: Helidon Config 99

Config Component	99
Signature	100
Create Method	100
Builder Pattern	101
Configuration Sources	102
Signatures	103
Configuration Loading	104
Configuration Mappers	105
Signatures	105

TABLE OF CONTENTS

Configuration Parsers 106

    Signatures 106

Configuration Filters 107

    Signatures 107

Loading Configuration 108

Putting It All Together 109

    Dependencies 111

    Application Class 112

    DirectorySources Class 112

    MergeSources Class 114

    MultipleConfigSources Class 115

    Build and Execute the Application 117

    Exercising the Application 118

Summary 119

Chapter 8: Helidon DB Client 121

DB Client Component 121

    Signature 122

    Create Method 122

    Builder Pattern 122

    Supporting Classes and Interfaces 122

    Configuration 124

Putting It All Together 125

    Dependencies 125

    Configuration 127

    PokemonService Class 129

    MongoDbApplication Class 130

    Build and Execute the Application 132

    Exercising the Application 133

Summary 136

Chapter 9: Helidon Security 137

Security Component 137

    Signature 138

    Create Method 138

    Builder Pattern 138

    Configuration 138

Putting It All Together 141

    Dependencies 141

    ConfigAuthenticationApplication Class 142

    Build and Execute the Application 146

    Exercising the Application 147

Summary 150

Part III: Helidon MP 151

Chapter 10: Creating a Small Working Project with Helidon MP 153

Prerequisites 153

Quickstarts 155

    Generate the Application 155

    Build the Application 158

    Initiate the Application 159

    The Client URL and JSON Pretty Printer Utilities 159

    Exercise the Application via the Command Line 160

    Exercise the Application via the Browser 161

    Server Shutdown 162

Command-Line Interface 162

    Installation 162

Project Starter 168

Summary 174

TABLE OF CONTENTS

Chapter 11: Helidon Metrics 175
Instrumenting Your Application 175
Helidon Metrics Scopes and Corresponding REST Endpoints 176
Base Metrics 176
Metric Registries and the MetricRegistry API 179
Helidon Metrics Annotations 179
@Counted Annotation 180
@Gauge Annotation 180
@Timed Annotation 181
Annotation Parameters 182
Putting It All Together 182
Dependencies 183
Using the @Counted and @Timed Annotations 184
Histogram Metric 185
Using a Gauge 188
Prometheus Format 189
Build and Execute the Application 190
Exercising the Application 190
Summary 198

Chapter 12: Helidon Fault Tolerance 199
Helidon Fault Tolerance Annotations 199
@Retry 200
@Timeout 202
@CircuitBreaker 203
@Bulkhead 205
@Fallback 206
@Asynchronous 208
Putting It All Together 208
Dependencies 208
Fallback 209
Retry 211

Build and Execute the Application	212
Exercising the Application	213
Summary	214

Chapter 13: Helidon Health Checks 215

Helidon Health Checks Types and REST Endpoints	215
HealthCheck Interface	217
Putting It All Together	217
Dependencies	217
System Resources	218
System Liveness	219
System Readiness	220
System Startup	221
Build and Execute the Application	223
Exercising the Application	223
Summary	229
Conclusion	230

Appendix A: MicroProfile Release History 231

Appendix B: The Jakarta EE Specifications 255

Appendix C: Helidon Reactive WebServer Component 271

Index 281

About the Author

Michael P. Redlich has been an active member within the Java community for the past 25 years. He founded the Garden State Java User Group (formerly the ACGNJ Java Users Group) in 2001 where he serves as one of the directors. Since 2016, Mike has served as a Java community news editor for InfoQ where his contributions include the weekly Java news roundup, news items, technical articles, and technical reviews from external authors. He is currently the lead Java Queue editor. Mike joined Payara as a contract Developer Advocate and Technical Writer in the summer of 2023.

He has presented at venues such as Devnexus, Oracle Code One, JCON World, Emerging Technologies for the Enterprise, Trenton Computer Festival (TCF), TCF IT Professional Conference, and numerous Java User Groups. Mike serves as a committer on the Jakarta NoSQL and Jakarta Data specifications and the Eclipse JNoSQL project. He also participates on the leadership council of the Jakarta EE Ambassadors. Mike was named a Java Champion in April 2023.

Mike retired from ExxonMobil Technology & Engineering in June 2023 with 33.5 years of service. His experience included developing custom scientific laboratory and web applications, polymer physics, chemometrics, infrared spectroscopy, and automotive testing. He also has experience as a Technical Support Engineer at Ai-Logix, Inc. (now AudioCodes) where he provided technical support and developed telephony applications for customers.

About the Technical Reviewer

Sunil Kumar Muppirala is a passionate technology enthusiast with over 18 years of experience driving digital transformation and innovation and designing modern applications in consulting and engineering teams. He specializes in distributed computing, cloud architecture, and micro services and has experience across multiple cloud platforms.

He also has a passion for teaching and simplifying technology concepts. He is an enthusiastic proponent of emerging technologies and stays current by reading books and engineering blogs. He resides in Frisco, TX, and spends his free time with family and watching and playing various sports.

PART I

Getting Started

CHAPTER 1

Introduction to Project Helidon

In September 2018, Oracle introduced its new microservices framework, Project Helidon. Originally named J4C (Java for Cloud), Helidon is an open source framework and collection of Java libraries for creating microservices-based applications.

Helidon, a Greek word for a swallow (a small bird with dark, glossy-blue backs, red throats, pale underparts, and long tail streamers), is unique because it was designed to be simple and fast and ships with two programming models: **Helidon SE** and **Helidon MP**.

Helidon is also observable and resilient and offers full support for MicroProfile, GraalVM, and persistence.

In this first chapter, you will be introduced to Helidon that includes a brief description of each programming model, its architecture and release history, and some examples on how Helidon has quickly become embedded in the Java community. You will learn more details about Helidon SE and Helidon MP and their corresponding components in Part II and Part III of this book, respectively.

Helidon SE

Helidon SE provides core functional-style APIs for building microservices-based applications. An application server is not required as Helidon SE provides a virtual web server. Let's take a sneak peek at the components that comprise Helidon SE as shown in Table 1-1.

Table 1-1. *The list of components in Helidon SE*

• Ahead-of-Time (AoT) Compilation	• Open API
• Config	• Reactive Messaging
• Cross-Origin Resource Sharing (CORS)	• Reactive Streams
• DB Client	• Security
• GraphQL	• Tracing
• gRPC	• WebClient
• Health Checks	• WebServer
• Metrics	• WebSocket

NOTE Helidon SE originally offered a reactive web server based on Netty, an asynchronous event-driven network application framework. With the release of Helidon 4.0 in October 2023, Helidon introduced Helidon Níma, a ground-up web server implementation based on virtual threads as defined in Project Loom.

You will learn more details about Helidon SE and some of these components in Part II of this book.

Functional Style

Helidon SE uses a functional programming style that has the following properties:

- Functional style APIs
- Reactive and nonblocking (Helidon 1.0 through Helidon 3.0)
- Virtual threads (Helidon 4.0 and beyond)
- Tiny memory footprint
- No annotations
- No dependency injection
- No enterprise Java standards support

Let's see how this looks in starting the Helidon web server as shown in Listing 1-1.

Listing 1-1. *The functional style for starting the Helidon web server*

```
Routing routing = Routing.builder()
    .get("/hello", (req, res) -> res.send("Hello World"))
    .build();
WebServer.create(routing)
    .start();
```

An instance of the **Routing** interface is created by using its builder pattern; then the **create()** and **start()** methods from the **WebServer** interface are chained together to get things going. Using this example as a starting point, you can incrementally build a more complex way to create and start a web server using configuration, routing, and media support.

Helidon MP

Helidon MP is an implementation of the MicroProfile specifications (as described in Chapter 2) for building microservices-based applications. MicroProfile 6.1 is the current supported version. Let's take a sneak peek at the components that comprise Helidon MP as shown in Table 1-2.

Table 1-2. *The list of components in Helidon MP*

• Ahead-of-Time (AoT) Compilation	• JWT Authentication
• Config	• Long-Running Actions
• Contexts and Dependency Injection (CDI) Extensions	• Metrics
• Cross-Origin Resource Sharing (CORS)	• Open API
• Fault Tolerance	• Reactive Messaging
• GraphQL	• Reactive Streams
• gRPC	• REST Client
• Health Checks	• Security
• JAX-RS/Jersey	• Tracing
• Java Persistence Architecture (JPA)	• WebSocket

You will learn more details about Helidon MP and some of these components in Part III of this book.

Declarative Style (Helidon MP)

Helidon MP uses a declarative style that has the following properties:

- Declarative style APIs
- Blocking and synchronous
- Small memory footprint
- Heavy use of annotations
- Jakarta Contexts and Dependency Injection (CDI)
- Full support of MicroProfile and partial support of Jakarta EE

Let's see how this looks in starting the Helidon web server as shown in Listing 1-2.

Listing 1-2. The declarative style for starting the web server

```
@Path("hello")
@ApplicationScoped
public class HelloWorld {
    @GET
    public String hello() {
        return "Hello World";
        }
    }
```

I'm sure you've already noticed the differences in this declarative style from the functional style as there are three annotations, **@Path**, **@ApplicationScoped**, and **@GET**, that are used to start this web server.

The **@ApplicationScoped** annotation is, as the name suggests, a scope annotation that tells the container which context to associate the instance of a managed bean. In this case, it is the **HelloWorld** class. In this particular case, a single bean instance is created for the application and used by all other beans that inject Translator.

You learned about functional style in Helidon SE and declarative style in Helidon MP. The comparisons are summarized in Table 1-3.

CHAPTER 1 INTRODUCTION TO PROJECT HELIDON

Table 1-3. *A comparison of functional vs. declarative programming styles*

Helidon SE	Helidon MP
Functional style APIs	Declarative style APIs
Reactive, nonblocking (Helidon 1.0–3.0)	Blocking, synchronous
Tiny memory footprint	Small memory footprint
No annotations	Annotations are heavily used
No dependency injection	Jakarta Contexts and Dependency Injection (CDI)
No enterprise Java standards support	Full support of MicroProfile and partial support of Jakarta EE

Helidon Architecture

The original Helidon WebServer component was an asynchronous and reactive API that ran on top of Netty, an asynchronous event-driven network application framework. With the release of Helidon 4.0 in October 2023, the WebServer component was rebuilt from the ground up and is now based on virtual threads.

Figure 1-1 shows the Helidon architecture from versions 1.x through 3.x.

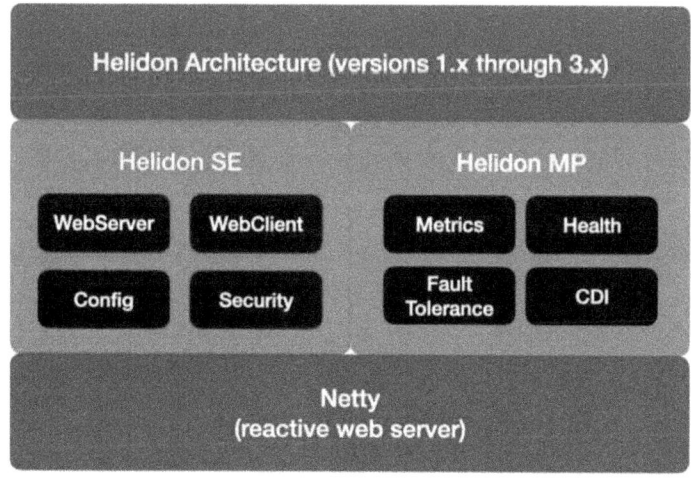

Figure 1-1. *The Helidon architecture for Helidon versions 1.x through 3.x*

7

Figure 1-2 shows Helidon's architecture for version 4.x and beyond.

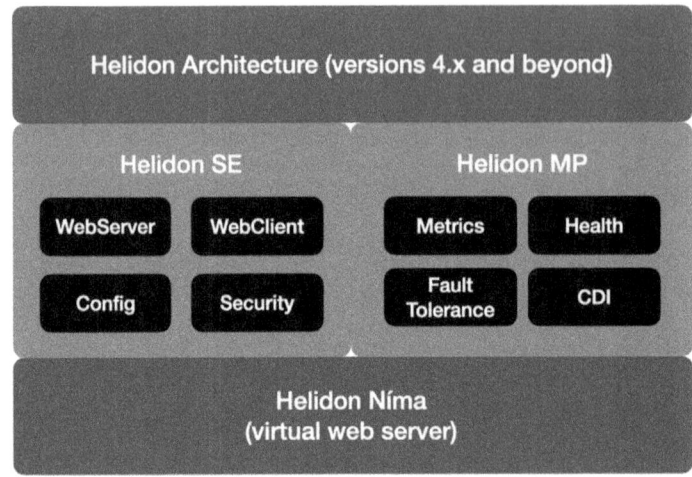

Figure 1-2. *The Helidon architecture for Helidon versions 4.x and beyond*

Helidon Landscape

Helidon is just one of many popular microservices frameworks in the Java space. Figure 1-3 shows how Helidon SE and Helidon MP align among different categories of these frameworks.

Figure 1-3. *The categories of microservices frameworks*

As you can see, Helidon SE aligns with the smaller end of micro-frameworks while Helidon MP aligns with the MicroProfile-based application servers.

Getting Started

You can easily get started building a Helidon application using one of these following methods:

- Helidon Quickstarts
- Helidon Command-Line Interface
- Helidon Project Starter

Let's take a sneak peek into these methods. You will be more formally introduced to these methods in Chapter 4 for Helidon SE and in Chapter 10 for Helidon MP.

Helidon Quickstarts

Oracle provides simple Quickstarts that download and generate a small, working Representational State Transfer (REST) application that is complete with **/greet** and **/simple-greet** endpoints and displays a default greeting of "Hello World!".

These Quickstarts are initiated via the popular Apache Maven build tool to accomplish this task. Quickstarts are available for both the Helidon SE and Helidon MP programming models.

Helidon CLI

The Helidon Command-Line Interface (CLI), a new feature with the release of Helidon 2.0.0, allows you to easily create a Helidon project by selecting a particular archetype. The CLI supports a developer loop, similar to the dev mode in Quarkus, that performs continuous compilation and application restart whenever you update your source code.

The Helidon CLI is distributed as a stand-alone executable. It is available for Linux, macOS, and Windows.

Helidon Project Starter

Similar to existing starter projects such as Spring Initializr, MicroProfile Starter, Jakarta Starter, and Quarkus Code, the Helidon Project Starter (*https://helidon.io/starter/4.1.0*), a new feature with the release of Helidon 3.0.0, is a customizable web application for generating Helidon projects for your specific needs.

Helidon and the Java Community

Helidon has grown in popularity since it was introduced and has made a significant impact on the Java community. These next few sections will provide you with some examples.

Helidon and GraalVM

Shortly after the release of Helidon 1.0, Oracle released Helidon 1.0.3 that introduced support for GraalVM, a polyglot virtual machine and platform created by Oracle Labs that converts Java applications to native executable code via the **native-image** utility.

Helidon and Jakarta Persistence Specification

In March 2020, the Helidon team announced support for the Jakarta Persistence 2.2 specification (*https://jakarta.ee/specifications/persistence/2.2/*) that was included in the September 2019 release of Jakarta EE 8. Jakarta Persistence, derived from heritage JSR 338, Java Persistence API (JPA) 2.2 (*https://jcp.org/en/jsr/detail?id=338*), defines a standard for management of persistence and object/relational mapping.

Helidon MP applications may take advantage of Jakarta Persistence to abstract away the tedious tasks of managing an **EntityManager** along with handling exceptions, thread safety, and transactions and rollbacks.

JPA 2.2 was included in Java EE 8, the last enterprise Java release by Oracle before Java EE was donated to the Eclipse Foundation. You will learn more details about Java EE/Jakarta EE in Chapter 3.

Helidon and Micronaut Data

With the release of Helidon 2.2.0 in December 2020, Oracle added support for Micronaut Data, a subproject of the Micronaut Framework (`https://micronaut.io/`), that provides a database access toolkit using Ahead-of-Time (AoT) compilation to pre-compute queries for repository interfaces that are executed by a thin, lightweight runtime layer. This reinforces Helidon's support for the Jakarta EE and MicroProfile specifications in Helidon MP.

Helidon and Kotlin

In the first of what would be significant support for IntelliJ IDEA, you can convert a Helidon project written in Java to a Kotlin application using the *Convert to Kotlin* menu option. The converted project can then be built and executed.

Helidon and MicroStream

With the release of Helidon 2.4.0 in November 2021, Oracle has integrated Helidon into MicroStream (`https://microstream.one/`), a Java-native persistence framework, which includes support for the Health, Metrics, and Caching components.

Helidon and Log4j2

On December 9, 2021, the Java community learned that a zero-day vulnerability had been discovered in Log4j2, the popular Java logging library. Many developers endured long days (and nights) ensuring that this vulnerability wasn't going to affect their applications.

At that time, Oracle stated that, by default, Log4j2 is not used in Helidon applications, but they do, however, support Log4j2 by providing a **helidon-logging-log4** module.

Improved Helidon Support in IntelliJ IDEA

JetBrains has improved support for Helidon in IntelliJ IDEA Ultimate Edition. You can take advantage of the configuration key completion in **.properties** and **.yaml** files, and there is support for the *Go to Declaration* and *Quick Doc* actions.

Release History

The remainder of this chapter is dedicated to providing a brief overview of the initial and major releases. Oracle uses the semantic version paradigm, that is, **MAJOR.MINOR.PATCH**.

Please note that only the most significant new features and improvements in each of these releases will be discussed. Otherwise. this would be an extremely long chapter! You should also assume that each release includes bug fixes along with improvements and new features.

Helidon 0.10.0

Released in September 2018, Helidon 0.10.0 provided updates to the WebServer and Security components. For the former, refactored HTTP-related classes were moved from the original **io.helidon.webserver** package to a new package, **io.helidon.common.http**. This created a breaking change requiring developers to update their **import** statements. For the latter, this release improved subject mapping for Oracle's Identity and Cloud Service (IDCS).

Helidon 1.0.0

Within five months of its introduction to the Java community, Helidon 1.0.0 was released in February 2019. This release provided greater API stability and support for the MicroProfile 1.2 specification.

New features supporting the WebServer component included the Java API for JSON Binding (JSON-B) specification (with Eclipse Yasson as the compatible implementation) and the Jackson JSON processing library.

Hystrix Fault Tolerance was upgraded to version 1.5.18 to support a simpler and easier-to-understand circuit breaker strategy.

And finally, the quickstart examples were updated such that the HTTP **PUT** request method uses JSON and not a **PATH** parameter that was previously practiced. The latter does not follow REST best practices. For example, to change the greeting from *"Hello"* to *"Guten Tag,"* the **curl** command, as shown in Listing 1-3, is necessary.

Listing 1-3. Using the curl command to change a greeting from "Hello" to "Guten Tag"

```
~ » curl -X PUT -H "Content-Type: application/json" -d '{"greeting" : "Guten Tag"}' http://localhost:8080/greet/greeting
```

Helidon 2.0.0

During an Oracle Live Webcast in June 2020, Helidon 2.0.0 was formally introduced to the Java community. With a new baseline of JDK 11 and Jakarta EE, Helidon 2.0.0 delivered a host of new significant features such as support for reactive messaging and streams; a new command-line tool; a new WebClient API for Helidon SE; support for GraalVM in Helidon MP, a new reactive database client; support for the Jakarta WebSocket specification; support for Cross-Origin Resource Sharing (CORS); easy generation of **jlink** custom runtime images that includes CDS archives for improved startup performance; improved discovery and handling of JAX-RS applications; and a new MediaSupport API

The new WebClient API complements the original three core Helidon SE APIs – Web Server, Configuration, and Security – to complete the minimal set of components for Helidon SE.

In previous versions, there was no support for GraalVM in Helidon MP due to the use of reflection. However, this limitation was removed as it is now possible to create a GraalVM native image from a Helidon MP application.

Helidon 3.0.0

Released in July 2022, Helidon 3.0.0 was made available after two milestone releases in February and May 2022. New features included support for MicroProfile 5.0 and Jakarta EE 9.1 and JDK 17+; JEP 290 security hardening; an updated Helidon SE Routing API; and a new Helidon Starter project (as described earlier in this chapter).

Support for MicroProfile 5.0 and Jakarta EE 9.1 includes the migration of the **javax** namespace from Java EE 8/Jakarta EE 8 to the **jakarta** namespace. This was necessary as the **javax** namespace is an Oracle brand. You will learn more about this in Chapter 3.

For additional protection, JEP 290: Filter Incoming Serialization Data (*https://openjdk.org/jeps/290*), delivered in JDK 9, was updated such that deserialization is disabled by default. You can still use deserialization in your application, but additional configuration is required.

The design of the multiprotocol part of the Helidon SE Routing API was improved and simplified when specifying routes for different protocols such as WebSocket, HTTP/1, and HTTP/2.

JDK 17 is a minimal version to use Helidon 3.0.0 in your applications. JDK 11 will, therefore, no longer be supported.

Helidon 4.0.0

Released in October 2023, the most significant change delivered in Helidon 4.0.0 was the introduction of the Helidon Níma (`https://helidon.io/nima`), a ground-up web server implementation based on virtual threads from JEP 444: Virtual Threads (`https://openjdk.org/jeps/444`), delivered in JDK 21 and Project Loom (`https://wiki.openjdk.org/display/loom/Main`).

This new server replaces the original Helidon reactive web server based on Netty (`https://netty.io/`), an asynchronous event-driven network application framework. However, the reactive web server is still supported in the Helidon 3.0.0 and 2.0.0 release trains.

Helidon 4.0.0 also supports MicroProfile 6.0.

JDK 21 is a minimal version to use Helidon 4.0.0 in your applications. JDK 11 will, therefore, no longer be supported.

Summary

In this chapter, you were introduced to Helidon, its architecture, its landscape relative to other microservices frameworks, the Helidon CLI, the Helidon Project Starter, its impact on the Java community, and a brief description of the major releases.

In Chapter 2, you will be introduced to the MicroProfile specifications.

CHAPTER 2

The MicroProfile Specifications

MicroProfile is a full suite of specifications for optimizing enterprise Java in a microservices architecture. In this chapter, you will be introduced to MicroProfile that includes its history, an overview of its releases, and a brief description of the specifications. It's important for you to become familiar with these specifications since Helidon MP supports MicroProfile.

In mid-2016, two new initiatives, MicroProfile and the Java EE Guardians (now the Jakarta EE Ambassadors), had formed as a direct response to Oracle having stagnated their efforts with the release of Java EE 8. The Java community felt that enterprise Java had fallen behind with the emergence of web services technologies for building microservices-based applications.

Introduced at Red Hat's DevNation conference on June 27, 2016, MicroProfile was created as a collaboration of Java middleware vendors – IBM, Red Hat, Tomitribe, and Payara – and the London Java Community to deliver microservices for enterprise Java. These founding vendors offered their own microservices frameworks, namely, Open Liberty (IBM), WildFly Swarm (Red Hat), TomEE (Tomitribe), and Payara Micro (Payara), respectively, that supported the MicroProfile initiative.

The founding members collaborated on building MicroProfile with these goals in mind:

- An open standard platform that enables vendors to compete on implementation, price, or business model
- A collaborative standard and process that is driven by many vendors and individual developers rather than a single vendor

- A consistent and holistic vision for all architectural tiers of the application

- A strong focus on adherence to the standard and compatibility between vendor implementations and versions of the specifications

In early-2018, Red Hat renamed WildFly Swarm to Thorntail to provide their microservices framework with its own identity. As Bob McWhirter, Senior Distinguished Engineer at Red Hat, speaking to InfoQ in May 2018, explained:

> While we lived with "WildFly Swarm" as a name for a few years, we noticed that "Swarm" is fairly overloaded, with many companies and projects using it. Additionally, as we move forward with a new architecture for the project, including "WildFly" in the name started to make less sense. When we started, we were absolutely an extension to the core WildFly project, but we've grown into our own, and needed our own identity. Given both of those reasons, we decided a new name was in order.

However, less than a year later, Red Hat introduced Quarkus, a "Kubernetes Native Java stack tailored for OpenJDK HotSpot and GraalVM, crafted from the best-of-breed Java libraries and standards." Dubbed "Supersonic Subatomic Java," Quarkus quickly gained popularity in the Java community to the point that interest in Thorntail had waned. Red Hat ultimately announced Thorntail's end-of-life in July 2020.

Quarkus joined the relatively new frameworks at the time, Micronaut and Helidon, that were introduced to the Java community less than a year earlier. With the exception of Micronaut, all of these microservices-based frameworks support the MicroProfile initiative.

MicroProfile Joins the Eclipse Foundation

In search of a foundation for MicroProfile, the founding members debated between the Apache Software Foundation and the Eclipse Foundation. Announced on December 14, 2016, by Mike Milinkovich, executive director at the Eclipse Foundation, MicroProfile joined the Eclipse Foundation as an incubator project to ensure that MicroProfile remained vendor-neutral and be able to leverage the resources and momentum of the Eclipse Foundation.

Eclipse Working Groups

The Eclipse Working Groups (*https://www.eclipse.org/org/workinggroups/about.php*) provide a common and consistent standard for projects under the auspices of the Eclipse Foundation. In particular, Table 2-1 displays what these working groups offer.

Table 2-1. Eclipse Working Group standards

• Vendor-Neutral Governance	• Specification Development
• Ecosystem Development and Marketing	• Branding and Compatibility
• Collaborative Management	• Research

There are currently 19 such working groups that include

- MicroProfile Working Group (*https://www.eclipse.org/org/workinggroups/microprofile-charter.php*)
- Jakarta EE Working Group (*https://www.eclipse.org/org/workinggroups/jakarta_ee_charter.php*)
- OSGi Working Group (*https://www.eclipse.org/org/workinggroups/osgi-charter.php*)
- Adoptium Working Group (formerly the AdoptOpenJDK initiative) (*https://www.eclipse.org/org/workinggroups/adoptium-charter.php*)

MicroProfile Working Group

Operating independently since its inception in 2016, there were a total of 12 MicroProfile releases (MicroProfile 1.0 through 3.3) by a dedicated group of contributors from within the Java community. In early 2020, the Eclipse Foundation mandated that it was time for MicroProfile to establish their own working group. An initial set of founding organizations – IBM, Red Hat, Payara, Tomitribe, Jelastic, and Atlanta JUG – started the process to form a steering committee and define the MicroProfile Specification Process. Working throughout the pandemic with weekly meetings that were open to the Java community, the working group was formally established in October 2020. Since then, other organizations have joined the MicroProfile Working Group, namely, Oracle, Fujitsu, Microsoft, Garden State JUG, and iJUG.

John Clingan, Senior Principal Product Manager at Red Hat Eclipse and MicroProfile Co-founder and Committer, speaking to InfoQ in November 2020, explained:

> The primary driver behind creating the MicroProfile Working Group is to close intellectual property gaps identified by the Eclipse Foundation for specification projects. So, there are more legal protections in place now that MicroProfile is a Working Group.
>
> A Working Group also places more processes on MicroProfile. Historically, MicroProfile moved quickly with minimal process and late-binding decisions. It was quite an agile project that delivered specifications at quite a quick pace. However, I personally feel like we were reaching a point where adding **some** process can benefit the project. For instance, we now have to put more thought and formality up-front into planning a specification, which requires a Steering Committee vote. Better planning gives implementers, tool vendors, and the community more up-front visibility into what is coming and to prepare. However, we codified "limited processes" in the MicroProfile Charter to keep processes to a minimum.

Due to the amount of time required to form this working group, the release of MicroProfile 4.0 was delayed until December 2020.

Compatible Implementations

A compatible implementation is a process for an organization to certify that their implementation of the MicroProfile specifications (or any Java-related specifications for that matter) has passed a series of tests known as the Technology Compatibility Kit (TCK). These tests check for correctness and consistency of all the MicroProfile specifications. Once these tests have passed, the organization may submit a Compatibility Certification Request (CCR) to the MicroProfile Working Group for approval.

CHAPTER 2 THE MICROPROFILE SPECIFICATIONS

MicroProfile Release History

The release of MicroProfile 1.0, announced on September 19, 2016, at JavaOne 2016, consisted of three JSR-based APIs from Java EE 7 that were considered minimal for creating microservices:

- JSR-346: Contexts and Dependency Injection (CDI) 1.1
- JSR-353: Java API for JSON Processing (JSON-P) 1.0
- JSR-339: Java API for RESTful Web Services (JAX-RS) 2.0

These specifications are shown in Figure 2-1.

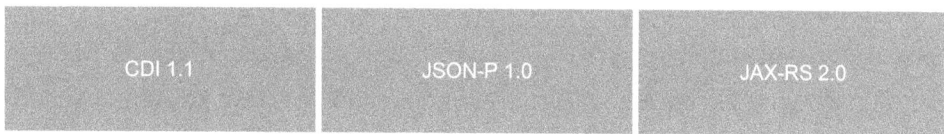

Figure 2-1. *The MicroProfile 1.0 specifications*

SouJava (`https://soujava.org.br/`), the largest Java Users Group from Brazil, also joined to support the MicroProfile initiative at that time.

Over the years since this initial release, the Java community contributed a number of specifications – Fault Tolerance, Metrics, and Health, among others – that were designed for cloud-native applications. If you're interested in the details of each MicroProfile release, head over to Appendix A.

MicroProfile 7.0

Released on August 22, 2024, MicroProfile 7.0, the latest release, delivered updates to four specifications – Open Telemetry 2.0, Open API 4.0, Rest Client 4.0, and Fault Tolerance 4.1 – as shown in Figure 2-2.

CHAPTER 2   THE MICROPROFILE SPECIFICATIONS

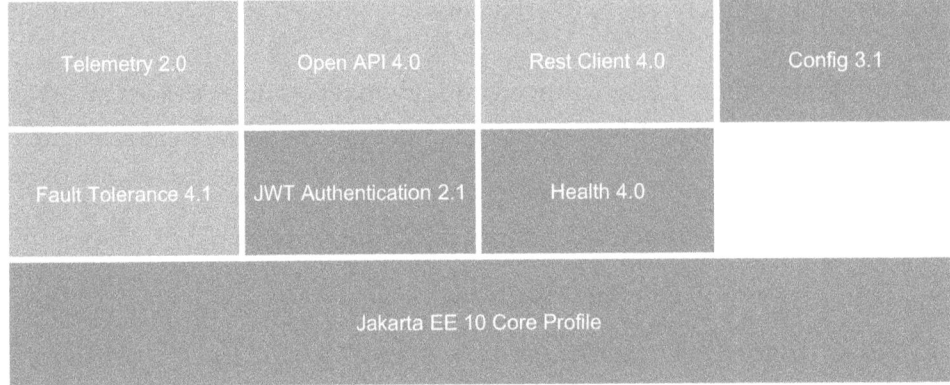

Figure 2-2. *The MicroProfile 7.0 core specifications*

The specifications in Figure 2-2 are part of the core set of specifications. MicroProfile also includes stand-alone specifications, shown in Figure 2-3, that you can use in your applications.

Figure 2-3. *The MicroProfile 7.0 stand-alone specifications*

As you can see, much has changed with MicroProfile over the past eight years as the framework has significantly grown.

The Open Tracing specification, having once belonged in the core set of specifications, was moved to the stand-alone specifications with the release of MicroProfile 6.0 in January 2023. This was due to the OpenTelemetry specification (*https://opentelemetry.io/*) having been created as a merger between the Open Tracing (*https://opentracing.io/*) and OpenCensus (*https://opencensus.io/*) specifications in May 2019. As a result, the MicroProfile Telemetry specification was formed.

The Metrics specification, also having once belonged in the core set of specifications, was moved to the stand-alone specifications with the release of MicroProfile 7.0 in August 2024. This was due to some vendors deciding not to implement the Metrics specification. Instead, those vendors implemented the Micrometer Metrics (*https://micrometer.io/*) specification.

The lone compatible implementation for MicroProfile 7.0 is

- Open Liberty 24.0.0.9-beta

The Jakarta EE 10 Core Profile, introduced with the release of Jakarta EE 10 in September 2022, includes seven specifications that include the updated versions of the original three JSR-related specifications from Java EE 7 as listed in Figure 2-1.

Table 2-2. *The Jakarta EE specifications defined in the Jakarta EE 10 Core Profile*

• Jakarta RESTful Web Services 3.1	• Jakarta Interceptors 2.1
• Jakarta JSON Processing 2.1	• Jakarta Dependency Injection 2.0
• Jakarta JSON Binding 3.0	• Jakarta Contexts and Dependency Injection 4.0
• Jakarta Annotations 2.1	

Meet the MicroProfile Specifications

Now that you have become familiar with a brief release history, it's time to get acquainted with the individual specifications. Please note that some of the specification names have changed over the past six years, so you will be introduced to the current specification names.

Jakarta Contexts and Dependency Injection (CDI)

Introduced in MicroProfile 1.0 and originally based on JSR 346, Contexts and Dependency Injection (CDI) 1.1, this specification, currently at version 4.1 (for Jakarta EE 11), manages the life cycle of stateful components though type-safe injection into client objects. This is accomplished by using the **@Inject** annotation as shown in the code snippet in Listing 2-1.

Listing 2-1. Using the **@Inject** annotation

```
@Inject
public MovieResource(MovieRepository movies) {
    this.movies = movies;
}
```

Since its initial release, this specification has evolved in major MicroProfile releases, and you will see how they are aligned with corresponding JSRs and Java EE/Jakarta EE versions as shown in Table 2-3.

Table 2-3. *Evolution of Jakarta Contexts and Dependency Injection specification*

MicroProfile 2.0	MicroProfile 4.0	MicroProfile 5.0	MicroProfile 6.0
Java EE 8 (JSR 365)	Jakarta EE 8	Jakarta EE 9.1	Jakarta EE 10
CDI 2.0	Jakarta CDI 2.0	Jakarta CDI 3.0	Jakarta CDI 4.0

You will learn more about Jakarta Contexts and Dependency Injection in Chapter 3.

Jakarta JSON Processing (JSON-P)

Introduced in MicroProfile 1.0 and originally based on JSR 353, Java API for JSON Processing (JSON-P) 1.0, this specification, currently at version 2.1, processes JSON messages that produce and consume streamed JSON text in binding with Java objects.

Since its initial release, this specification has evolved in major MicroProfile releases, and you will see how they are aligned with corresponding JSRs and Java EE/Jakarta EE versions as shown in Table 2-4.

Table 2-4. *Evolution of Jakarta JSON Processing specification*

MicroProfile 2.0	MicroProfile 4.0	MicroProfile 5.0	MicroProfile 6.0
Java EE 8 (JSR 374)	Jakarta EE 8	Jakarta EE 9.1	Jakarta EE 10
JSON-P 1.1	Jakarta JSON-P 1.1	Jakarta JSON-P 2.0	Jakarta JSON-P 2.1

You will learn more about Jakarta JSON Processing in Chapter 3.

Jakarta RESTful Web Services (JAX-RS)

Introduced in MicroProfile 1.0 and originally based on JSR 339, Java API for RESTful Web Services (JAX-RS) 2.0, this specification, currently at version 4.0 (for Jakarta EE 11), provides support for creating web services as defined by the Representational State Transfer (REST) architectural pattern.

CHAPTER 2   THE MICROPROFILE SPECIFICATIONS

Since its initial release, this specification has evolved in major MicroProfile releases, and you will see how they are aligned with corresponding JSRs and Java EE/Jakarta EE versions as shown in Table 2-5.

Table 2-5. *Evolution of Jakarta RESTful Web Services specification*

MicroProfile 2.0	MicroProfile 4.0	MicroProfile 5.0	MicroProfile 6.0
Java EE 8 (JSR 370)	Jakarta EE 8	Jakarta EE 9.1	Jakarta EE 10
JAX-RS 2.1	Jakarta JAX-RS 2.1	Jakarta JAX-RS 3.0	Jakarta JAX-RS 4.0

You will learn more about Jakarta RESTful Web Services in Chapter 3.

Config

Introduced in MicroProfile 1.1, the Config specification, currently at version 3.1, is a framework to define and manage configurations through environment variables, system properties, or property files. This specification is designed to externalize configuration from microservices and inject configuration values at runtime.

The de facto standard for naming property files is usually **microprofile-config.properties**, but other file names, such as the popular **application.properties**, may be used. Config externalizes the specific environment/stage configuration differences away from the application so that there is no need to repackage or rebuild the application when moving through the stages of the software development lifecycle.

Consider the properties file in Listing 2-2.

Listing 2-2. A typical properties file for a MicroProfile application

```
# Application properties. This is the default greeting
app.greeting=Hello

# Microprofile server properties
server.port=8080
server.host=0.0.0.0
```

The value defined in app.greeting may be used in conjunction with the **@ConfigProperty** annotation as shown in the code snippet in Listing 2-3.

Listing 2-3. Applying the **@ConfigProperty** annotation

```
@Inject
public GreetingProvider(@ConfigProperty(name = "app.greeting") String message) {
    this.message.set(message);
}
```

Fault Tolerance

Introduced in MicroProfile 1.2, the Fault Tolerance specification, currently at version 4.1, leverages strategies to guide the execution and result of business logic upon some failure within the application. The Fault Tolerance specification introduces new policies with corresponding annotations that may be added to any class or method:

- **@Timeout** – Defines a required timeout period
- **@Retry** – Defines criteria for when a retry is necessary
- **@Fallback** – Provides an alternative solution for a failed execution
- **@Bulkhead** – Prevents a system overload or an indefinite wait
- **@CircuitBreaker** – Isolates a failure allowing the rest of the system to function

Metrics

Introduced in MicroProfile 1.2, the Metrics specification, currently at version 5.1, provides well-known monitoring endpoints and metrics for each computing process. It introduces the following built-in annotations that may be added to any class or method:

- **@Counted** – Marks a method, constructor, or type as a counter
- **@Gauge** – Marks a method as a gauge
- **@Metered** – Marks a method or constructor as metered and tracks how frequently they are called
- **@Timed** – Marks a method or constructor of an annotated object as timed and tracks how long invocations of those annotated objects take to complete
- **@Metric** – Requests that a metric should be injected or registered

JWT Propagation

Introduced in MicroProfile 1.2, the JWT Propagation specification, currently at version 2.1, is a token-based authentication/authorization system that includes a set of standards for interoperability. Application callers have the ability to authenticate themselves using a JSON Web Token (JWT) token.

A JWT token consists of three parts – the header, the body, and the signature – and each part is separated with a dot (.). You can use the **base64** utility in UNIX to decode this token.

Consider the example as shown in Listing 2-4.

Listing 2-4. A typical JWT token

```
eyJhbGci0iJIUzI1NiIsInR5cCI6IkpXVCIsImtpZCI6ImY1ODg5MGQx0SJ9.eyJhdWQi0
iI4NWEwMzg2Ny1kY2NmLTQ40DItYWRkZS0xYTc5YWVlYzUwZGYiLCJleHAi0jE2NDQ40DQ
x0DUsImlhdCI6MTY0ODg4MDU4NSwiaXNzIjoiYWNtZS5jb20iLCJzdWIi0iIwMDAwMDAwM
CowMDAwLTAwMDAtMDAwMCowMDAwMDAwMDAwMDEiLCJqdGki0iIzZGQ2NDMoZCo3OWE5LTR
kMTUt0ThiNS03YjUxZGJiMmNkMzEiLCJhdXRoZW50aWNhdGlvbiR5cGUi0iJQQVNTV09SR
CIsImVtYWlsIjoiYWRtaW5AZnVzaW9uYXV0aC5pbyIsImVtYWlsX3ZlcmlmaWVkIjp0cnV
lLCJhcHBsaWNhdGlvbklkIjoi0DVhMDM4NjctZGNjZi00ODgyLWFkZGUtMWE3OWFlZWM1M
GRmIiwicm9sZXMi0lsiY2VvIl19.dee-Ke6RzR0G9avaLNRZf1GUCDfe8Zbk9L2c7yaqKME
```

The header is the first part that contains metadata about this token, including the key identifier and the algorithm used for sign-in as shown in Listing 2-5.

Listing 2-5. The header section of the JWT token

```
eyJhbGci0iJIUzI1NiIsInR5cCI6IkpXVCIsImtpZCI6ImY1ODg5MGQx0SJ9
```

As shown in Listing 2-6, the body, or as it may be referred to as the payload, contains the data that this token was created to transport. User data, such as authorization, to access certain data or functionality, the payload contains user data such as roles or other authorization information.

Listing 2-6. The payload section of the JWT token

```
eyJhdWQi0iI4NWEwMzg2Ny1kY2NmLTQ40DItYWRkZS0xYTc5YWVlYzUwZGYiLCJleHAi0jE
2NDQ40DQx0DUsImlhdCI6MTY0ODg4MDU4NSwiaXNzIjoiYWNtZS5jb20iLCJzdWIi0iIw
MDAwMDAwMCowMDAwLTAwMDAtMDAwMCowMDAwMDAwMDAwMDEiLCJqdGki0iIzZGQ2NDMoZCo30
```

```
WE5LTRkMTUtOThiNSO3YjUxZGJiMmNkMzEiLCJhdXRoZW50aWNhdGlvblR5cGUiOiJQQVN
TV09SRCIsImVtYWlsIjoiYWRtaW5AZnVzaW9uYXV0aC5pbyIsImVtYWlsX3ZlcmlmaWVk
IjpOcnVlLCJhcHBsaWNhdGlvbklkIjoiODVhMDM4NjctZGNjZiOoODgyLWFkZGUtMWE3OWF1
ZWM1MGRmIiwicm9sZXMiOlsiY2VvIl19
```

And finally, as shown in Listing 2-7, the signature is the most crucial part of this token as it guarantees the integrity of the body and the header and it must be verified before any other operation is performed.

Listing 2-7. The signature section of the JWT token

```
dee-Ke6RzROG9avaLNRZf1GUCDfe8Zbk9L2c7yaqKME
```

Health

Introduced in MicroProfile 1.2, the Health Check specification, currently at version 4.0, determines if a computing node, or microservice, is on the brink of termination or shutdown and will replace that node with a fresh, healthy instance. It includes a built-in class annotation, **@Health**, and the class must implement the **HealthCheck** interface and override the **call()** method.

Open Tracing

Introduced in MicroProfile 1.3, the Open Tracing specification, currently at version 3.0, enables tracing of all JAX-RS methods by default for easier tracing of the flow of a request across service boundaries in a microservices environment. To further control and customize these traces, use the **@Traced** annotation to enable and disable tracing of particular methods. You can also inject a custom Tracer object to create and customize spans.

A third-party distributed tracing system, such as Zipkin or Jaeger, is required.

Open API

Introduced in MicroProfile 1.3, the Open API specification, currently at version 4.0 and derived from the Open API standard, provides a set of interfaces and programming models for Java developers to natively produce Open API documents from their JAX-RS applications.

The Open API standard defines a consistent, language-agnostic interface to RESTful APIs which allows both humans and computers to discover and understand the capabilities of the service without access to source code, documentation, or through network traffic inspection.

By default, an **/openapi** endpoint is automatically generated in any compatible implementation of MicroProfile.

Rest Client

Introduced in MicroProfile 1.3, the Rest Client specification, currently at version 4.0, provides a type-safe approach to invoke RESTful services over HTTP.

As you will see in the **MovieResource** class shown in Listing 2-8, the endpoints, **/movies** and **/movies/{id}**, are defined using the **@Path** annotation to update, delete, or obtain a movie by its ID in the database.

Listing 2-8. The MovieResource class that demonstrates the MicroProfile Rest Client specification

```
@Path("/movies")
@RequestScoped
public class MovieResource {
    private final static Logger LOGGER = Logger.getLogger(MovieResource.
    class.getName());

    private final MovieRepository movies;

    @Context
    ResourceContext resourceContext;

    @Context
    UriInfo uriInfo;

    @Inject
    public MovieResource(MovieRepository movies) {
        this.movies = movies;
        }

    @GET
    @Produces(MediaType.APPLICATION_JSON)
```

```java
    public Response getAllMovies() {
        return ok(this.movies.all()).build();
        }

    @POST
    @Consumes(MediaType.APPLICATION_JSON)
    public Response savePost(@Valid Movie movie) {
        Movie saved = this.movies.save(Movie.of(movie.getId(),movie.
        getTitle(),movie.getYear()));
        return created(
                uriInfo.getBaseUriBuilder()
                        .path("/movies/{id}")
                        .build(saved.getId())
        ).build();
        }

    @Path("{id}")
    @GET
    @Produces(MediaType.APPLICATION_JSON)
    public Response getMovieById(@PathParam("id") final int id) {
        Movie movie = this.movies.getById(id);
        if (movie == null) {
            throw new MovieNotFoundException(id);
            }
        return ok(movie).build();
        }

    @Path("{id}")
    @PUT
    @Consumes(MediaType.APPLICATION_JSON)
    public Response updateMovie(@PathParam("id") final int id, @Valid Movie
    movie) {
        Movie existed = this.movies.getById(id);
        existed.setTitle(movie.getTitle());
        existed.setYear(movie.getYear());

        Movie saved = this.movies.save(existed);
```

```
        return noContent().build();
    }

    @Path("{id}")
    @DELETE
    public Response deleteMovie(@PathParam("id") final int id) {
        this.movies.deleteById(id);
        return noContent().build();
    }
}
```

Jakarta JSON Binding (JSON-B)

Introduced in MicroProfile 2.0 and originally based on JSR 367, the Java API for JSON Binding (JSON-B), the Jakarta JSON-B specification, currently at version 3.0, provides a standard binding layer for converting Java objects to/from JSON messages.

Since its initial release, this specification has evolved in major MicroProfile releases, and you will see how they are aligned with corresponding JSRs and Java EE/Jakarta EE versions as shown in Table 2-6.

Table 2-6. *Evolution of Jakarta JSON Binding specification*

MicroProfile 2.0	MicroProfile 4.0	MicroProfile 5.0	MicroProfile 6.0
Java EE 8 (JSR 367)	Jakarta EE 8	Jakarta EE 9.1	Jakarta EE 10
JSON-B 1.0	Jakarta JSON-B 1.0	Jakarta JSON-B 2.0	Jakarta JSON-B 3.0

You will learn more about Jakarta JSON Binding in Chapter 3.

Jakarta Annotations

Introduced in MicroProfile 4.1, the Jakarta Annotations specification, currently at version 3.0 (for Jakarta EE 11), defines a collection of annotations that represent a common set of semantic concepts that enable a declarative style of programming that applies across a variety of Java technologies.

Reactive Messaging

Initially released in June 2019 as a 1.0 release in July 2019, the Reactive Messaging specification, currently at version 3.0, provides asynchronous interactions with different services and resources that can be implemented using Reactive Messaging. The goal of this specification is to provide a way to connect event-driven microservices and provide asynchronous messaging support for the Reactive Streams Operators specification.

Reactive Streams Operators

Initially released in August 2018 as a 1.0 release in January 2019, the Reactive Streams Operators specification, currently at version 3.0, provides a set of operators to create new reactive streams to process and consume data. You should know that this specification was not designed to be used directly by application developers. The semantics defined by this specification are very strict and nontrivial to implement correctly, especially when it comes to thread safety.

You are expected to use third-party libraries that provide the tools necessary to manipulate and control streams. Examples of this include Akka Streams, RxJava, and Reactor.

In the code example, as shown in Listing 2-9, a list of strings are converted to uppercase and displayed on the terminal window.

Listing 2-9. A simple MicroProfile Streams Operators example

```java
public class QuickStart {
    public static void main(String[] args) {
        // create a stream of words
        ReactiveStreams.of("hello", "from", "smallrye", "reactive",
        "stream", "operators")
                .map(String::toUpperCase) // transform the words
                .filter(s -> s.length() > 4) // filter items
                .forEach(word -> System.out.println(">> " + word))
                // terminal operation
                .run(); // run it (create the streams, subscribe to
                it, etc.)
```

Context Propagation

Initially released in April 2019 as a 1.0 release in July 2019, the Context Propagation specification, currently at version 1.3, provides a set of APIs for propagating contexts across units of work (classes and interfaces such as **CompletionStage**, **CompletableFuture**, **Function**, **Runnable**) that are thread agnostic. These are backed by threads that are managed by the container, also known as managed threads.

GraphQL

Initially introduced in May 2019 as a 1.0 release in February 2020, the GraphQL specification, currently at version 2.0, enables developers to build portable GraphQL-based applications. This solves the issue of over-fetching or under-fetching data. Over-fetching is fetching all the data from an endpoint, but using only a portion of that data for, say, a mobile application. This requires filtering and leaving the remaining data unused. Under-fetching is fetching all the data from an endpoint, but not having enough data. This usually requires a call to a second endpoint.

Long-Running Actions (LRA)

Initially introduced in April 2021 as a 1.0 release in May 2021, the Long-Running Actions specification, currently at version 2.0, "introduces an API for loosely coupled services to coordinate long-running activities in such a way as to guarantee a globally consistent outcome without the need to take locks on data."

Telemetry

Introduced in January 2023 as a 1.0 release, the Telemetry specification, currently at version 2.0, adopts the OpenTelemetry specification that standardizes data portability and instrumentation maintenance. Telemetry data in the Telemetry specification include tracing, logging, metrics, and baggage.

CHAPTER 2   THE MICROPROFILE SPECIFICATIONS

MicroProfile Starter

Inspired by the Spring Initializr utility, some of the folks in the MicroProfile community collaborated to build MicroProfile Starter (*https://start.microprofile.io/*), a website that allows you to generate and download a new MicroProfile project based on your selected custom options.

This utility allows you to specify your project's coordinates (**groupId** and **artifactId**), your desired version of MicroProfile, MicroProfile and JDK versions, your favorite build tool (Maven or Gradle), and desired specifications. Figure 2-4 shows the main MicroProfile Starter page with a few options selected.

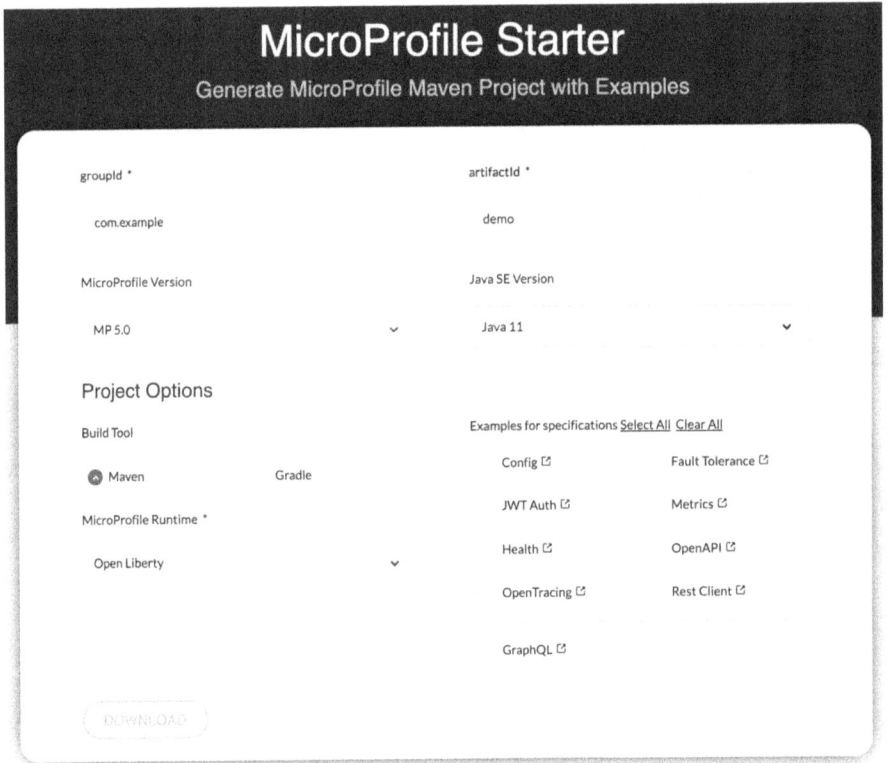

Figure 2-4. The MicroProfile Starter page

Summary

In this chapter, you were introduced to MicroProfile, its history, a brief description of the specifications, and how to get started with MicroProfile using MicroProfile Starter. Should you be interested to learn more, please visit the MicroProfile website (*https://microprofile.io/*).

You will be introduced to the Jakarta EE specifications in Chapter 3.

CHAPTER 3

The Jakarta EE Specifications

In this chapter, you will be introduced to Jakarta EE (*https://jakarta.ee/*), a set of specifications for building enterprise Java applications. You will learn about the history related to the migration from Java EE, the Jakarta EE releases, and a brief overview of the specifications.

After the much anticipated release of Java EE 8 on August 31, 2017, Oracle donated the Java EE specifications to the Eclipse Foundation with the intent of open-sourcing the platform. While Oracle still maintains Java EE 8 for their customers, there will never be a Java EE 9 or above.

Due to Oracle branding policies, the Java EE name could not be used for this new open source platform. The search for the new name included soliciting the Java community. The name, *Jakarta*, named after the retired Apache Jakarta Project that was sunset in 2011, was the ultimate favorite.

Founded in 1999, the Apache Jakarta Project was home to a number of popular open source solutions such as Ant, Maven, JAMES, and Velocity. However, in an effort to evolve a flatter Apache Software Foundation, these projects started to migrate to full, top-level Apache projects to the point where the Jakarta Project was no longer necessary.

The new name is also appropriate since Jakarta is the capital of Indonesia that is located on the northwest coast of the island of Java. The Java community also participated in selecting the new logo, which was unveiled in April 2018.

Similarly, the **javax** namespace, typically used for Java EE package names for classes, interfaces, and annotations, also falls under the auspices of Oracle branding. This means that you can no longer import **javax.enterprise.context.ApplicationScoped**, for example, in your Jakarta EE applications.

Java Users Groups are encouraged to adopt one or more specifications through the Adopt a Spec program (`https://jakarta.ee/community/adopt-a-spec/`) for developers who are interested in contributing and advocating for Jakarta EE.

Evolution of Java EE/Jakarta EE

Jakarta EE has a rich history that dates back to the initial release of the specification as J2EE 1.2 in December 1999. The J2EE naming convention matched with its Java SE counterpart, namely, J2SE. This naming convention lasted until the release of Java EE 5 in May 2006.

From J2EE to Java EE to Jakarta EE, you can see the evolution of this platform in Figure 3-1.

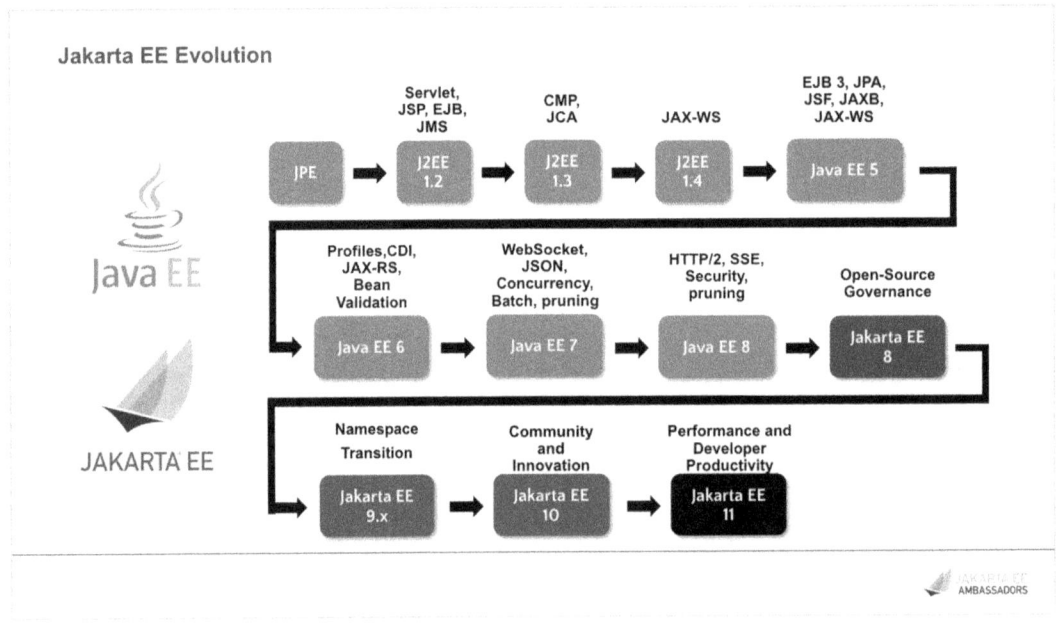

Figure 3-1. Evolution of Java/Jakarta EE (image courtesy of the Jakarta EE Ambassadors)

Eclipse Working Groups

The Eclipse Working Groups (`https://www.eclipse.org/org/workinggroups/about.php`) provide a common and consistent standard for projects under the auspices of the Eclipse Foundation. In particular, Table 3-1 displays what these working groups offer.

Table 3-1. Eclipse Working Group standards

• Vendor-Neutral Governance	• Specification Development
• Ecosystem Development and Marketing	• Branding and Compatibility
• Collaborative Management	• Research

There are currently 19 such working groups that include

- MicroProfile Working Group (`https://www.eclipse.org/org/workinggroups/microprofile-charter.php`)

- Jakarta EE Working Group (`https://www.eclipse.org/org/workinggroups/jakarta_ee_charter.php`)

- OSGi Working Group (`https://www.eclipse.org/org/workinggroups/osgi-charter.php`)

- Adoptium Working Group (formerly the AdoptOpenJDK initiative) (`https://www.eclipse.org/org/workinggroups/adoptium-charter.php`)

Jakarta EE Working Group

Similar to the MicroProfile Working Group, the Jakarta EE Working Group was established in 2018 as part of the process to migrate Java EE to Jakarta EE. The Founding organizations were Oracle, IBM, and Red Hat. Since then, the working group membership has grown to over 25 organizations and Java User Groups.

Compatible Implementations

A compatible implementation is a process for an organization to certify that their implementation of the Jakarta EE specifications (or any Java-related specifications for that matter) has passed a series of tests known as the Technology Compatibility Kit (TCK). These tests check for correctness and consistency of all Jakarta EE specifications. Once these tests have passed, the organization may submit a Compatibility Certification Request (CCR) to the Jakarta EE Working Group for approval.

CHAPTER 3   THE JAKARTA EE SPECIFICATIONS

Jakarta EE Profiles

There are three Jakarta EE profiles: **Platform**, **Web Profile**, and the new **Core Profile** that was introduced with the release of Jakarta EE 10. What follows is a brief introduction to each profile and a list of the specifications contained within it.

Platform

The Jakarta EE Platform defines a standard platform for hosting all Jakarta EE applications. It is designed for developers who require the full set of Jakarta EE specifications for developing enterprise applications.

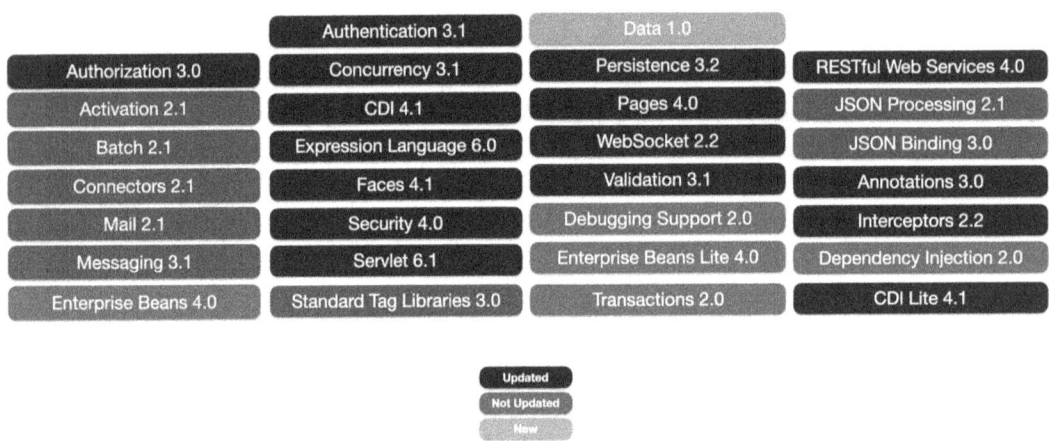

Figure 3-2. *The specifications included in the Jakarta EE Platform (image courtesy of the Eclipse Foundation)*

Web Profile

The Web Profile defines a subset of the Jakarta EE Platform that contains web technologies specifically targeted for developing web applications. The 23 specifications, as shown in Figure 3-3, are included in the Web Profile.

CHAPTER 3 THE JAKARTA EE SPECIFICATIONS

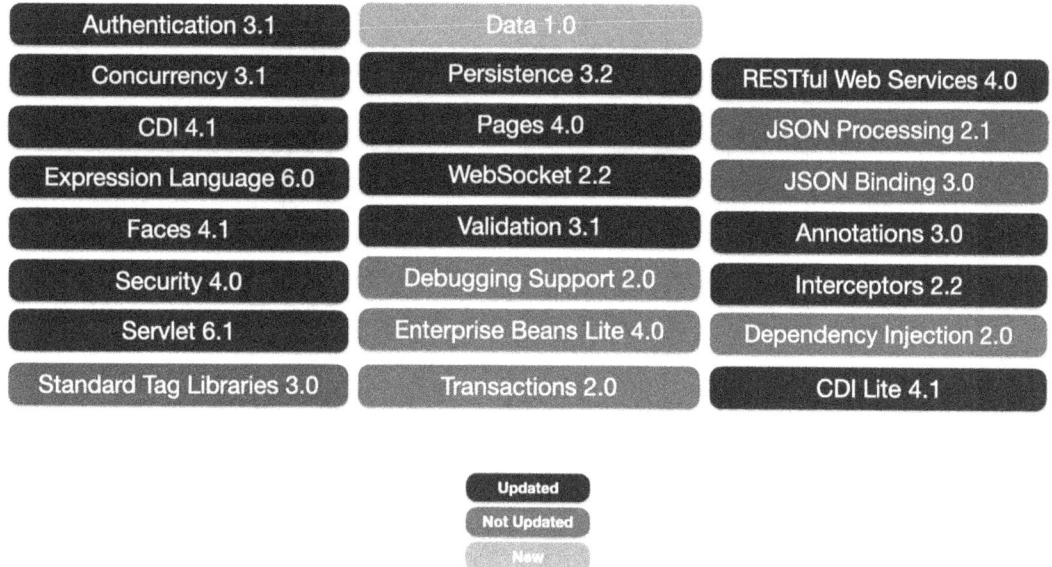

Figure 3-3. The specifications included in the Jakarta EE Web Profile (image courtesy of the Eclipse Foundation)

Core Profile

The new Core Profile, available with the release of Jakarta EE 10, defines a subset of the Jakarta EE Platform specifications focused on providing a minimal basis for cloud-native runtimes, including runtimes that support build time applications.

It contains a set of Jakarta EE specifications targeting smaller runtimes suitable for microservices and ahead-of-time compilation. The eight specifications, as shown in Figure 3-4, are included in the Core Profile.

39

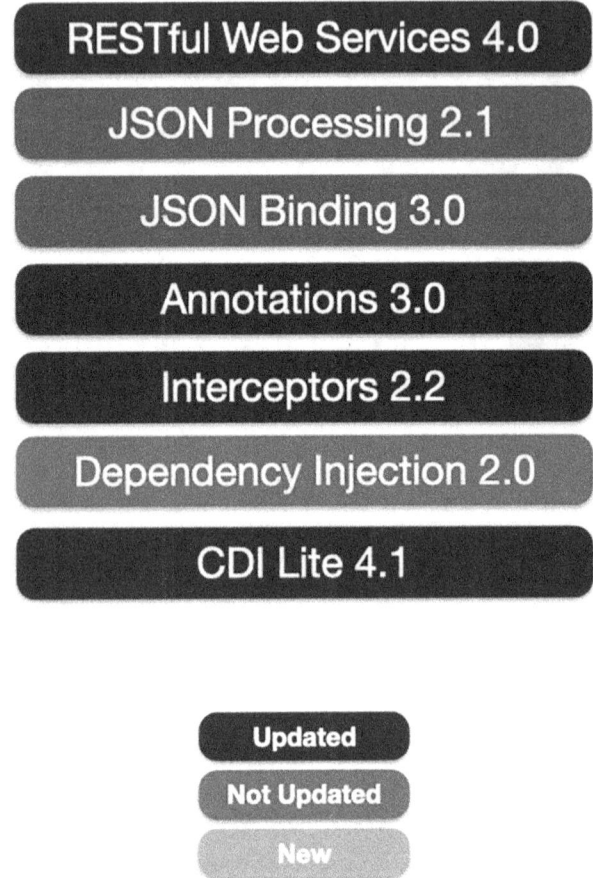

Figure 3-4. The specifications included in the Jakarta EE Core Profile (image courtesy of the Eclipse Foundation)

Jakarta EE Release History

To give you an appreciation on how Jakarta EE has evolved since 2019, what follows next is a brief overview of each release.

Jakarta EE 8

Jakarta EE 8, released on September 10, 2019, was essentially an open source version of Java EE 8. Use of the **javax** namespace was still allowed for this release; however, the Eclipse Foundation was ultimately required to implement a new namespace.

Jakarta EE 9

Jakarta EE 9, released on December 8, 2020, featured the implementation of the new **jakarta** namespace to replace the **javax** namespace. Therefore, developers had to change their imports from **javax.exterprise.context.ApplicationScoped** to the corresponding **jakarta.enterprise.context.ApplicationScoped**.

There was much debate over the process to implement this significant change. There were two approaches: (a) implement the change all at once and (b) implement the change one specification at a time. Option (a), coined "the big bang," was ultimately chosen as the way to proceed.

Tools, such as the Eclipse Transformer (*https://github.com/eclipse/transformer/blob/main/README.md*) project and the Apache Tomcat Migration Tool (*https://github.com/apache/tomcat-jakartaee-migration/blob/main/README.md*), helped developers update the specifications and applications.

Jakarta EE 9.1

Jakarta EE 9.1, released on May 25, 2021, was the first incremental release of Jakarta EE. This is the first incremental point release in which you may now

- Develop and deploy Jakarta EE 9.1 applications on JDK 11 and JDK 8
- Take advantage of Java SE 11 features and new technologies added since Java SE 8
- Move existing Jakarta EE 9 applications to Java SE 11 without changes
- Migrate existing Java EE and Jakarta EE 8 applications to Jakarta EE 9.1 using the same straightforward process available for migration to Jakarta EE 9

Jakarta EE 10

Jakarta EE 10, released on September 22, 2022, delivered a set of 20 updated specifications and a new Core profile that defined a subset of the Jakarta EE specifications focused toward microservices development, smaller runtimes, and ahead-of-time (AOT) compilation.

CHAPTER 3   THE JAKARTA EE SPECIFICATIONS

Jakarta EE 11

Jakarta EE 11, scheduled to be released in 3Q2024, will be the fourth major and fifth overall and latest release of Jakarta EE by the Jakarta EE Working Group since Oracle donated Java EE to the Eclipse Foundation in 2017. This release will deliver 16 updated specifications for building modernized, simplified, and lightweight cloud-native Java applications across the spectrum of Jakarta EE technologies.

Meet the Updated Jakarta EE Specifications

There are 42 Jakarta EE specifications, but only 30 of them are part of the Jakarta EE Platform. Some specifications haven't been updated since Jakarta EE 8. The remainder of this chapter is dedicated to providing you with a brief introduction to the 16 updated specifications that have passed their ballots for Jakarta EE 11.

Jakarta Annotations

The **Jakarta Annotations** specification (*https://jakarta.ee/specifications/annotations/*), currently at version 3.0, defines a collection of annotations representing common semantic concepts that enable a declarative style of programming that applies across a variety of Java technologies.

The compatible implementation for this specification is **Eclipse GlassFish 8.0.0-M3**.

Jakarta Authentication

The **Jakarta Authentication** specification (*https://jakarta.ee/specifications/authentication/*), currently at version 3.1, defines a general low-level SPI for authentication modules, which are controllers that interact with a caller and the environment of a container to acquire the caller's credentials, validate them, and pass an authenticated identity to the container.

The compatible implementations for this specification are **Eclipse Epicyro 3.1.0** and **Eclipse GlassFish 8.0.0-M6**.

Jakarta Authorization

The **Jakarta Authorization** specification (`https://jakarta.ee/specifications/authorization/`), currently at version 3.0, defines a low-level SPI for authorization modules, which are repositories of permissions facilitating subject-based security by determining whether a given subject has a defined permission, and algorithms to transform security constraints for specific containers (such as Jakarta Servlet or Jakarta Enterprise Beans) into these permissions. The compatible implementations for this specification are **Eclipse Exousia 3.0.0-M3** and **Eclipse GlassFish 8.0.0-M5**.

Jakarta Concurrency

The **Jakarta Concurrency** specification (`https://jakarta.ee/specifications/concurrency/`), currently at version 3.1, provides a mechanism for using concurrency from application components without compromising container integrity while still preserving the fundamental benefits of the Jakarta EE Platform.

The compatible implementation for this specification is **Open Liberty 22.0.0.6-beta**.

Jakarta Contexts and Dependency Injection

The **Jakarta Contexts and Dependency Injection** specification (`https://jakarta.ee/specifications/cdi/4.1/`), currently at version 4.1, specifies a means for obtaining objects in such a way to maximize reusability, testability, and maintainability as compared to traditional approaches such as constructors, factories, and service locators like the Java Naming and Directory Interface (JNDI).

The compatible implementation for this specification is **Weld 6.0.0.Beta1**.

Jakarta Data

The **Jakarta Data** specification (`https://jakarta.ee/specifications/data/`), at version 1.0, provides an API that allows easy access to database technologies. A Java developer can split the persistence from the model with several features, such as the ability to compose custom query methods on a **Repository** interface where the framework will implement it.

The compatible implementations for this specification are **Hibernate ORM 6.6.0** and **Open Liberty 24.0.0.6**.

Jakarta Expression Language

The **Jakarta Expression Language** specification (*https://jakarta.ee/ specifications/expression-language/6.0/*), currently at version 6.0, defines a simple language to meet the needs of the presentation layer in web applications that features a simple syntax restricted to the evaluation of expressions; variables and nested properties; relational, logical, arithmetic, conditional, and empty operators; and functions implemented as static methods on Java classes.

The compatible implementation for this specification is **Tomcat 11.0.0-M18**.

Jakarta Faces

The **Jakarta Faces** specification (*https://jakarta.ee/specifications/faces/*), formerly known as *Jakarta Server Faces* and currently at version 4.1, defines a Model-View-Controller (MVC) framework for building user interfaces for web applications that include UI components, state management, event handling, input validation, page navigation, and support for internationalization and accessibility.

The compatible implementations for this specification are **Eclipse Mojarra 4.1.0** and **Eclipse GlassFish 8.0.0-M6**.

Jakarta Interceptors

The **Jakarta Interceptors** specification (*https://jakarta.ee/specifications/ interceptors/*), currently at version 2.2, defines a means of interposing on business method invocations and specific events, such as lifecycle and timeout events, that occur on instances of Jakarta EE components and other managed classes.

The compatible implementation for this specification is **Weld 6.0.0.Beta1**.

Jakarta Pages

The **Jakarta Pages** specification (*https://jakarta.ee/specifications/pages/*), formerly known as *Jakarta Server Pages* and currently at version 4.0, defines a template engine for web applications that supports mixing of textual content (including HTML and XML) with custom tags, expression language, and embedded Java code, which is ultimately compiled into a Jakarta Servlet.

The compatible implementation for this specification is **Apache Tomcat 11.0.0-M20**.

Jakarta Persistence

The **Jakarta Persistence** specification (`https://jakarta.ee/specifications/persistence/`), currently at version 3.2, defines a standard for the management of persistence and object/relational mapping in a Java environment.

The compatible implementations for this specification are **EclipseLink 5.0.0-B02** and **Hibernate ORM 7.0.0.Alpha2**.

Jakarta RESTful Web Services

The **Jakarta RESTful Web Services** specification (`https://jakarta.ee/specifications/restful-ws/`), currently at version 4.0, provides a foundational API to develop web services following the Representational State Transfer (REST) architectural pattern.

The compatible implementation for this specification is **Eclipse RESTEasy 7.0.0.Alpha1** and **Eclipse Jersey 4.0.0-M1**.

Jakarta Security

The **Jakarta Security** specification (`https://jakarta.ee/specifications/security/`), currently at version 4.0, defines a standard for creating secure Jakarta EE applications in modern application paradigms.

The compatible implementation for this specification is **Eclipse Soteria 4.0.0** and **Eclipse GlassFish 8.0.0-M6**.

Jakarta Servlet

The **Jakarta Servlet** specification (`https://jakarta.ee/specifications/servlet/`), currently at version 6.1, defines a server-side API for handling HTTP requests and responses.

The compatible implementation for this specification is **Tomcat 11.0.0-M20**.

Jakarta Validation

The **Jakarta Validation** specification (*https://jakarta.ee/specifications/bean-validation/*), formerly known as *Jakarta Bean Validation* and currently at version 3.1, provides an object-level constraint declaration and validation facility as well as a constraint metadata repository and query API. It also offers method and constructor validation facilities to ensure constraints on their parameters and return values.

The compatible implementation for this specification is **Hibernate Validator 8.0.1.Final**.

Jakarta WebSocket

The **Jakarta WebSocket** specification (*https://jakarta.ee/specifications/websocket/*), currently at version 2.2, defines an API for client and server endpoints for the WebSocket protocol as defined by the Internet Engineering Task Force (IETF) RFC6455.

The compatible implementation for this specification is **Eclipse Tyrus 2.2.0-M1** and **Apache Tomcat 11.0.0-M20**.

Summary

In this chapter, you were introduced to Jakarta EE where you learned some background, the history, the three profiles, and all of the specifications.

There are 42 specifications in the Jakarta EE ecosystem, but they are in various stages of development and maintenance.

Java User Groups are encouraged to adopt a specification (or two) by advocating and contributing to Jakarta EE.

PART II

Helidon SE

CHAPTER 4

Creating a Small Working Project with Helidon SE

Helidon SE is a microframework that features three core components required to create a microservice – a web server, configuration, and security – for building microservices-based applications. It is a small, functional style API that is reactive, simple, and transparent in which an application server is not required. A web client that complements the original three components was added as a new feature in Helidon 2.0.

You can easily get started with Project Helidon in three ways: the Quickstarts, the command-line utility, and the Helidon Project Starter. In this chapter, you will learn how to use all three of these.

Prerequisites

Throughout this book, you will be extensively using a terminal window and commands such as **mvn**, **curl**, and **json_pp** to generate, build, and execute the example applications. If you're not familiar with any of these commands, don't worry, you will learn all about them!

Before you do anything, however, let's ensure that you have the minimal versions of the JDK and other build tools:

- JDK 21
- Maven 3.8.0
- Docker 18.09
- Kubernetes 1.16.5

CHAPTER 4   CREATING A SMALL WORKING PROJECT WITH HELIDON SE

> **Note** Details on the use of Docker and Kubernetes are beyond the scope of this book. For more information, please visit the Helidon website.

You can easily check for the versions installed on your computer workstation by executing the commands as shown in Listing 4-1.

Listing 4-1. The commands to check for versions of Java, Maven, Docker, and Kubernetes

```
$ » java -version
openjdk version "21" 2023-09-19
OpenJDK Runtime Environment (build 21+35-2513)
OpenJDK 64-Bit Server VM (build 21+35-2513, mixed mode, sharing)

$ » mvn -version
Apache Maven 3.9.9 (8e8579a9e76f7d015ee5ec7bfcdc97d260186937)
Maven home: /Users/mpredli01/.sdkman/candidates/maven/current
Java version: 21, vendor: Oracle Corporation, runtime: /Library/Java/
JavaVirtualMachines/jdk-21.jdk/Contents/Home
Default locale: en_US, platform encoding: UTF-8
OS name: "mac os x", version: "10.15.7", arch: "x86_64", family: "mac"

$ » docker --version

$ » kubectl version
```

Quickstarts

The Quickstarts for Helidon SE and Helidon MP have been available to the Java community since the initial release of Project Helidon in 2018. As Helidon has evolved, so too have the Quickstarts.

You can initiate a Quickstart example through Maven by using **archetype:generate** and its corresponding attributes. This will download and generate the example that is complete with **/greet** and **/simple-greet** endpoints and displays a default greeting of *"Hello World!".*

So without further ado, let's get started!

CHAPTER 4 CREATING A SMALL WORKING PROJECT WITH HELIDON SE

Generate the Application

In your terminal window, execute the Maven command as shown in Listing 4-2.

Listing 4-2. The Maven command to download and generate the Quickstarts application

```
$ » mvn -U archetype:generate -DinteractiveMode=false \
    -DarchetypeGroupId=io.helidon.archetypes \
    -DarchetypeArtifactId=helidon-quickstart-se \
    -DarchetypeVersion=4.1.0 \
    -DgroupId=io.helidon.examples \
    -DartifactId=helidon-quickstart-se \
    -Dpackage=io.helidon.examples.quickstart.se
```

This will download and create the application in a directory named **helidon-quickstart-se**, using all of the parameters in the command for the directory structure and resulting **pom.xml** file as specified in the Maven command. The directory structure is shown in Listing 4-3.

Listing 4-3. The directory structure generated using the Maven build tool

```
.
├── Dockerfile
├── Dockerfile.jlink
├── Dockerfile.native
├── README.md
├── app.yaml
├── pom.xml
└── src
    ├── main
    │   ├── java
    │   │   └── io
    │   │       └── helidon
    │   │           └── examples
    │   │               └── quickstart
    │   │                   └── se
```

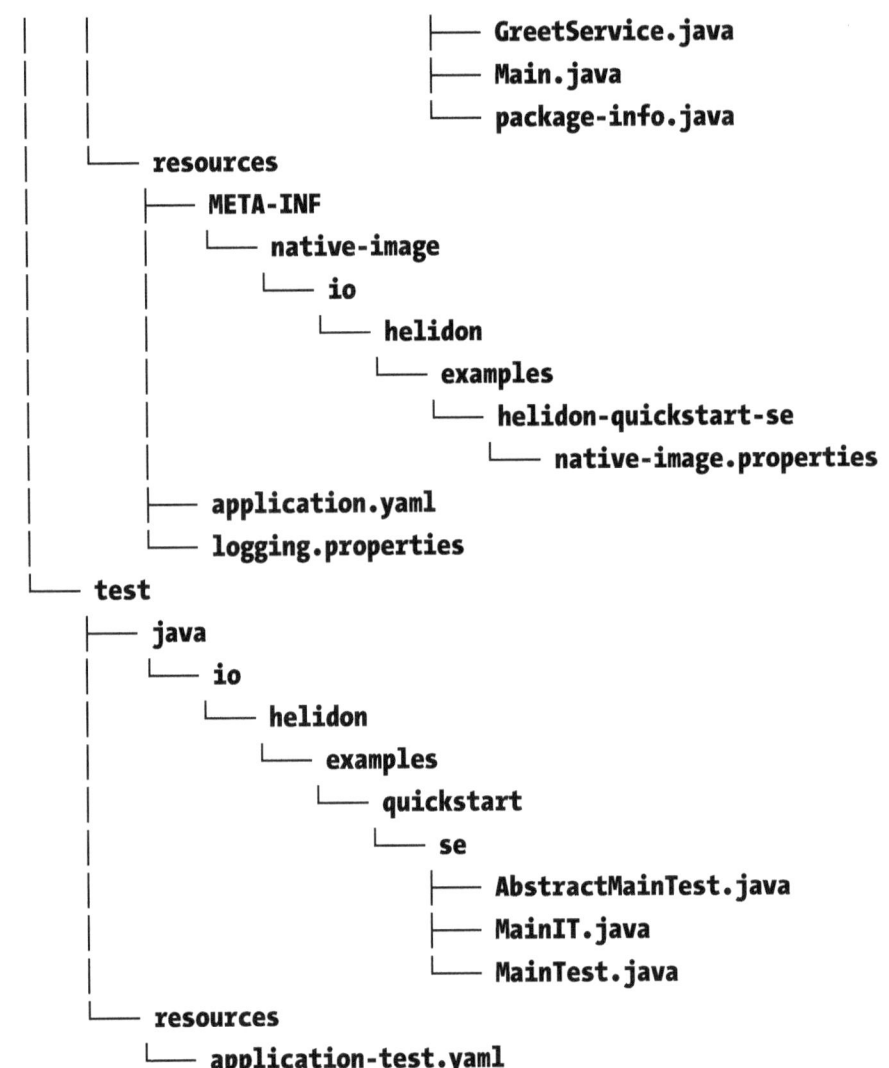

```
                            ├── GreetService.java
                            ├── Main.java
                            └── package-info.java
        └── resources
            ├── META-INF
            │   └── native-image
            │       └── io
            │           └── helidon
            │               └── examples
            │                   └── helidon-quickstart-se
            │                       └── native-image.properties
            ├── application.yaml
            └── logging.properties
    └── test
        ├── java
        │   └── io
        │       └── helidon
        │           └── examples
        │               └── quickstart
        │                   └── se
        │                       ├── AbstractMainTest.java
        │                       ├── MainIT.java
        │                       └── MainTest.java
        └── resources
            └── application-test.yaml
```

`23 directories, 16 files`

Let's break down this directory tree.

First, the **README.md** file contains a wealth of information on how to build and execute the application including details on using Docker and Kubernetes for containerizing and orchestrating, respectively.

Three Docker files – **Dockerfile**, **Dockerfile.jlink** and **Dockerfile.native** – provide all the commands to build and execute the application from Docker. The **Docker.jlink** file uses the **jlink** tool to create a custom Java runtime image, resulting in a smaller and more efficient Docker image. The **Docker.native** file builds a container image that runs a native executable that is commonly used with GraalVM Native Image.

CHAPTER 4   CREATING A SMALL WORKING PROJECT WITH HELIDON SE

The **app.yml** file contains the required configuration for container orchestration with Kubernetes.

The **application.yaml** file, located in the **src/main/resources** folder, contains configuration for the server and the application as shown in Listing 4-4.

Listing 4-4. The contents of the **application.yaml** file used for configuration

```
server:
  port: 8080
  host: 0.0.0.0

app:
   greeting: "Hello"
```

Two Java files - **Main.java** and **GreetService.java** - located in the **src/main/java/io/helidon/examples/quickstart/se** folder, make up the application.

The **Main** class is the entry point into the application that adds configuration and routing and then starts the web server.

The **GreetService** class implements the Helidon built-in **HttpService** interface and defines all the methods for handling the default and custom greetings. As you will see when you exercise the application, you can change the default greeting and add a name after the **/greet** endpoint. This class also reads the specification configuration under the **app** section of the **application.yaml** file.

You will learn more details about the Helidon WebServer component in Chapter 5.

Build the Application

Now, change directory to **helidon-quickstart-se** where the application resides and execute the Maven command as shown in Listing 4-5.

Listing 4-5. The commands to change directory into the root of the application and build the application

```
~ » cd helidon-quickstart-se
helidon-quickstart-se » mvn clean package
```

> **Note** On this initial build, you don't have to include the **clean** parameter, but this is a good practice to ensure a fresh application is built.

Upon successful compilation, a JAR file named **helidon-quickstart-se.jar** is generated, and from here, you can initiate the application via the command line or the browser.

Initiate the Application

In your terminal window, execute the **java** command to initiate the application as shown in Listing 4-6 along with the resulting response.

Listing 4-6. Initiating the application and the resulting output

```
$ helidon-quickstart-se » java -jar target/helidon-quickstart-se.jar
2024.08.27 19:03:46.625 Logging at runtime configured using classpath:
/logging.properties
2024.08.27 19:03:47.458 Helidon SE 4.1.0 features: [Config, Encoding,
Health, Media, Metrics, Observe, WebServer]
2024.08.27 19:03:47.485 [0x04e2fa50] http://0.0.0.0:8080 bound for socket
'@default'
2024.08.27 19:03:47.497 Started all channels in 44 milliseconds. 1164
milliseconds since JVM startup. Java 21+35-2513
WEB server is up! http://localhost:8080/simple-greet
```

Notice the last line in which the application provides the URL that you will use to exercise the application.

The Client URL and JSON Pretty Printer Utilities

The **curl** command, a portmanteau for Client URL, is a popular built-in command-line tool in the UNIX/Linux environments that enables data transfer over various network protocols. It communicates with a web or application server by specifying a relevant URL and the data that need to be sent or received.

Note The **curl** command is highly configurable with many options. Therefore, the most basic use of **curl** will be demonstrated throughout this book.

The **json_pp** command, an acronym for JSON Pretty Printer (*https://github.com/deftek/json_pp/blob/master/README.md*), prints JSON data in legible, indented format in the terminal window.

Exercise the Application via the Command Line

First, you will need to open a new terminal window since the first one is occupied running the server.

Let's start with the **/simple-greet** endpoint. The application defined this endpoint to be simple, unconfigurable, with a response that doesn't support JSON.

As shown in Listing 4-7, you can execute the **curl** command, and you should see the resulting response.

Listing 4-7. Executing the **curl** command with the **/simple-greet** endpoint and corresponding response

```
~ » curl http://localhost:8080/simple-greet

Hello World!
```

Now, let's use the **/greet** endpoint that has many options.

As shown in Listing 4-8, you can execute the **curl** and **json_pp** command, and you should see the resulting response in JSON format.

Listing 4-8. Executing the **curl** command with the **/greet** endpoint and corresponding response

```
~ » curl -s http://localhost:8080/greet/ | json_pp
{
   "message" : "Hello World!"
}
```

The application was built to accept a named parameter after the **/greet** endpoint. This allows you to personalize the greeting. The endpoint and its named parameter are in the form of **/greet/{name}**. Let's experiment with this by passing in "*Mike*" as the named parameter as shown in Listing 4-9.

Listing 4-9. Executing the **curl** command with the **/greet/Mike** endpoint and resulting response

```
~ » curl -s http://localhost:8080/greet/Mike | json_pp
{
   "message" : "Hello Mike!"
}
```

But wait, there is more! You can change the salutation from "*Hello*" to "*Guten Tag*" by executing a more complex version of the **curl** command as shown in Listing 4-10.

Listing 4-10. Executing a more complex curl command to change the greeting from "Hello" to "Guten Tag"

```
~ » curl -X PUT -H "Content-Type: application/json" -d '{"greeting" : "Guten Tag"}' http://localhost:8080/greet/greeting
```

Note that there is no response when you execute this command.
Now let's use "*Dieter*" as the named parameter as shown in Listing 4-11.

Listing 4-11. Executing the curl command with the **/greet/Dieter** endpoint and resulting response

```
~ » curl -s GET http://localhost:8080/greet/Dieter | json_pp
{
   "message" : "Guten Tag Dieter!"
}
```

Exercise the Application via the Browser

If you would prefer not to type all of those commands on the command line, you can simply use the browser! To exercise the application in the browser, simply add the URL in the address bar as shown in Listing 4-12.

Listing 4-12. Executing the application in the browser

`http://localhost:8080/greet/Dieter`

The resulting JSON response may be formatted differently depending on whether you have a JSON parser utility installed on your browser.

Server Shutdown

To shut down the server, return to your first terminal window and simply use **CTRL-C** and you will be returned to your command-line prompt.

Command-Line Interface

Introduced in Helidon 2.0, you can create, build, and run Helidon applications via the Helidon Command-Line Interface (CLI) tool. A separate download and installation is required to use the CLI tool.

Installation

You can install the Helidon CLI from the usual operating system environments.

In macOS, you can use the **curl** command, as shown in Listing 4-13, to install the Helidon CLI utility, set the appropriate permissions, and move the executable to the **/usr/local/bin** directory.

Listing 4-13. Install the Helidon CLI utility on macOS.

```
~ » curl -L -O https://helidon.io/cli/latest/darwin/helidon
chmod +x ./helidon
sudo mv ./helidon /usr/local/bin/
```

Similarly in Linux, you can use the **curl** command, as shown in Listing 4-14, to install the Helidon CLI utility, set the appropriate permissions, and move the executable to the **/usr/local/bin** directory. Note that the URL is slightly different from that of the macOS installation.

Listing 4-14. Install the Helidon CLI utility on Linux.

```
~ » curl -L -O https://helidon.io/cli/latest/linux/helidon
chmod +x ./helidon
sudo mv ./helidon /usr/local/bin/
```

For those of you using the Windows environment, you can use the PowerShell command, as shown in Listing 4-15, to install the Helidon CLI utility.

Listing 4-15. Install the Helidon CLI utility on Windows.

```
C:> PowerShell -Command Invoke-WebRequest -Uri "https://helidon.io/cli/latest/windows/helidon.exe" -OutFile "C:\Windows\system32\helidon.exe"
```

You will now have a new **helidon** command installed on your computer workstation to generate a Helidon application. Now that you have the CLI installed, let's start using it!

Upon executing the **helidon** command by itself, you will be provided with a simple help screen as shown in Listing 4-16.

Listing 4-16. Executing the **helidon** command

```
~ » helidon

Helidon command line tool

Usage: helidon [OPTIONS] COMMAND

Options

  -D<name>=<value>    Define a system property
  --verbose           Produce verbose output
  --debug             Produce debug output
  --error             Print error stack traces
  --plain             Do not use color or styles in output
  --args-file         Path to a file with arguments for Helidon CLI tool
  --props-file        Path to a properties file with user inputs for
                      Helidon CLI tool

Commands
  build               Build the application
  dev                 Continuous application development
```

CHAPTER 4 CREATING A SMALL WORKING PROJECT WITH HELIDON SE

```
info               Print project information
init               Generate a new project
version            Print version information
```
Run helidon COMMAND --help for more information on a command.

Now let's explore the **init** option to generate a Helidon application. As you will see, this is configurable for your application needs, and there are options that weren't available in the Quickstarts. For now, let's just invoke the default values.

In Listing 4-17, you are presented with the latest versions in the Helidon 4.0, Helidon 3.0, and Helidon 2.0 release trains.

Listing 4-17. The list of available Helidon versions

```
/usr/local/apps/helidon-apps » helidon init
Looking up default Helidon version
Helidon versions
   (1) 4.1.0
   (2) 3.2.8
   (3) 2.6.7
   (4) Show all versions
Enter selection (default: 1):
```

In Listing 4-18, you have a choice to generate a Helidon SE or Helidon MP application. In the Quickstarts section, you generated a Helidon SE application using the appropriate Maven command. Generating the Helidon MP equivalent is essentially the same, but you will learn more about that in more detail in Chapter 10.

Listing 4-18. The list of available Helidon flavors

```
Helidon version: 4.1.0

| Helidon Flavor

Select a Flavor
   (1) se | Helidon SE
   (2) mp | Helidon MP
Enter selection (default: 1):
```

As you will see in Listing 4-19, here is where things look different from the Quickstarts. As you can see, a Quickstart example is still an available option, but you can also generate Database and Custom applications. Let's continue to focus on building Quickstart for now and discuss the Database and Custom examples when you learn about the Helidon components.

Listing 4-19. The list of available application types

```
| Application Type

Select an Application Type
  (1) quickstart | Quickstart
  (2) database   | Database
  (3) custom     | Custom
Enter selection (default: 1):
```

Now select your preferred media support type as shown in Listing 4-20. The default is the Jakarta JSON Processing library, also known as JSON-P.

Listing 4-20. The list of available media types

```
| Media Support

Select a JSON library
  (1) jsonp   | JSON-P
  (2) jackson | Jackson
  (3) jsonb   | JSON-B
Enter selection (default: 1):
```

And, finally, you can customize your project with your preferred **groupId**, **artifactId**, version number, and package name as shown in Listing 4-21.

Listing 4-21. The list of custom options for your Helidon project

```
| Customize Project

Project groupId (default: me.mpredli01-helidon):
Project artifactId (default: quickstart-se):
Project version (default: 1.0-SNAPSHOT):
```

CHAPTER 4   CREATING A SMALL WORKING PROJECT WITH HELIDON SE

Java package name (default: me.mpredli01.se.quickstart):

Switch directory to /usr/local/apps/helidon-apps/quickstart-se to use CLI

Start development loop? (default: n):

You can provide your own **groupId**, **artifactId**, **version**, and **package name** if you'd like. For example, I normally use **org.redlich** as the **groupId** and the name of the project as the **artifactId**. Let's continue to use the default values.

Start development loop? (default: n):

The development loop is similar to the hot reloading provided by Quarkus (**quarkus:dev**). This monitors your source files for changes and automatically triggers a restart of the application.

When you choose the default value of **n**, the example application will be downloaded and generated in the same manner as the Quickstarts and you will be returned to the command prompt. Otherwise, you will do the same, but then automatically build and execute the application for you.

Listing 4-22 displays the resulting directory structure. Other than some of the directory names, this looks familiar, right?

Listing 4-22. The resulting directory structure after executing the **helidon init** command

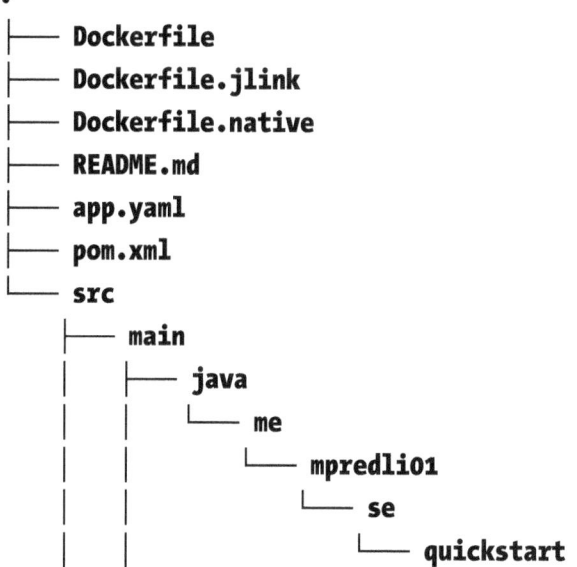

CHAPTER 4 CREATING A SMALL WORKING PROJECT WITH HELIDON SE

```
|       |                               ├── GreetService.java
|       |                               ├── Main.java
|       |                               └── package-info.java
|       └── resources
|           ├── META-INF
|           │   └── native-image
|           │       └── me
|           │           └── mpredli01-helidon
|           │               └── quickstart-se
|           │                   └── native-image.properties
|           ├── application.yaml
|           └── logging.properties
└── test
    ├── java
    │   └── me
    │       └── mpredli01
    │           └── se
    │               └── quickstart
    │                   ├── AbstractMainTest.java
    │                   ├── MainIT.java
    │                   └── MainTest.java
    └── resources
        └── application-test.yaml

20 directories, 16 files
```

Now, let's build the application using the **build** option as shown in Listing 4-23. But first, you should change the directory to where the application resides, that is, the **quickstart-se** directory.

Listing 4-23. Executing the **helidon build** command

```
/usr/local/apps/helidon-apps » cd quickstart-se
/usr/local/apps/helidon-apps/quickstart-se » helidon build
```

At this point, you can exercise the application in the same manner as with the Quickstarts.

CHAPTER 4   CREATING A SMALL WORKING PROJECT WITH HELIDON SE

Now that you have completed exploring the Helidon CLI, let's make our way over to the Helidon Project Starter.

Project Starter

Introduced in Helidon 3.0, Project Starter (*https://helidon.io/starter/*) is a web-based application for generating Helidon applications. This is essentially an online GUI version of the Helidon CLI.

Let's go through each of the sections and, once again, select the default values as shown in Figure 4-1 through Figure 4-4.

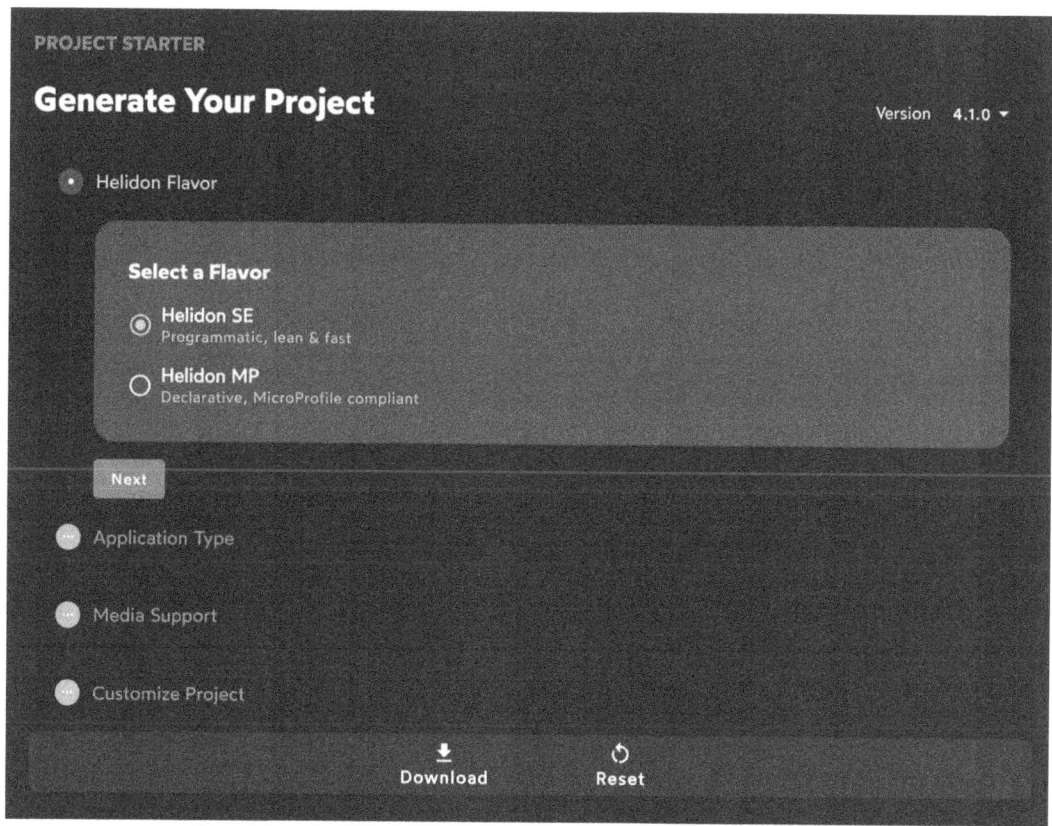

Figure 4-1. *The Helidon flavor section of the Helidon Starter page*

Click "*Next*".

CHAPTER 4 CREATING A SMALL WORKING PROJECT WITH HELIDON SE

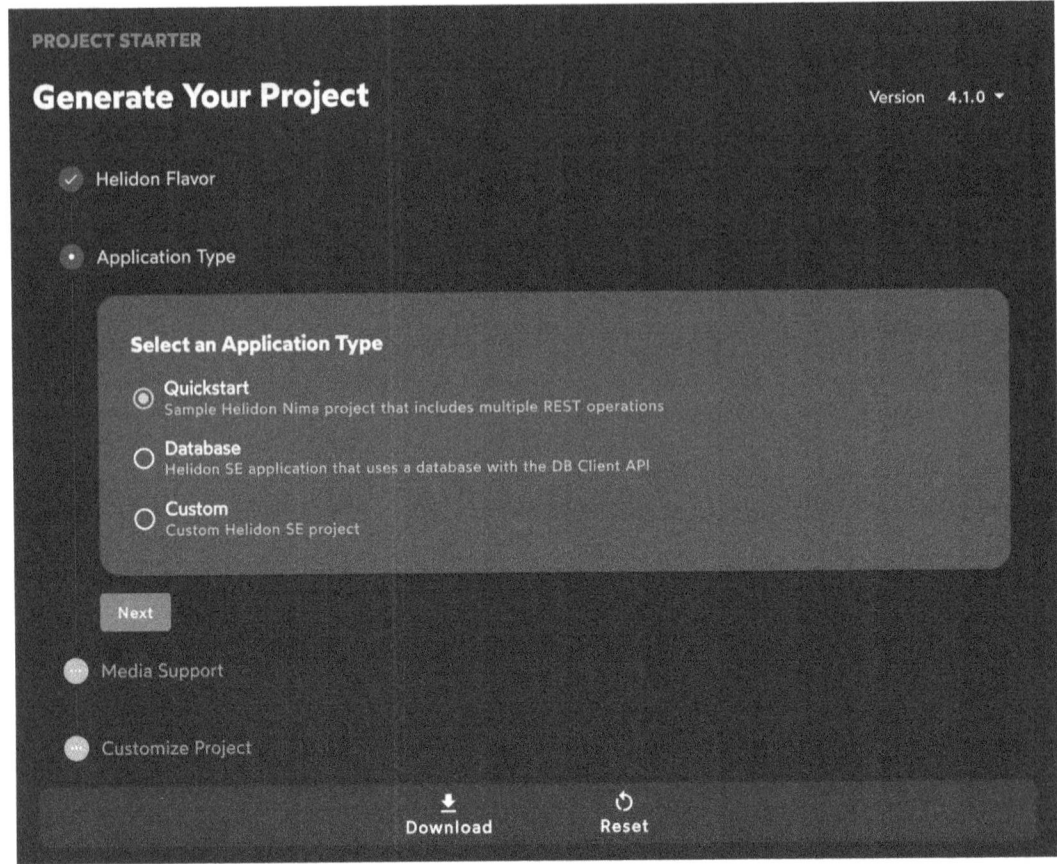

Figure 4-2. *The application type section of the Helidon Starter page*

Click "*Next*".

CHAPTER 4 CREATING A SMALL WORKING PROJECT WITH HELIDON SE

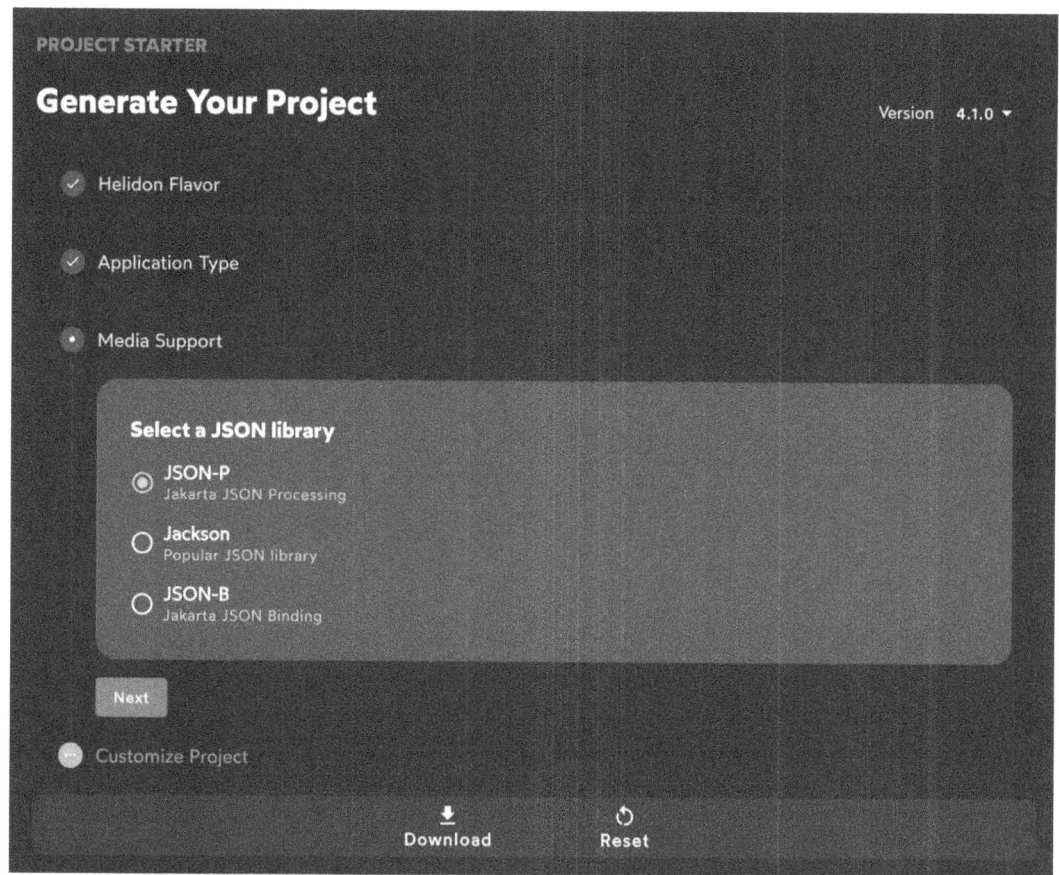

Figure 4-3. *The media support section of the Helidon Starter page.*

Click "*Next*".

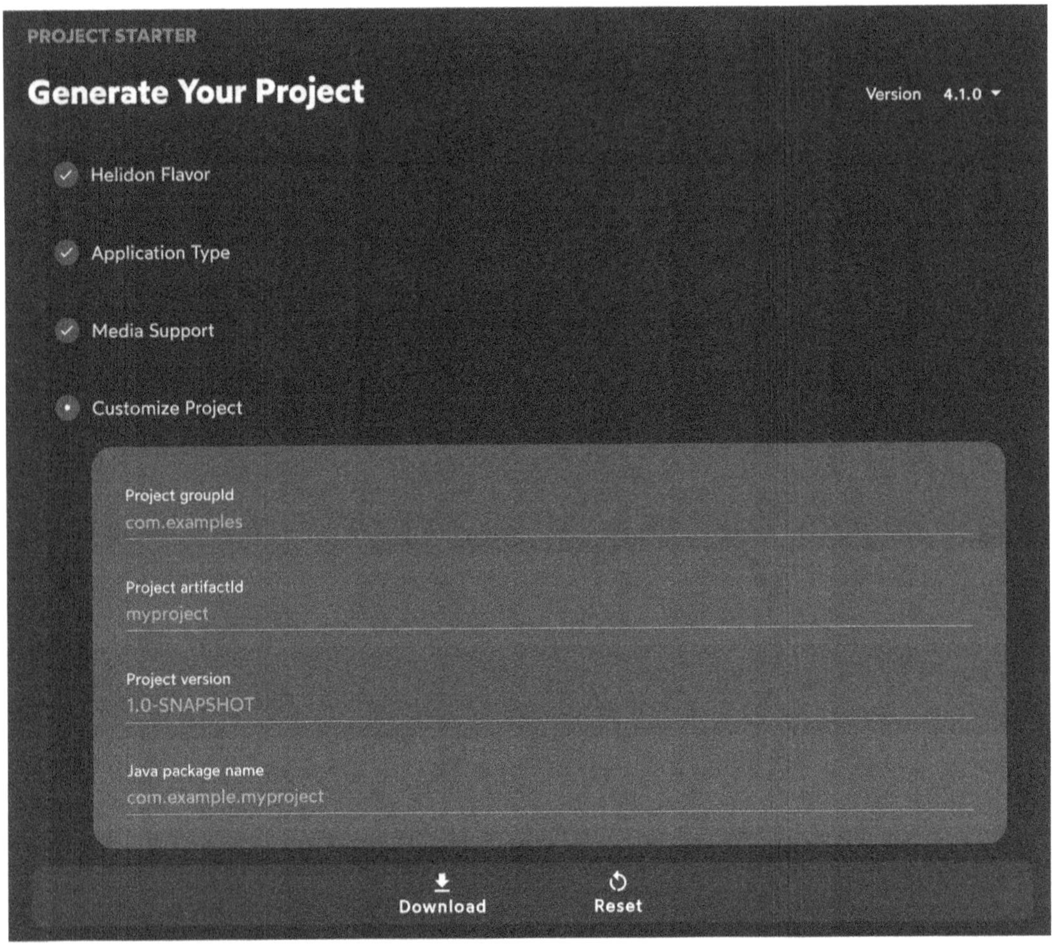

CHAPTER 4 CREATING A SMALL WORKING PROJECT WITH HELIDON SE

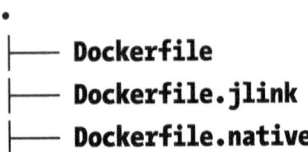

Figure 4-4. The customize project section of the Helidon Starter page

You can now click the "Download" button. You will be provided with a **myproject.zip** file in your default downloads directory. Once you extract the ZIP file, a **myproject** folder will be created and you will see the resulting directory structure as shown in Listing 4-24.

Listing 4-24. The resulting directory structure from unzipping the **myproject.zip** file

```
.
├── Dockerfile
├── Dockerfile.jlink
├── Dockerfile.native
```

CHAPTER 4 CREATING A SMALL WORKING PROJECT WITH HELIDON SE

```
├── README.md
├── app.yaml
├── pom.xml
└── src
    ├── main
    │   ├── java
    │   │   └── com
    │   │       └── example
    │   │           └── myproject
    │   │               ├── GreetService.java
    │   │               ├── Main.java
    │   │               └── package-info.java
    │   └── resources
    │       ├── META-INF
    │       │   └── native-image
    │       │       └── com
    │       │           └── examples
    │       │               └── myproject
    │       │                   └── native-image.properties
    │       ├── application.yaml
    │       └── logging.properties
    └── test
        ├── java
        │   └── com
        │       └── example
        │           └── myproject
        │               ├── AbstractMainTest.java
        │               ├── MainIT.java
        │               └── MainTest.java
        └── resources
            └── application-test.yaml

18 directories, 16 files
```

This, too, looks familiar, right? As with the Quickstarts, you can build the application with Maven and initiate the project using the **java** command as shown in Listing 4-25.

67

Listing 4-25. Initiate and execute the application.

```
myproject » mvn clean package
myproject » java -jar target/myproject.jar
```

Summary

In this chapter, you learned how to get started with Helidon SE by working with a small example that can be generated with your choice of Quickstarts, the Helidon CLI, or Helidon Project Starter.

The next five chapters in Part II will cover Helidon SE components: WebServer, WebClient, Config, DBClient, and Security.

CHAPTER 5

Helidon WebServer

Inspired by Node.js and other Java frameworks, the original Helidon WebServer component was an asynchronous and reactive API that ran on top of Netty, an asynchronous event-driven network application framework. With the release of Helidon 4.0 in October 2023, the WebServer component was rebuilt from the ground up and is now based on virtual threads. In this chapter, you will learn about the Helidon 4.0 WebServer component.

> **Note** Oracle still maintains the Helidon 2.0 and 3.0 release trains. As such, details on the original reactive WebServer component may be found in Appendix C.

As you can imagine, the Helidon WebServer component is the cornerstone to Helidon applications because you will always need to spin up an instance of a web server for any Helidon SE application and its related testing.

WebServer Component

The WebServer component represents an immutably configured web server. The **WebServer** interface is at the heart of this component and provides basic server lifecycle and monitoring enhanced by configuration, routing, error handling, and building metrics and health endpoints.

Signature

The WebServer interface has the following signature as shown in Listing 5-1.

Listing 5-1. The **WebServer** interface signature

```
public interface WebServer extends RuntimeType.Api<WebServerConfig>
```

Let's break down the classes and interfaces from which the **WebServer** interface extends as this is much different from the heritage asynchronous and reactive **WebServer** interface.

- The **RuntimeType** class holds all runtime types that are configured from prototypes.
- The **Prototype** class holds all types related to generating prototypes from a blueprint.
- The **Prototype.Api** interface is a marker for the Prototype API that serves as a parent interface to the **WebServer** and **WebClient** interfaces, among others.
- The **RuntimeType.Api<T extends Prototype.Api>** interface is created from a specific prototype. In this case, as shown in Listing 5-1, the prototype is an instance of the **WebServerConfig** interface.

Create Method

The **WebServer** interface defines two overloaded **create()** methods to build a web server handling configuration and routing information that return a static instance of the **WebServer** interface as shown in Listing 5-2.

Listing 5-2. The overloaded **create()** methods

- **create(WebServerConfig serverConfig)** creates a new web server from its configuration.
- **create(Consumer<WebServerConfig.Builder> builderConsumer)** creates a new web server customizing its configuration.

The first **create()** method accepts an instance of the **WebServerConfig** interface, a **WebServer** configuration bean, and has the signature as shown in Listing 5-3.

Listing 5-3. The **WebServerConfig** interface signature

```
public interface WebServerConfig extends Prototype.Api, ListenerConfig
```

The **WebServerConfig** interface and its corresponding **WebServerConfig.Builder** class replace the original **WebServer.Builder** class that was once part of the **WebServer** interface.

The **ListenerConfig** interface provides configuration of a server listener (server socket).

The second **create()** method accepts an instance of **Consumer<WebServerConfig. Builder>**. **Consumer<T>** is a functional interface in Java SE that may be used as the assignment target for a lambda expression or method reference. Type **T** (**WebServerConfig.Builder** in this case) is a generic that represents the type of results supplied by this consumer.

Builder Pattern

The **WebServerConfig.Builder** class, its signature shown in Listing 5-4, provides a convenient way to implement an instance of the **WebServer** interface with multiple server sockets and optional multiple routings. As you progress through this chapter, you will learn how all of this works.

Listing 5-4. The **WebServerConfig.Builder** class signature

```
public static class WebServerConfig.Builder
extends WebServerConfig.BuilderBase<WebServerConfig.Builder,
WebServerConfig> implements Builder<WebServerConfig.Builder, WebServer>
```

Configuration

You can configure the web server directly or through the Helidon Config component. You will learn more about the Config component in Chapter 7, but let's take a sneak peek on how it works here.

Direct Configuration

You can take advantage of a number of methods defined in the **WebServer.Builder** class to directly configure your web server. Consider the example in Listing 5-5.

Listing 5-5. Building the web server using direct configuration

```
WebServer server = WebServer.builder() ❶
        .port(8080) ❷
        .routing(BasicMain::routing) ❸
        .build() ❹
        .start(); ❺
```

> ❶ The **builder()** method creates a fluent API builder of the **WebServer** interface and returns a static instance of **WebServerConfig.Builder** from which the following methods are used in this example.
>
> ❷ The **port(int port)** method configures a server port on which to listen with the server socket. If the port is set to **0**, then any available ephemeral port will be used.
>
> ❸ The **routing()** method returns an instance of **HttpRouting.Builder** for defining custom routes in an application.
>
> ❹ The **build()** method builds an instance of the **WebServer** interface using this configuration by this builder and its parameters.
>
> ❺ And finally, the **start()** method starts the server.

External Configuration

A configuration file may also be used to create your web server. In Helidon, the default configuration file is **application.yaml** located in the **src/main/resources** folder. However, you can use other commonly used file names, such as **application.properties** or **microprofile-config.properties**. A typical server configuration, defined in YAML format, is shown in Listing 5-6.

Listing 5-6. A typical server configuration defined in YAML format

```
server:
  port: 8080
  host: 0.0.0.0
```

Assuming you're using the default **application.yaml** file, you can load the file by creating an instance of the **Config** interface as shown in Listing 5-7.

Listing 5-7. Loading configuration properties from the **application.yaml** file

```
Config config = Config.create();
```

Then, to extract the contents of the **server** section, you can use either the **get(Config.Key key)** or **get(String key)** method. Let's use the second **get()** method as shown in Listing 5-8.

Listing 5-8. Extracting the contents from the **server** section of the YAML file

```
Config greeting = config.get("server");
```

Routing and HttpRouting

The **Routing** and **HttpRouting** interfaces represent composition of HTTP request-response handlers with rules for routing. This allows for request matching criteria to bind requests to a handler that will implement your custom business logic.

Signature

The **Routing** and **HttpRouting** interfaces have the signature as shown in Listings 5-9 and 5-10, respectively.

Listing 5-9. The **Routing** interface signature

```
public interface Routing extends ServerLifecycle
```

Listing 5-10. The **HttpRouting** interface signature

```
public interface HttpRouting extends Routing, Prototype.Api
```

This interface extends the **ServerLifecycle** interface that defines basic server lifecycle operations and declares two methods: **beforeStart()** and **afterStart()**. Routing also has its own builder pattern and declares a method, **route(ConnectionContext, RoutingRequest, RoutingResponse)**, that processes minimal request and response relative to a server connection context.

Builder Pattern

The **Routing.Builder** class builds an instance of the **Routing** interface. Here is a basic example as shown in Listing 5-11.

Listing 5-11. Building an instance of the **Routing** interface

```
static void routing(HttpRouting.Builder routing) {
    routing
            .register("/greet", new GreetService())
            .get("/simple-greet", (request, response) -> response
            .send("Hello World!"));   }
```

The **routing()** method creates a fluent API builder of the **Routing** interface and returns a static instance of **HttpRouting.Builder** from which the following methods are used in this example.

There are three overloaded versions of the **get()** method as shown in Listing 5-12.

Listing 5-12. Building an instance of the **Routing** interface

- **get(Handler... requestHandlers)** routes all **GET** requests to provided handler(s).
- **get(PathMatcher pathMatcher, Handler... requestHandlers)** routes all **GET** requests with the corresponding path via the **PathMatcher** interface to the provided handler(s).
- **get(String pathPattern, Handler... requestHandlers)** routes all **GET** requests with the corresponding path via a **String** to the provided handler(s).

In Listing 5-8, the third **get()** method from Listing 5-12 is being used to define a **/hello** endpoint to print "*Hello World!*".

HttpRouting.Builder also provides corresponding overloaded methods, similar to the **get()** method, for handling other HTTP requests as shown in Table 5-1.

Table 5-1. *List of HTTP requests and corresponding methods*

HTTP Request	Corresponding Routing.Builder Method
GET	.get()
PUT	.put()
POST	.post()
HEAD	.head()
Any request	.any()

Putting It All Together

Now that you've learned how to create and start a web server, let's put it all together and build an application! You can find the full source code and relevant documentation at the **helidon-book** GitHub repository (*https://github.com/mpredli01/helidon-book*) under the **wsvirtual** module. Inspiration for these examples was adapted from the Helidon examples GitHub repository (*https://github.com/helidon-io/helidon-examples/*).

To demonstrate the Helidon WebServer component in action, let's look at the **Application** and **GreetService** classes.

Dependencies

Let's start with Maven and Gradle dependencies that you would use in your application:

> **Note** The examples associated with this book use Maven as a build tool. The Gradle dependency is listed here for completeness and for the possibility of adding Gradle as a build tool in the future.

If Maven is your build tool, use the dependency as shown in Listing 5-13.

CHAPTER 5   HELIDON WEBSERVER

Listing 5-13. *The Maven dependency for the Helidon WebServer component*

```xml
<dependency>
    <groupId>io.helidon.webserver</groupId>
    <artifactId>helidon-webserver</artifactId>
    <version>4.1.0</version>
</dependency>
```

If Gradle is your build tool, use the dependency as shown in Listing 5-14.

Listing 5-14. *The Gradle dependency for the Helidon WebServer component*

```
implementation group: 'io.helidon.webserver', name: 'helidon-webserver', version: '4.1.0'
```

The **Application** class is the entry point into the application as shown in Listing 5-15. Let's take a closer look at what this does.

Listing 5-15. *The **Application** class*

```java
public class Application {

    private Application() {
    }

    public static void main(String[] args) {

        // load logging configuration
        LogConfig.configureRuntime();

        // initialize global config from default configuration
        Config config = Config.create(); ❶
        Config.global(config);

        WebServer server = WebServer.builder() ❷
                .config(config.get("server")) ❸
                .routing(Application::routing) ❹
                .build() ❺
                .start(); ❻

        System.out.println("WEB server is up! http://localhost:" + server
        .port() + "/simple-greet");
```

```
    }
    static void routing(HttpRouting.Builder routing) { ❼
        routing
                .register("/greet", new GreetService()) ❽
                .get("/simple-greet", (req, res) -> res.send("Hello
                World!")); ❾
    }
}
```

❶ The **create()** method, defined in the **Config** interface, loads the default configuration file as defined in the **application.yaml** file.

❷ The **builder()** method, defined in the **WebServer** interface, returns new builder to set up server.

❸ The **config()** method, defined in the **WebServerConfig.BuilderBase** class, returns a config node used to configure this builder or empty if not configured. The return type is **Optional<Config>** for type safety.

❹ The **routing()** method, also defined in the **WebServerConfig.BuilderBase** class, adds custom HTTP routing as defined in the local **routing()** method.

❺ The **build()** method, defined in the **WebServerConfig.Builder** class, builds the instance from this builder. The return type is **WebServer**.

❻ The **start()** method, defined in the **WebServer** interface, starts the server.

❼ The local **routing()** method in the **Application** class that defines the custom routes for this application.

❽ The overloaded **register()** method, defined in the **HttpRouting.Builder** interface, registers a service by defining the endpoint, **/greet**, and creates an instance of the **GreetService** class.

❾ The **get()** method, also defined in the **HttpRouting.Builder** interface, adds a **GET** route by defining the **/simple-greet** endpoint and using a server request and defines the response of *"Hello World!"*.

Let's now examine the **GreetService** class as shown in Listing 5-16.

Listing 5-16. The **GreetService** class

```java
class GreetService implements HttpService {

    private static final JsonBuilderFactory JSON = Json.createBuilder
    Factory(Collections.emptyMap());

    private final AtomicReference<String> greeting = new
    AtomicReference<>(); ❶

    GreetService() {
        this(Config.global().get("app")); ❷
    }

    GreetService(Config appConfig) {
        greeting.set(appConfig.get("greeting").asString().orElse("Ciao"));
    }

    @Override
    public void routing(HttpRules rules) {
        rules
                .get("/", this::getDefaultMessageHandler) ❸
                .get("/{name}", this::getMessageHandler) ❹
                .put("/greeting", this::updateGreetingHandler); ❺
    }

    private void getDefaultMessageHandler(ServerRequest request,
    ServerResponse response) { ❻
        sendResponse(response, "World");
    }

    private void getMessageHandler(ServerRequest request, ServerResponse
    response) { ❼
```

```
        String name = request.path().pathParameters().get("name");
        sendResponse(response, name);
    }

    private void sendResponse(ServerResponse response, String name) {
        String msg = String.format("%s %s!", greeting.get(), name);

        JsonObject returnObject = JSON.createObjectBuilder()
                .add("message", msg)
                .build();
        response.send(returnObject);
    }

    private void updateGreetingFromJson(JsonObject jo, ServerResponse
    response) { ❽

        if (!jo.containsKey("greeting")) {
            JsonObject jsonErrorObject = JSON.createObjectBuilder()
                    .add("error", "No greeting provided")
                    .build();
            response.status(Status.BAD_REQUEST_400)
                    .send(jsonErrorObject);
            return;
        }

        greeting.set(jo.getString("greeting"));
        response.status(Status.NO_CONTENT_204).send();
    }

    private void updateGreetingHandler(ServerRequest request,
    ServerResponse response) {
        updateGreetingFromJson(request.content().as(JsonObject.class),
        response);
    }
}
```

❶ Instantiating the **greeting** variable of type **AtomicReference <String>**, defined in Java SE, used to get and set various greetings.

❷ The **get()** method, defined in the **Config** interface, that obtains the values from the **application.yaml** file. The default constructor that is called from the **register()** method, defined in the **Application** class.

❸ This **get()** method, tied to an HTTP **GET**, defines the **/** endpoint and calls the **getDefaultMessageHandler()** method.

❹ This **get()** method, also tied to an HTTP **GET**, defines the **/{name}** endpoint and calls the **getMessageHandler()** method.

❺ This **put()** method, tied to an HTTP **PUT**, defines that the **/greeting** endpoint should be changed and calls the **updateGreetingHandler()** method.

❻ The **getDefaultMessageHandler()** method that establishes the **/** endpoint.

❼ The **getMessageHandler()** method that establishes the **/{name}** endpoint.

❽ The **updateGreetingHandler()** method that resets the **/greeting** endpoint from the default "*Hello*" to a user-defined greeting, such as "*Buenos Días.*"

Build and Execute the Application

From the command line, you can build and execute the application with Maven as shown in Listing 5-17.

Listing 5-17. Build and execute the application with Maven.

```
~ » mvn clean compile exec:java
```

Notice the **exec:java** at the end of the command line. Normally, the **-Dexec.mainClass=<fully-qualified-class-name>** flag would be required right after the **exec:java**. However, adding the Exec Maven Plugin (*https://www.mojohaus.org/exec-maven-plugin/*) to your **pom.xml** file eliminates the need to add the **-Dexec.mainClass** flag. Simply add the Maven plug-in as shown in Listing 5-18.

Listing 5-18. The Exec Maven Plugin

```xml
<build>
    <plugins>
        <plugin>
            <groupId>org.codehaus.mojo</groupId>
            <artifactId>exec-maven-plugin</artifactId>
            <version>3.4.1</version>
            <configuration>
                <mainClass>${mainClass}</mainClass> ❶
            </configuration>
        </plugin>
    </plugins>
</build>
```

❶ The **${mainClass}** corresponds to the fully qualified class name for this application, namely, **org.redlich.wsvirtual.Application**.

Exercising the Application

First, you will need to open a new terminal window since the first one is occupied running the server.

Let's start with the **/simple-greet** endpoint. The application defined this endpoint to be simple, unconfigurable, with a response that doesn't support JSON.

As shown in Listing 5-19, you can execute the **curl** command, and you should see the resulting response.

Listing 5-19. Executing the **curl** command with the **/simple-greet** endpoint and corresponding response

```
~ » curl http://localhost:8080/simple-greet
Hello World!
```

Now, let's use the **/greet** endpoint that has many options.

As shown in Listing 5-20, you can execute the **curl** and **json_pp** commands, and you should see the resulting response in JSON format.

CHAPTER 5   HELIDON WEBSERVER

Listing 5-20. Executing the **curl** command with the **/greet** endpoint and corresponding response

```
~ » curl -s http://localhost:8080/greet/ | json_pp
{
   "message" : "Hello World!"
}
```

The application was built to accept a named parameter after the **/greet** endpoint. This allows you to personalize the greeting. The endpoint and its named parameter are in the form of **/greet/{name}**. Let's experiment with this by passing in "*Mike*" as the named parameter as shown in Listing 5-21.

Listing 5-21. Executing the **curl** command with the **/greet/Mike** endpoint and resulting response

```
~ » curl -s http://localhost:8080/greet/Mike | json_pp
{
   "message" : "Hello Mike!"
}
```

But wait, there is more! You can change the salutation from "*Hello*" to "*Buenos Días*" by executing a more complex version of the **curl** command as shown in Listing 5-22.

Listing 5-22. Executing a more complex curl command to change the greeting from "Hello" to "Buenos Días"

```
~ » curl -X PUT -H "Content-Type: application/json" -d '{"greeting"
: "Buenos Días"}' http://localhost:8080/greet/greeting
```

Note that there is no response when you execute this command.

Now let's use "*Carlos*" as the named parameter as shown in Listing 5-23.

Listing 5-23. Executing the curl command with the **/greet/Carlos** endpoint and resulting response

```
~ » curl -s GET http://localhost:8080/greet/Carlos | json_pp
{
   "message" : "Buenos Días Carlos!"
}
```

Summary

In this chapter, you were introduced to the WebServer component that includes the **WebServer**, **Routing**, and **Config** interfaces, how to establish routing and configuration, and an examination on how it all fits together in a Helidon application.

In the next chapter, you will learn about the WebClient component that was introduced in Helidon 2.0.

CHAPTER 6

Helidon WebClient

The release of Helidon 2.0 in June 2020 delivered a host of new significant features such as support for reactive messaging and streams; a new command-line tool, GraalVM support for Helidon MP, a new reactive database client; and a new HTTP client, WebClient, for Helidon SE.

To complement the original three core Helidon SE component APIs – WebServer, Config, and Security – the new WebClient API completed the set for Helidon SE. WebClient processes HTTP requests and responses related to a specified endpoint.

WebClient Component

The WebClient component represents an HTTP client for Helidon SE. Just like the WebServer component, WebClient was originally designed to be reactive so it didn't have to wait for a response from asynchronous and reactive WebServer that is available in the Helidon 2.0 and 3.0 release trains. With the release of Helidon 4.0 in October 2023, the Helidon WebClient component now uses a blocking approach to synchronously process requests.

Other features include: a builder pattern to create an instance of WebClient; and a redirect chain that performs requests on the correct endpoint and provides automatic metrics, tracing, and security to your application.

Signature

The `WebClient` interface has the signature as shown in Listing 6-1.

Listing 6-1. The `WebClient` interface signature

```
public interface WebClient extends RuntimeType.Api<WebClientConfig>,
HttpClient<HttpClientRequest>
```

Let's break down the classes and interfaces from which the **WebClient** interface extends as this is much different from the heritage asynchronous and reactive **WebClient** interface.

- The **RuntimeType** class holds all runtime types that are configured from prototypes.
- The **Prototype** class holds all types related to generating prototypes from a blueprint.
- The **Prototype.Api** interface is a marker for the Prototype API that serves as a parent interface to the **WebServer** and **WebClient** interfaces, among others.
- The **RuntimeType.Api<T extends Prototype.Api>** interface is created from a specific prototype. In this case, as shown in Listing 5-1, the prototype is an instance of the **WebClientConfig** interface.

Create Method

There are three defined overloaded **create()** methods for defining configuration and routing information that return a static instance of the **WebClient** interface as shown in Listing 6-2.

Listing 6-2. The overloaded **get()** methods

- **create()** creates a new default instance of the **WebClient** interface.
- **create(WebClientConfig config)** creates a new instance from the provided configuration.
- **create(Consumer<WebClientConfig.Builder> consumer)** creates a new instance of **WebClient**, customizing its configuration.

Consumer<T> is a functional interface in Java SE that may be used as the assignment target for a lambda expression or method reference. Type **T** is a generic that represents the type of results supplied by this consumer.

Builder Pattern

The **WebClient.Builder** class provides a convenient way to implement an instance of the **WebClient** interface. As you progress through this chapter, you will learn how all of this works.

Configuration

Similar to the WebServer component, you can configure the web client directly or through the Helidon Config component. You will learn more details about the Helidon Config component in Chapter 7, but you'll get a sneak peek on how it works here.

Direct Configuration

You can take advantage of a number of methods defined in the **WebServer.Builder** class to directly configure your web server. Consider the example as shown in Listing 6-3.

Listing 6-3. Building the web client using direct configuration

```
WebClientService clientService = WebClientMetrics.counter()
        .methods(Method.GET)
        .nameFormat("example.metric.%1$s.%2$s")
        .build();

WebClient client = WebClient.builder() ❶
        .baseUri("http://localhost") ❷
        .config(config) ❸
        .addService(clientService) ❹
        .build(); ❺
```

> ❶ The **builder()** method creates a fluent API builder of the **WebClient** interface and returns a static instance of **WebClient.Builder** from which the following methods are used in this example.
>
> ❷ The **baseUri()** method establishes a base URI for each request.

❸ The **config()** method adds defined configuration for the web client.

Then finally, the **build()** method builds an instance of the **WebClient** interface using this configuration by this builder and its parameters.

❹ The **addService()** method adds the **clientService** variable.

❺ And finally, the **build()** method builds an instance of the **WebClient** interface using this configuration by this builder and its parameters.

External Configuration

A configuration file may also be used to create your web server. In Helidon, the default configuration file is **application.yaml** located in the **src/main/resources** folder. However, you can use other commonly used file names, such as **application. properties** or **microprofile-config.properties**. A typical client configuration, defined in YAML format, is shown in Listing 6-4.

Listing 6-4. A typical **application.yaml** file

```
client:
  connect-timeout-millis: 2080
  read-timeout-millis: 2000
  follow-redirects: true
  max-redirects: 5
  cookies:
    automatic-store-enabled: true
    default-cookies:
name: "env"
value: "dev"
  headers:
name: "Accept"
value: ["application/json","text/plain"]
  services:
    config:
```

```
    metrics:
methods: ["PUT","POST","DELETE"]
Type: METER
```

As you can see, there are many more configuration options with the WebClient client vs. the WebServer component. Assuming you're using the default **application.yaml** file, you can load the file by creating an instance of the **Config** interface as shown in Listing 6-5.

Listing 6-5. Loading configuration properties from the **application.yaml** file

```
Config config = Config.create();
```

Then, to extract the contents of the **config** section, you can use either the **get(Config.Key key)** or **get(String key)** method. In our case, let's use the second one as shown in Listing 6-6.

Listing 6-6. Extracting the contents from the **client** section of the YAML file

```
Config greeting = config.get("client");
```

Putting It All Together

Now that you've learned how to create and start a web client, let's put it all together and build an application! You can find the full source code and relevant documentation at the **helidon-book** GitHub repository (*https://github.com/mpredli01/helidon-book*) under the **webclient** module. Inspiration for these examples was adapted from the Helidon examples GitHub repository (*https://github.com/helidon-io/helidon-examples/*).

To demonstrate the Helidon WebClient component in action, let's take a look at a small working example that has one service to start the web server and a second service to execute the client. The application consists of three main classes: **ServerApplication**, **ClientApplication**, and **SimpleGreetService**. The **GreetService** class defines endpoints, **/greeting** and **greeting/{name}**, that you already know from the Quickstart examples. So, that leaves the other two classes as the main focus of this example application.

Note The application generates a random server port so that there is no clash with port 8080. This is accomplished by setting the **port** property in the **application.yaml** file to **-1**.

Dependencies

Let's start with Maven and Gradle dependencies that you would use in your application.

Note The examples associated with this book use Maven as a build tool. The Gradle dependency is listed here for completeness and for the possibility of adding Gradle as a build tool in the future.

If Maven is your build tool, use the dependency as shown in Listing 6-7.

Listing 6-7. The Maven dependency for the Helidon WebClient component

```xml
<dependency>
    <groupId>io.helidon.webclient</groupId>
    <artifactId>helidon-webclient</artifactId>
    <version>4.1.0</version>
</dependency>
```

If Gradle is your build tool, use the dependency as shown in Listing 6-8.

Listing 6-8. The Gradle dependency for the Helidon WebClient component

```
implementation group: 'io.helidon.webclient', name: 'helidon-webclient',
version: '4.1.0'
```

ServerApplication Class

The **ServerApplication** class, shown in Listing 6-9, configures routing and starts the web server.

Listing 6-9. The **ServerApplication** class

```
public final class ServerApplication {

    private ServerApplication() {
    }

    public static void main(String[] args) {
        Config config = Config.create();   ❶
        Config.global(config);

        WebServerConfig.Builder builder = WebServer.builder();
        setup(builder);
        WebServer server = builder.build().start();
        server.context().register(server);
        System.out.println("WEB server is up! http://localhost:" + server
        .port() + "/greet");
    }

    static void setup(WebServerConfig.Builder server) {   ❷
        Config config = Config.global();
        server.config(config.get("server"))
                .routing(ServerApplication::routing);
    }

    private static void routing(HttpRouting.Builder routing) {   ❸
        routing.register("/greet", new GreetService());
    }
}
```

> ❶ The **create()** method to read the default **application.yaml** file.
>
> ❷ The **setup()** method to establish configuration for the web server and call the **routing()** method.
>
> ❸ The **routing()** method to establish the /greet endpoint and create a new instance of the **GreetService** class.

ClientApplication Class

The **ClientApplication** class, shown in Listing 6-10, establishes a web client and provides all the methods to interact with the web server.

Listing 6-10. The **ClientApplication** class

```java
public class ClientApplication {

    private static final MeterRegistry METER_REGISTRY = Metrics
    .globalRegistry();
    private static final JsonBuilderFactory JSON_BUILDER = Json
    .createBuilderFactory(Map.of());
    private static final JsonObject JSON_NEW_GREETING;

    static {
        JSON_NEW_GREETING = JSON_BUILDER.createObjectBuilder()
                .add("greeting", "Hola")
                .build();
    }

    private ClientApplication() {
    }

    public static void main(String[] args) {
        Config config = Config.create();
        String url;
        if (args.length == 0) {
            ConfigValue<Integer> port = config.get("server.port").asInt();
            if (!port.isPresent() || port.get() == -1) {
                throw new IllegalStateException("Unknown port! Please
                specify port as a main method parameter "
                        + "or directly to config server.port");
            }
            url = "http://localhost:" + port.get() + "/greet";
        }
        else {
            url = "http://localhost:" + Integer.parseInt(args[0]) + "/greet";
        }
```

```
    WebClient client = WebClient.builder()  ❶
            .baseUri(url)
            .config(config.get("client"))
            .build();

    performPutMethod(client);
    performGetMethod(client);
    followRedirects(client);
    getResponseAsAnJsonObject(client);
    saveResponseToFile(client);
    clientMetricsExample(url, config);
}

static Status performPutMethod(WebClient client) {  ❷
    System.out.println("Put request execution.");
    try (HttpClientResponse response = client.put("/greeting")
    .submit(JSON_NEW_GREETING)) {
        System.out.println("PUT request executed with status:
        " + response.status());
        return response.status();
        }
    }

static String performGetMethod(WebClient client) {  ❸
    System.out.println("Get request execution.");
    String result = client.get().requestEntity(String.class);
    System.out.println("GET request successfully executed.");
    System.out.println(result);
    return result;
    }

static String followRedirects(WebClient client) {  ❹
    System.out.println("Following request redirection.");
    try (HttpClientResponse response = client.get("/redirect").
    request()) {
        if (response.status() != Status.OK_200) {
            throw new IllegalStateException("Follow redirection
            failed!");
```

```
            }
        String result = response.as(String.class);
        System.out.println("Redirected request successfully
        followed.");
        System.out.println(result);
        return result;
        }
    }

    static void getResponseAsAnJsonObject(WebClient client) { ❺
        System.out.println("Requesting from JsonObject.");
        JsonObject jsonObject = client.get().requestEntity
        (JsonObject.class);
        System.out.println("JsonObject successfully obtained.");
        System.out.println(jsonObject);
        }

    static void saveResponseToFile(WebClient client) { ❻
        Path file = Paths.get("test.txt");
        try {
            Files.deleteIfExists(file);
            }
        catch (IOException e) {
            e.printStackTrace();
            }

        System.out.println("Downloading server response to file: " + file);
        try (HttpClientResponse response = client.get().request()) {
            Files.copy(response.entity().inputStream(), file);
            System.out.println("Download complete!");
            }
        catch (IOException e) {
            throw new UncheckedIOException(e);
            }
        }

    static String clientMetricsExample(String url, Config config) { ❼
```

```
        String counterName = "example.metric.GET.localhost";
        Counter counter = METER_REGISTRY.getOrCreate(Counter.builder
        (counterName));
        System.out.println(counterName + ": " + counter.count());

        WebClientService clientService = WebClientMetrics.counter()
                .methods(Method.GET)
                .nameFormat("example.metric.%1$s.%2$s")
                .build();

        WebClient client = WebClient.builder()
                .baseUri(url)
                .config(config)
                .addService(clientService)
                .build();

        String result = performGetMethod(client);
        System.out.println(counterName + ": " + counter.count());
        return result;
    }
}
```

- ❶ Using the **builder()** method to create an instance of the WebClient.

- ❷ The **performPutMethod()** method that initiates an HTTP **PUT** for changing the greeting to the **/greeting** endpoint from "*Hello*" to "*Hola*".

- ❸ The **performGetMethod()** method that initiates an HTTP **GET** and calls the **requestEntity()** method defined in the **ClientRequest** class. The response is **{"message":"Hola World!"}**.

- ❹ The **followRedirects()** method that follows the **/redirect** endpoint, defined in the **GreetService** class, and changes the HTTP status to **302**, Permanently Moved. The response is **{"message":"Hello World!"}**.

- ❺ The **getResponseAsAnJsonObject()** method initiates an HTTP **GET** and calls the **requestEntity()** method to request a JSON object. The response is **{"message":"Hola World!"}**.

- ❻ The **saveResponseToFile()** method gets the file named **test.txt**, tests that it can be deleted, copies a client response to the file, and then downloads it.

- ❼ The **clientMetricsExample()** method

  - Establishes a **counterName** variable with the value **example.metric.GET.localhost**
  - Creates a new metric that will count all the **GET** requests with a format of **example.metric.GET.localhost**
  - Registers the new metric to the web client
  - Performs any **GET** requests using this newly created instance of **WebClient**

Build and Execute the Application

From the command line, you can build and package the application as a JAR file with Maven as shown in Listing 6-11.

Listing 6-11. Build and package the application as a JAR file with Maven

```
~ » mvn clean package
```

Now you can invoke the JAR file using the **java** command as shown in Listing 6-12. Note the last part of the response that displays the URL and JVM startup time.

Listing 6-12. Invoke the application with the **java** command

```
~ » java -jar target/webclient.jar
Sep 05, 2024 8:22:30 PM io.helidon.common.features.HelidonFeatures features
INFO: Helidon SE 4.1.0 features: [Config, Encoding, Media, Metrics,
Observe, WebClient, WebServer]
Sep 05, 2024 8:22:30 PM io.helidon.webserver.ServerListener start
```

```
INFO: [0x4d7700c8] http://0.0.0.0:63988 bound for socket '@default'
There is no Helidon logging implementation on classpath, skipping log
configuration.
Sep 05, 2024 8:22:30 PM io.helidon.webserver.LoomServer startIt
INFO: Started all channels in 63 milliseconds. 921 milliseconds since JVM
startup. Java 21+35-2513
WEB server is up! http://localhost:63988/greet
```

Notice that the web server is running on port 63988. The web client will use this port to connect to the server.

Exercising the Application

First, you will need to open a new terminal window since the first one is occupied running the server. Now you can connect to the server using the **java** command as shown in Listing 6-13.

Listing 6-13. The server response upon invoking the client

```
/usr/local/publications/helidon-book/webclient (master*) »
java -cp "target/classes:target/libs/*" org.redlich.webclient.
ClientApplication 63988
Put request execution.
PUT request executed with status: 204 No Content
Get request execution.
GET request successfully executed.
{"message":"Hola World!"}
Following request redirection.
Redirected request successfully followed.
{"message":"Hola World!"}
Requesting from JsonObject.
JsonObject successfully obtained.
{"message":"Hola World!"}
Downloading server response to file: test.txt
Download complete!
example.metric.GET.localhost: 0
Get request execution.
```

```
GET request successfully executed.
{"message":"Hola World!"}
example.metric.GET.localhost: 1
```

Summary

In this chapter, you were introduced to the WebClient component that includes the `WebClient` and `WebClientRequestBuilder` interfaces, how to establish configuration, and an examination on how it all fits together in a Helidon application.

In the next chapter, you will be introduced to the Helidon Config component that is used for configuration for many of the Helidon components.

CHAPTER 7

Helidon Config

Configuration in microservices applications should be based on a runtime environment. Therefore, it is absolutely necessary to modify configuration data from outside the application such that the application itself does not need to be repackaged and redeployed. Helidon SE supports various configuration formats and provides the relevant implementations.

Config Component

The Config component provides a comprehensive and flexible configuration system to load and process configuration data from various sources into a configuration object that may be used in a Helidon application. This is accomplished through the **Config** interface to read configuration properties from a defined properties file in various formats.

These are the main parts of the Helidon configuration system:

- A configuration system that allows you to read configuration data in a Helidon application

  - The **Config** interface is used for this purpose.

- A configuration source containing configuration data such as a file, map, properties, etc.

  - The **ConfigSource** interface is used for this purpose.

- A configuration parser that can transform bytes into configuration data

  - This would include formats such as JSON and YAML.

  - The **ConfigParser** interface is used for this purpose.

CHAPTER 7   HELIDON CONFIG

Figure 7-1 describes the working parts of the Config component.

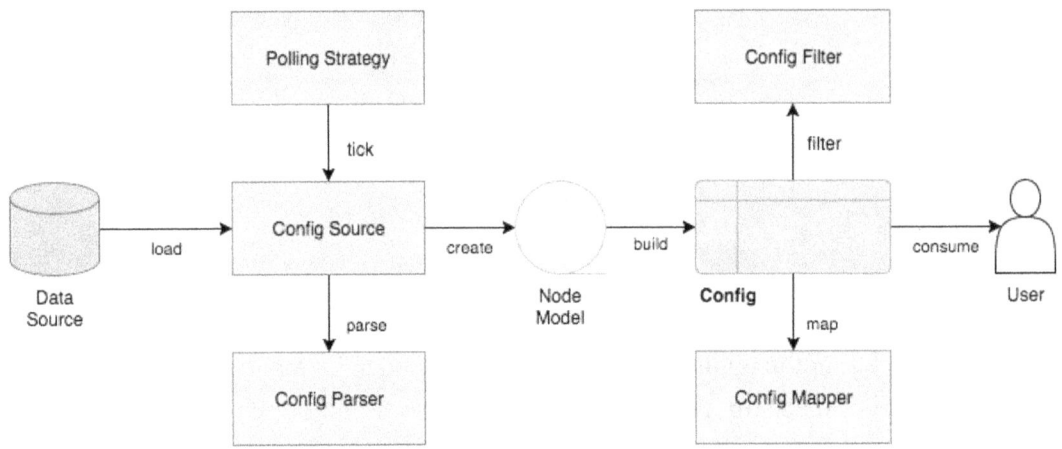

Figure 7-1. *The anatomy of the Config component (image from Helidon Config documentation)*

Signature

The **Config** interface has the signature as shown in Listing 7-1.

Listing 7-1. The **Config** interface signature

public interface Config

This interface is an immutable tree structure that loads and processes configuration properties.

Create Method

You can use the **create()** method to establish configuration for your Helidon application. There are two defined overloaded **create()** methods, as shown in Listing 7-2, that return a static instance of the **Config** interface.

Listing 7-2. The overloaded **create()** methods

- **create()** returns a new default instance of **Config** loaded from configuration files available on the classpath and/or using the runtime environment.

- **create(Supplier<? extends ConfigSource>... configSources)** creates a new instance of **Config** that is loaded from environment variables, system properties, and specified configuration sources.

Builder Pattern

The **Config.Builder** interface provides a convenient way to define various configuration characteristics:

- Sources

    - Sources of configuration that you can implement to support various aspects of a configuration source.

    - The **ConfigSource** interface and **ConfigSources** class are used for this purpose.

- Mappers

    - An ordered list of mapper functions. It is also possible to disable loading of configuration mapping providers as a service.

    - The **ConfigMapper** and **ConfigMapperProvider** interfaces are used for this purpose.

- Parsers

    - An ordered list of configuration content parsers. It is also possible to disable loading of configuration parsers as a service.

    - The **ConfigParser** interface is used for this purpose.

- Filters

    - An ordered list of configuration value filters. It is also possible to disable loading of configuration filters as a service.

    - The **ConfigFilter** interface and **ConfigFilters** class are used for this purpose.

- Overrides

    - Provide an alternate, or overriding, value for a configuration element based on the element's key.

    - The **OverrideSource** interface is used for this purpose.

- Token References

    - Provide the ability to resolve reference tokens.

    - A token is defined as a key starting with **$** and optionally enclosed between curly braces, that is, **$ref** or **${ref}**.

    - A key composed of more than one token can be referenced in another key, that is, **${env.ref}**.

- Caching

    - Provides the ability to disable or enable caching a configuration filter. Caching is enabled by default.

    - With caching disabled, registered filters are always applied, and you can access the elementary configuration values.

    - With caching enabled, registered filters are applied just once per unique configuration node or key.

Configuration Sources

As mentioned earlier, Helidon supports various configuration sources and formats:

- Environment variables

    - A name/value pair

- Java properties

    - a name/value pair

- Resources in the classpath

    - The contents of the resource are parsed according to its inferred format.

- File
  - The contents of the file are parsed according to its inferred format.
- Directory
  - Each non-directory file in the directory becomes a configuration entry.
  - The file name is the key, and the contents of that file are used as the corresponding configuration string value.
- URL resource
  - The contents are parsed according to its inferred format.
- A variety of in-memory data structures
  - Strings, maps, properties, etc.

Signatures

The **ConfigSource** interface provides sources of configuration via the **Source** interface. There is a set of defined interfaces that you may implement to support various aspects of a configuration source. It has the following signature as shown in Listing 7-3.

Listing 7-3. The **ConfigSource** interface signature

```
public interface ConfigSource extends Supplier<ConfigSource>, Source
```

The **ConfigSources** class provides access to built-in implementations of the **ConfigSource** interface. It has the signature as shown in Listing 7-4.

Listing 7-4. The **ConfigSources** class signature

```
public final class ConfigSources extends Object
```

CHAPTER 7 HELIDON CONFIG

Configuration Loading

A defined set of specific interfaces to support various aspects of a configuration source are also available for you to implement. These can be categorized in two groups: eagerness of loading data and mutability of data.

Eagerness of Loading Data

These configuration sources either load all data on demand or separately load each key. The former is the preferred method for loading data. The following interfaces are available for this purpose:

- **ParsableSource**
  - An eager source that provides an input stream with data to be parsed based on its content type
- **NodeConfigSource**
  - An eager source that provides an instance of the **ConfigNode.ObjectNode** interface with its configuration tree
- **LazyConfigSource**
  - A lazy source that provides values key-by-key

Mutability of Data

The configuration source may be immutable, by default, or provide a means for change. The following interfaces are available for this purpose:

- **PollableSource**
  - A source that can generate a "signature" of the data that can be used to check for possible changes in the underlying data, such as a file digest, a timestamp, and data version
- **WatchableSource**
  - A source that is based on data that has a specific change watcher that can notify the configuration framework of changes without the need for regular polling, such as file

- **EventConfigSource**
    - A source that can directly notify about changes

Each of these interfaces contains a corresponding inner class with a builder interface.

The **AbstractConfigSource** class implements a super set of all the configuration methods from all interfaces with the **protected** access specifier so you can use them in your implementation.

The **AbstractConfigSourceBuilder** class implements the configuration methods, so you can simply extend it with your builder and implement all the builders that make sense for your configuration source type.

Configuration Mappers

Configuration mappers are an ordered list of mapper functions that convert a **Config** subtree to specific Java types. The configuration system automatically loads an instance of the **ConfigMapperProvider** interface using the Java **ServiceLoader** class mechanism, and by default, the configuration system automatically registers all instances of the **ConfigMapper** interface from all providers with every **Config.Builder**. The application can suppress auto-registration of loaded mappers by invoking the **disableMapperServices()** method defined in the **Config.Builder** interface.

Signatures

The **ConfigMapper** interface is provided to the **ConfigMapperProvider** to help transformation of complex structures. It has the signature as shown in Listing 7-5.

Listing 7-5. The **ConfigMapper** interface signature

```
public interface ConfigMapper
```

The **ConfigMappers** class provides utility methods for converting configuration to Java types. It has the signature as shown in Listing 7-6.

Listing 7-6. The **ConfigMappers** class signature

```
public final class ConfigMappers extends Object
```

The **ConfigMapperProvider** interface provides mapping functions that convert a **Config** subtree to specific Java types. It has the signature as shown in Listing 7-7.

Listing 7-7. The **ConfigMapperProvider** interface signature

```
@FunctionalInterface
public interface ConfigMapperProvider
```

Please note that **ConfigMapperProvider** is a functional interface and may be used as an assignment target for a lambda expression or method reference.

Configuration Parsers

The Config component includes several built-in parsers, such as Java properties, YAML, JSON, and HOCON formats, to translate configuration text to in-memory data structures.

Helidon supports various Maven artifacts to search for, and read, formats other than the default configuration and Java properties.

Please note that the default configuration stops once it finds one of the files listed in Table 7-1 that shows the priority order of default configuration files and their corresponding Maven **artifactId**, under the **io.helidon.config groupdId**, for your **pom.xml** or **build.gradle** file.

Table 7-1. *Default configuration files (most to the least important)*

Configuration File	Maven artifactId	Format
application.yaml	**helidon-config-yaml**	YAML
application.conf	**helidon-config-hocon**	HOCON
application.json	**helidon-config-hocon**	JSON
application.properties	**helidon-config**	Java properties

Signatures

The **ConfigParser** interface can register parsers for an application on a builder using the **Config.Builder.addParser(ConfigParser)** method. It has the signature as shown in Listing 7-8.

Listing 7-8. The **ConfigParser** interface signature

```
public interface ConfigParser
```

The **ConfigParsers** class provides access to built-in implementations of the **ConfigParser** interface. It has the signature as shown in Listing 7-9.

Listing 7-9. The **ConfigParsers** class signature

```
public final class ConfigParsers extends Object
```

You can create your own custom configuration parser by implementing the **ConfigParser** interface and then construct using the **addParser()** method defined in the **Config.Builder** interface passing an instance of your custom parser.

Configuration Filters

Helidon provides parsers that translate text it reads from configuration files into in-memory data structures representing that configuration.

Your application can explicitly add configuration filters and overrides to a configuration builder, and by default, the configuration system will use the Java **ServiceLoader** class mechanism to locate all available filters and overrides, and automatically add them to configuration builders unless you choose to disable that behavior.

Each configuration filter accepts a key and corresponding value and returns the value to be used. The filter is designed to leave the value unchanged or, if necessary, change it.

Signatures

The **ConfigFilter** interface transforms elementary configuration values, namely, strings, before they are returned via the Config component. It has the signature as shown in Listing 7-10.

Listing 7-10. The **ConfigFilter** interface signature

```
@FunctionalInterface
public interface ConfigFilter
```

Please note that, just like the **ConfigMapperProvider** interface, **ConfigFilter** is a functional interface and may be used as an assignment target for a lambda expression or method reference.

The **ConfigFilters** class provides access to built-in implementations of the **ConfigFilter** interface. It has the signature as shown in Listing 7-11.

Listing 7-11. The **ConfigFilters** class signature

```
public final class ConfigFilters extends Object
```

Loading Configuration

The easiest way to load configuration for your application is to use the default properties file, **application.yaml**, and use the **create()** method, defined in the **Config** interface, as shown in Listing 7-12.

Listing 7-12. Using the **create()** method to load configuration from the default **application.yaml** file

```
Config config = Config.create();
```

Now let's consider an **application.yaml** file, as shown in Listing 7-13, that will provide configuration for the application, server, and security.

Listing 7-13. A typical **application.yaml** file

```
app:
  greeting: "Greetings from the web server!"
server:
  port: 8080
  host: 0.0.0.0
security:
  config:
    require-encryption: false

  providers:
    - http-basic-auth:
```

```
      realm: "helidon"
      users:
        - login: "mike"
          password: "${CLEAR=password}"
          roles: ["user", "admin"]
        - login: "rowena"
          password: "${CLEAR=password}"
          roles: ["user"]
  - http-digest-auth:
```

There are three main sections, or nodes, within this **application.yaml** file: **app**, **server**, and **security**. The first two nodes are straightforward. The **greeting** subnode defines the server response. The **port** subnode defines port 8080 for the web server to use upon startup. However, you should have noticed that the **security** node is a bit more complex utilizing YAML's sequence of mappings to define multiple entries. Separated by the "**-**" character, two security providers, **http-basic-auth** and **http-digest-auth**, and two users, **mike** and **rowena**, have been defined. You will learn more details on security in Chapter 9.

Also note that this configuration allows for clear-text passwords as the **config.require-encryption** subsection is set to **false**. You would obviously set this value to **true** in a production environment so that any attempt to pass a clear-text password would throw an exception.

Putting It All Together

Now that you've learned how to configure a Helidon application, let's put it all together and build an application! You can find the full source code and relevant documentation at the **helidon-book** GitHub repository (*https://github.com/mpredli01/helidon-book*) under the **config** module. Inspiration for these examples was adapted from the Helidon examples GitHub repository (*https://github.com/helidon-io/helidon-examples/*).

To demonstrate the Helidon Config component in action, let's take a look at a small working example that shows how to use configuration from multiple sources. The application consists of four main classes: **Application**, **DirectorySources**, **MergeSources**, and **MultipleConfigSources**.

CHAPTER 7   HELIDON CONFIG

To fully appreciate the location of these multiple source files, let's take a look at the directory structure as shown in Listing 7-14.

Listing 7-14. The directory structure for the application

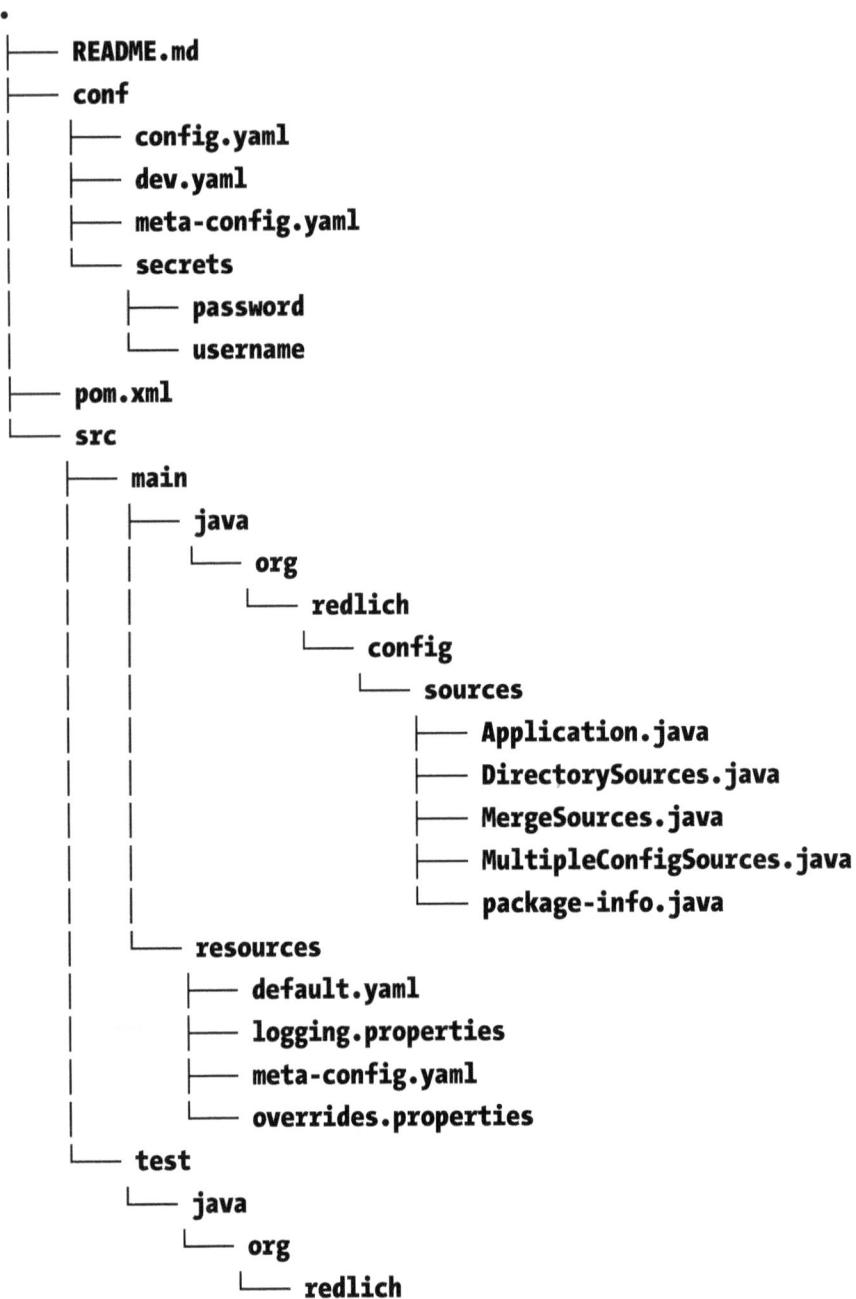

```
    └── config
        └── sources
            ├── TestDirectorySources.java
            ├── TestMergeSources.java
            └── TestMetaConfigSources.java
```

16 directories, 19 files

As you can see, there are configuration files located in the **conf** and the usual **src/main/resources** folders.

Dependencies

Let's start with Maven and Gradle dependencies that you would use in your application.

> **Note** The examples associated with this book use Maven as a build tool. The Gradle dependency is listed here for completeness and for the possibility of adding Gradle as a build tool in the future.

If Maven is your build tool, use the dependency as shown in Listing 7-15.

Listing 7-15. The Maven dependency for the Helidon Config component

```
<dependency>
    <groupId>io.helidon.config</groupId>
    <artifactId>helidon-config</artifactId>
    <version>4.1.0</version>
</dependency>
```

If Gradle is your build tool, use the dependency as shown in Listing 7-16.

Listing 7-16. The Gradle dependency for the Helidon Config component

```
implementation group: 'io.helidon.config', name: 'helidon-config', version: '4.1.0'
```

CHAPTER 7 HELIDON CONFIG

Application Class

The **Application** class, as shown in Listing 7-17, simply calls the **main()** methods defined in the other three classes.

Listing 7-17. The **Application** class

```
public class Application {

    private Application() {
    }

    public static void main(String[] args) {
        LogConfig.configureRuntime();
        DirectorySources.main(args);      ❶
        MergeSources.main(args);          ❷
        MultipleConfigSources.main(args); ❸
    }
}
```

❶ Calls and executes the **main()** method in the **DirectorySources** class

❷ Calls the executes the **main()** method in the **MergeSources** class

❸ Calls and executes the **main()** method in the **MultipleConfigSources** class

DirectorySources Class

The **DirectorySources** class, as shown in Listing 7-18, loads configuration from the **conf/secrets** folder containing a **username** and **password**.

Listing 7-18. The **DirectorySources** class

```
import static io.helidon.config.ConfigSources.directory;

public class DirectorySources {
```

```
    private DirectorySources() {
    }

    public static void main(String... args) {
        displaySplashScreen();

        // creates a config from files from specified directory
        Config secrets = Config.builder(directory("conf/secrets"))  ❶
                .disableEnvironmentVariablesSource()  ❷
                .disableSystemPropertiesSource()  ❸
                .build();

        String username = secrets.get("username").asString().get();  ❹
        String password = secrets.get("password").asString().get();  ❺

        System.out.println("[APP] Username: " + username);
        System.out.println("[APP] Password: " + password);
        System.out.println();
    }
}
```

❶ Using the **directory()** method, defined in the **ConfigSources** class as a parameter of the **builder()** method to establish the location of the **conf/secrets** folder.

❷ The **disableEnvironmentVariablesSource()** method disables the use of the system properties.

❸ The **disableSystemPropertiesSource()** method disables the use of the environmental properties.

❹ Using the **get()** method to obtain the value assigned to the **username** property.

❺ Using the **get()** method to obtain the value assigned to the **password** property.

CHAPTER 7 HELIDON CONFIG

MergeSources Class

The **MergeSources** class, as shown in Listing 7-19, merges various configuration source files.

Listing 7-19. The **MergeSources** class

```
import static io.helidon.config.ConfigSources.classpath;
import static io.helidon.config.ConfigSources.file;

public class MergeSources {

    private MergeSources() {
    }

    public static void main(String... args) {

        Config config = Config
                .builder(file("conf/dev.yaml").optional(),
                        file("conf/config.yaml").optional(),
                        classpath("default.yaml"))
                .addFilter((key, stringValue) -> key.name().equals("level") ?
                stringValue.toUpperCase() : stringValue)
                .build(); ❶

        ConfigValue<String> env = config.get("meta.env").asString(); ❷
        String appName = config.get("app.name").asString().get(); ❸
        int pageSize = config.get("app.page-size").asInt().get(); ❹
        // Applied filter (uppercase logging level), from dev.yaml:
        finest -> FINEST
        String level = config.get("component.audit.logging.level")
        .asString().get(); ❺

        env.ifPresent(e -> System.out.println("[APP] Environment: " + e));
        System.out.println("[APP] Name: " + appName);
        System.out.println("[APP] Page size: " + pageSize);
        System.out.println("[APP] Level: " + level);
        System.out.println();
    }
}
```

❶ Creates a configuration source composed of following sources:

- **conf/dev.yaml**, a developer-specific configuration, should not be placed in VCS.

- **conf/config.yaml**, a deployment-dependent configuration with values such as **prod**, **stage**, etc.

- **default.yaml**, application default values loaded from the classpath with a filter which converts values with keys ending with "*level*" to uppercase.

❷ Obtaining the value assigned to the **meta.env** property listed in the **dev.yaml** file

❸ Obtaining the value assigned to the **app.name** property listing in the **default.yaml** file

❹ Obtaining the **app.page-size** property from the **config.yaml** file

❺ Obtaining the **component.audit.logging.level** property from the **dev.yaml** file

MultipleConfigSources Class

The **MultipleConfigSources** class, as shown in Listing 7-20, uses multiple configuration files.

Listing 7-20. The **MultipleConfigSources** class

```
public class MultipleConfigSources {

    private MultipleConfigSources() {
    }

    public static void main(String... args) {

        Config metaConfig = Config.create(file("conf/meta-config.yaml")
        .optional(),
                classpath("meta-config.yaml"));  ❶
```

```
Config config = Config.builder()
        .config(metaConfig)
        .addFilter((key, stringValue) -> key.name().equals("level")
        ? stringValue.toUpperCase() : stringValue)
        .build();

ConfigValue<String> env = config.get("meta.env").asString(); ❷
env.ifPresent(e -> System.out.println("[APP] Environment: " + e));

String appName = config.get("app.name").asString().get(); ❸
System.out.println("[APP] Name: " + appName);

int pageSize = config.get("app.page-size").asInt().get(); ❹
System.out.println("[APP] Page size: " + pageSize);

// Applied filter (uppercase logging level), from dev.yaml:
finest -> FINEST
String level = config.get("component.audit.logging.level").
asString().get(); ❺
System.out.println("[APP] Level: " + level);
    }
}
```

- ❶ Creates configuration from a list of sources loaded from meta sources, namely:
  - **conf/meta-config.yaml**, a deployment-dependent meta-configuration file loaded from the file on the filesystem
  - **meta-config.yaml**, an application default meta-configuration file loaded from the classpath with a filter which converts values with keys ending with "*level*" to uppercase

- ❷ Obtaining the value assigned to the **meta.env** property listed in the **dev.yaml** file

- ❸ Obtaining the value assigned to the **app.name** property listing in the **default.yaml** file

❹ Obtaining the **app.page-size** property from the **config.yaml** file

❺ Obtaining the **component.audit.logging.level** property from the **dev.yaml** file

Build and Execute the Application

From the command line, you can build and execute the application with Maven as shown in Listing 7-21.

Listing 7-21. Build and execute the application with Maven.

`~ » mvn clean compile exec:java`

Notice the **exec:java** at the end of the command line. Normally, the **-Dexec.mainClass=<fully-qualified-class-name>** flag would be required right after the **exec:java**. However, adding the Exec Maven Plugin (*https://www.mojohaus.org/exec-maven-plugin/*) to your **pom.xml** file eliminates the need to add the **-Dexec.mainClass** flag. Simply add the Maven plug-in as shown in Listing 7-22.

Listing 7-22. The Exec Maven Plugin

```
<build>
    <plugins>
        <plugin>
            <groupId>org.codehaus.mojo</groupId>
            <artifactId>exec-maven-plugin</artifactId>
            <version>3.4.1</version>
            <configuration>
                <mainClass>${mainClass}</mainClass> ❶
            </configuration>
        </plugin>
    </plugins>
</build>
```

CHAPTER 7 HELIDON CONFIG

❶ The **${mainClass}** corresponds to the fully qualified class name for this application, namely, **org.redlich.config.sources.Application**.

Exercising the Application

After a successful build and execution of the application, you will see the output in your terminal window as shown in Listing 7-23.

Listing 7-23. The terminal output from executing the application on the command line

```
[APP] ----------------------------------
[APP]  Helidon Config Example (Sources)
[APP] ----------------------------------

[APP] --------------------------
[APP]  Directory Sources Example
[APP] --------------------------
[APP] Username: mike
[APP] Password: password

[APP] ---------------------
[APP]  Merge Sources Example
[APP] ---------------------
[APP] Environment: development
[APP] Name: Config Sources Example
[APP] Page size: 10
[APP] Level: FINE

[APP] --------------------------------
[APP]  Multiple Configuration Sources
[APP] --------------------------------
[APP] Environment: development
[APP] Name: Config Sources Example
[APP] Page size: 10

[APP] Level: FINE
```

Summary

In this chapter, you were introduced to the Config component that includes the **Config**, **ConfigSource**, **ConfigMapper**, **ConfigParser**, and **ConfigFilter** interfaces, how they all provide custom configuration, and an examination on how it all fits together in a Helidon application.

In the next chapter, you will be introduced to the DBClient component that provides a unified, reactive API for working with databases in a nonblocking way.

CHAPTER 8

Helidon DB Client

To address the challenges associated with reactive applications connecting to JDBC databases that, by design, are nonreactive, Helidon 2.0, released in June 2020, introduced the new DB Client component that provides consistent reactive database access and queries for Helidon SE applications. DB Client supports relational databases that connect via JDBC and reactive drivers for MongoDB.

DB Client features the ability to specify database connections and write native query code in a configuration file such that making database-related changes can easily be made without having to recompile code. Support for metrics, health checks, and tracing in DB Client is also included.

DB Client Component

The Helidon SE DB Client, supported by the **DbClient** interface, provides a unified, reactive API to simplify how you work with databases, both relational and NoSQL, by abstracting the type of the database in a nonblocking way.

You can use Helidon Config to specify database implementation-specific configuration without the need to use database implementation-specific APIs. This allows you to more easily switch between databases based on configuration. You can also use Helidon Config to define database-specific named statements that allow you to use different databases on different environments without changing your application source code.

DB Client supports the natively reactive driver for MongoDB and an executor service wrapped support for any JDBC driver. This allows you to seamlessly use the JDBC drivers in a reactive nonblocking environment, including support for backpressure in which the result set is processed as requested by the query subscriber.

Observability is also supported. DB Client supports observability in database applications with metrics, health checks, and tracing. Therefore, it is recommended to use named statements in database applications to allow for improved monitoring.

Signature

The **DbClient** interface has the signature as shown in Listing 8-1.

Listing 8-1. The **DbClient** interface signature

```
public interface DbClient extends AutoCloseable
```

Create Method

You can use the **create()** method to create a database handler builder for your Helidon application. There is one defined **create()** method that returns a static instance of the **DbClient** interface as shown in Listing 8-2.

Listing 8-2. The **create()** method

- ```
  create(Config config) returns a static instance of the DbClient
  interface and creates a Helidon database handler builder.
  ```

Builder Pattern

The **DbClient.Builder** class provides convenient ways to implement an instance of the **DbBuilder** interface; add configuration; add services such as metrics, health, and tracing via the **DbClientService** interface; and handle database statements and mappers. As you progress through this chapter, you will learn how all of this works.

Supporting Classes and Interfaces

There are a number of utility classes that are used in a database application to register metrics, health checks, and tracing. Let's take a look at a few of them.

DbClientService

The **DbClientService** interface has the signature as shown in Listing 8-3.
  ```

Listing 8-3. The **DbClientService** interface signature

```
@FunctionalInterface
public interface DbClientService
```

This is a functional interface that can be used as the assignment target for a lambda expression or method reference. Services can modify the data used to execute a statement as well as react on a statement result. The order of execution of services is based on the order in which they are registered in a builder, or by their priority when loaded from a Java Service loader.

DbClientMetrics

The **DbClientMetrics** interface has the signature as shown in Listing 8-4.

Listing 8-4. The **DbClientMetrics** class signature

```
public class DbClientMetrics extends Object
```

This is a utility class to obtain various types of metrics to register using the **addService(DbClientService)** method defined in the **DbClient.Builder** class. Metrics can be limited to a set of statement types or statement names and also configured to meter success, failure, or both.

DbClientHealthCheck

The **DbClientHealthCheck** interface has the signature as shown in Listing 8-5.

Listing 8-5. The **DbClientHealthCheck** class signature

```
public abstract class DbClientHealthCheck extends Object implements
HealthCheck
```

This is a utility class to obtain a database health check to register using the **addService(DbClientService)** method defined in the **DbClient.Builder** class. This class implements the **HealthCheck** interface from the MicroProfile Health specification.

DbClientTracing

The **DbClientTracing** interface has the signature as shown in Listing 8-6.

CHAPTER 8 HELIDON DB CLIENT

Listing 8-6. The **DbClientTracing** class signature

```
public class DbClientTracing extends DbClientServiceBase
```

This is a utility class to obtain a tracing interceptor. This interceptor is added through the Java Service loader.

Configuration

Basic configuration for using either a JDBC-connected or MongoDB client is shown in Listings 8-7 and 8-8. Please note that this configuration can be expanded to include named statements as you will see with the example application.

JDBC Client

Listing 8-7. Configuration for connecting to a JDBC database

```yaml
db:
  source: "jdbc"
  connection:
    url: "jdbc:mysql://127.0.0.1:3306/pokemon?useSSL=false"
    username: "user"
    password: "password"
  statements:
    ping: "DO 0"
    select-all-pokemons: "SELECT id, name FROM Pokemons"
```

MongoDB Client

Listing 8-8. Configuration for connecting to a MongoDB database

```yaml
db:
  source: "mongoDb"
  connection:
    url: "mongodb://127.0.0.1:27017/pokemon"
    username: "user"
    password: "password"
```

```
statements:
  ping: "DO 0"
  select-all-pokemons: "SELECT id, name FROM Pokemons"
```

As you can see, both configurations are very similar with the only differences being the **source** and **url** attributes as highlighted in blue.

Putting It All Together

Now that you've learned how to connect to databases using Helidon, let's put it all together and build an application! You can find the full source code and relevant documentation at the **helidon-book** GitHub repository (*https://github.com/mpredli01/helidon-book*) under the **dbclient** module. Inspiration for these examples was adapted from the Helidon examples GitHub repository (*https://github.com/helidon-io/helidon-examples/*).

To demonstrate the DB Client component in action, let's take a look at a Pokémon application using MongoDB as the database. The application consists of two main classes, **MongoDbApplication** and **PokemonService**, but there are a few behind-the-scenes helper classes that you need to know for this application.

Dependencies

Let's start with Maven and Gradle dependencies that you would use in your application.

> **Note** The examples associated with this book use Maven as a build tool. The Gradle dependency is listed here for completeness and for the possibility of adding Gradle as a build tool in the future.

If Maven is your build tool, use the dependency as shown in Listing 8-9.

Listing 8-9. The Maven dependency for the Helidon **DbClient** component

```
<dependency>
    <groupId>io.helidon.dbclient</groupId>
    <artifactId>helidon-dbclient</artifactId>
    <version>4.1.0</version>
</dependency>
```

If Gradle is your build tool, use the dependency as shown in Listing 8-10.

Listing 8-10. The Gradle dependency for the Helidon **DbClient** component

```
implementation group: 'io.helidon.dbclient', name: 'helidon-dbclient', version: '4.1.0'
```

Once this dependency is added to your application, you can choose your dependency of choice for client databases supported by JDBC or MongoDB.

JDBC Client

If Maven is your build tool, use the dependency as shown in Listing 8-11.

Listing 8-11. The Maven dependency for the JDBC

```
<dependency>
    <groupId>io.helidon.dbclient</groupId>
    <artifactId>helidon-dbclient-jdbc</artifactId>
    <version>4.1.0</version>
</dependency>
```

If Gradle is your build tool, use the dependency as shown in Listing 8-12.

Listing 8-12. The Gradle dependency for JDBC

```
implementation group: 'io.helidon.dbclient', name: 'helidon-dbclient-jdbc', version: '4.1.0'
```

MongoDB Client

If Maven is your build tool, use the dependency as shown in Listing 8-13.

Listing 8-13. The Maven dependency for using MongoDB

```xml
<dependency>
    <groupId>io.helidon.dbclient</groupId>
    <artifactId>helidon-dbclient-mongodb</artifactId>
    <version>4.1.0</version>
</dependency>
```

If Gradle is your build tool, use the dependency as shown in Listing 8-14.

Listing 8-14. The Gradle dependency for using JDBC

```
implementation group: 'io.helidon.dbclient', name: 'helidon-dbclient-mongodb',
version: '4.1.0'
```

Configuration

Now let's add the necessary database configuration for this application that is defined in an **application.yaml** file as shown in Listing 8-15.

Listing 8-15. An **application.yaml** file containing database configuration

```yaml
server:
  port: 8079
  host: 0.0.0.0
  features:
    print-details: true
db:
  source: "mongoDb"
  connection:
    url: "mongodb://127.0.0.1:27017/pokemon"
  health-check:
    type: "query"
    statementName: "health-check"
  statements:
    health-check: '{ ❶
            "operation": "command",
```

```
            "query": { ping: 1 }
    }'
insert2: '{  ❷
        "collection": "pokemons",
        "value": {
            "_id": $name,
            "type": $type
        }
    }'
select-all: '{
        "collection": "pokemons",
        "query": {}
    }'
select-one: '{
        "collection": "pokemons",
        "query": {
          "_id": ?
        }
    }'
delete-all: '{
        "collection": "pokemons",
        "operation": "delete"
    }'
update: '{
        "collection": "pokemons",
        "query": {
            "_id": $name
        },
        "value": {
            $set: { "type": $type }
        }
    }'
delete: '{
        "collection": "pokemons",
        "query": {
```

```
            "_id": ?
        }
    }'
```

❶ Health check statement that must be of type query.

❷ The **insert2** key defined here corresponds to the string provided in method names, such as **createNamedInsert()** and **createNamedDelete()**, that are defined in the **DbExecute** interface. In this instance, this insert operation contains the collection name, operation type, and data to be inserted via the **$name** and **$type** variable names. The same goes for the other key names, such as **select-one**, **select-all**, **update**, **delete-all**, etc.

PokemonService Class

The **PokemonService** class, as shown in Listing 8-16, is referenced in the **MongoDbApplication** class and triggers all the behind-the-scenes helper classes.

Listing 8-16. The **PokemonService** class

```java
public class PokemonService extends AbstractPokemonService { ❶

    PokemonService(DbClient dbClient) {
        super(dbClient); ❷
    }

    @Override
    protected void deleteAllPokemons(ServerRequest req,
    ServerResponse res) {
        long count = dbClient().execute().createNamedDelete("delete-all")
                .execute(); ❸
        res.send("Deleted: " + count + " values");
    }
}
```

- ❶ The **PokemonService** class extends the **Abstract PokemonService** class that defines a number of database methods for CRUD operations. There is, however, one method, **deleteAllPokemons()**, that is declared and implemented in the **PokemonService** class. The **AbstractPokemonService** class is located in a separate package as it is used for JDBC-connected applications.

- ❷ An instance of **DBClient** is passed to the **AbstractPokemonService** class that stores a copy.

- ❸ The **createNamedDelete()** method, defined in the **DbExecute** interface, creates a delete statement using a named statement, in this case: **delete-all** as defined in the **application.yaml** file.

MongoDbApplication Class

The MongoDbApplication class, as shown in Listing 8-17, serves as the entry point of the application and starts the Helidon web server.

Listing 8-17. The **MongoDbApplication** class

```
public final class MongoDbApplication {

    private MongoDbApplication() {
    }

    public static void main(String[] args) {
        startServer();
    }

    static WebServer startServer() { ❶

        // load logging configuration
        LogConfig.configureRuntime();

        WebServer server = setupServer(WebServer.builder());
```

```
        System.out.println("WEB server is up! http://localhost:" + server.
        port() + "/");
        return server;
    }

    static WebServer setupServer(WebServerConfig.Builder builder) {
        // By default, this will pick up application.yaml from the
        classpath
        Config config = Config.create(); ❷

        return builder.routing(routing -> routing(routing, config))
                .config(config.get("server"))
                .build()
                .start();
    }

    private static void routing(HttpRouting.Builder routing, Config
    config) {
        Config dbConfig = config.get("db");

        DbClient dbClient = DbClient.builder(dbConfig) ❸
                // add an interceptor to named statement(s)
                .addService(DbClientMetrics.counter().
                statementNames("select-all", "select-one"))
                // add an interceptor to statement type(s)
                .addService(DbClientMetrics.timer() ❹
                        .statementTypes(DbStatementType.DELETE,
                        DbStatementType.UPDATE, DbStatementType.INSERT))
                // add an interceptor to all statements
                .addService(DbClientTracing.create()) ❺
                .build();

        routing.register("/db", new PokemonService(dbClient)); ❻
    }
}
```

❶ This **startServer()** method shown here is relatively the same as to what you learned in Chapter 5.

❷ As you learned in Chapter 7, this will automatically find the **application.yaml** file from the classpath by default.

❸ Using the **builder()** method to establish an instance of **DbClient**.

❹ This **addService()** method adds an interceptor to named statements and registers a counter in the **DbClientMetrics** class that will count the number of instances of the **select-all** and **select-one** named statements that will be displayed upon calling the **/metrics** endpoint. The other addService() methods perform similar operations for statement types and for monitoring all statements, respectively.

❺ This **addService()** method creates a trace named "*mongo-db*" via the **TracerBuilder** interface that you will be able to monitor in a tracing tool such as Zipkin or Jaeger.

❻ This **register()** method registers the **/db** endpoint and associates it with the **PokemonService** class.

Now let's exercise the application!

Build and Execute the Application

From the command line, you can build and execute the application with Maven as shown in Listing 8-18.

Listing 8-18. Build and execute the application with Maven.

```
~ » mvn clean compile exec:java
```

Notice the **exec:java** at the end of the command line. Normally, the **-Dexec.mainClass=<fully-qualified-class-name>** flag would be required right after the **exec:java**. However, adding the Exec Maven Plugin (*https://www.mojohaus.org/exec-maven-plugin/*) to your **pom.xml** file eliminates the need to add the **-Dexec.mainClass** flag. Simply add the Maven plug-in as shown in Listing 8-19.

Listing 8-19. The Exec Maven Plugin

```xml
<build>
    <plugins>
        <plugin>
            <groupId>org.codehaus.mojo</groupId>
            <artifactId>exec-maven-plugin</artifactId>
            <version>3.4.1</version>
            <configuration>
                <mainClass>${mainClass}</mainClass> ❶
            </configuration>
        </plugin>
    </plugins>
</build>
```

❶ The **${mainClass}** corresponds to the fully qualified class name for this application, namely, **org.redlich.security. ConfigAuthenticationApplication**.

Exercising the Application

Once the application has started and the web server is running, you can exercise the application using the **curl** command in the examples below. Result set output will be in JSON format.

The command, as shown in Listing 8-20, will list all the Pokémons in the database. Assuming the database is empty, you should receive an empty set.

Listing 8-20. Retrieving Pokémons from the database

```
~ » curl http://localhost:8079/db
[]
```

Now let's add some Pokémons to the database. First, let's add "*Squirtle*" as shown in Listing 8-21.

CHAPTER 8 HELIDON DB CLIENT

Listing 8-21. Adding "Squirtle" to the database

```
~ » curl -i -X PUT -d '{"name":"Squirtle","type":"Water"}'
http://localhost:8079/db
HTTP/1.1 200 OK
Content-Type: text/plain
Date: Wed, 13 Sep 2023 06:54:47 -0400
connection: keep-alive
content-length: 18

Inserted: 1 values
```

Now let's add "*Caterpie*" to the database as shown in Listing 8-22.

Listing 8-22. Adding "Caterpie" to the database

```
~ » curl -i -X PUT -d '{"name":"Caterpie","type":"Bug"}'
http://localhost:8079/db
HTTP/1.1 200 OK
Content-Type: text/plain
Date: Wed, 13 Sep 2023 06:57:16 -0400
connection: keep-alive
content-length: 18

Inserted: 1 values
```

And finally, let's add "*Rattata*" to the database as shown in Listing 8-23.

Listing 8-23. Adding "Rattata" to the database

```
~ » curl -i -X PUT -d '{"name":"Rattata","type":"Dark"}'
http://localhost:8079/db
HTTP/1.1 200 OK
Content-Type: text/plain
Date: Wed, 13 Sep 2023 06:58:22 -0400
connection: keep-alive
content-length: 18

Inserted: 1 values
```

Let's try to retrieve all the Pokémons again as shown in Listing 8-24. There should now be three entries.

Listing 8-24. Retrieving all the Pokémons

```
~ » curl http://localhost:8079/db
[{"type":"Water","_id":"Squirtle"},{"type":"Bug","_id":"Caterpie"},{"type":"Dark","_id":"Rattata"}]
```

You can retrieve a single Pokémon of interest from the database. Let's find out more about "*Squirtle*" using the command as shown in Listing 8-25.

Listing 8-25. Retrieving information about "Squirtle"

```
~ » curl http://localhost:8079/db/Squirtle
{"type":"Water","_id":"Squirtle"}
```

You can delete a single Pokémon from the database. Let's delete "*Caterpie*" from the database using the command as shown in Listing 8-26.

Listing 8-26. Deleting "Caterpie" from the database

```
~ » curl -i -X DELETE http://localhost:8079/db/Caterpie
HTTP/1.1 200 OK
Content-Type: text/plain
Date: Wed, 13 Sep 2023 07:15:10 -0400
connection: keep-alive
content-length: 17

Deleted: 1 values
```

Let's get the list of Pokémons from the database as shown in Listing 8-27. There should only be two.

Listing 8-27. Retrieving all remaining Pokémons

```
~ » curl http://localhost:8079/db
[{"type":"Water","_id":"Squirtle"},{"type":"Dark","_id":"Rattata"}]
```

Now, let's delete all Pokémons from the database as shown in Listing 8-28.

Listing 8-28. Deleting the remaining Pokémons from the database

```
~ » curl -i -X DELETE http://localhost:8079/db
HTTP/1.1 200 OK
Content-Type: text/plain
Date: Wed, 13 Sep 2023 07:45:44 -0400
connection: keep-alive
content-length: 17

Deleted: 2 values
```

Now let's ensure that you once again have an empty set in the database as shown in Listing 8-29.

Listing 8-29. Retrieving Pokémons from the database

```
~ » curl http://localhost:8079/db
[]
```

The DB Client examples in the GitHub repository that accompanies this book contain four folders: **jdbc** for a JDBC-connected database example; **mongodb** for a MongoDB database example; **pokemons**, a database example in which you can switch between a JDBC client and a MongoDB database; and **common** that contains four utility class files that are used in all three examples.

Summary

In this chapter, you were introduced to the DB Client component featuring the **DbClient** interface and a number of supporting interfaces to perform database operations for your application.

DB Client supports relational databases that connect via JDBC and reactive drivers for MongoDB. You can use Config to specify database implementation-specific configuration without the need to use database implementation-specific APIs. This allows you to more easily switch between databases based on configuration. You can also use Helidon Config to define database-specific named statements that allow you to use different databases on different environments without changing your application source code.

In the next chapter, you will be introduced to the Helidon Security component.

CHAPTER 9

Helidon Security

Helidon's Security component provides authentication, authorization, audit, and outbound security.

Security Component

The Security component, defined through the **Security** interface, is used to bootstrap security and integrate it with other frameworks. It is also the main runtime entry point for the **SecurityContext** interface.

Support for a number of implemented security providers for use in Helidon applications provides a number of options:

- HTTP Basic Authentication
- HTTP Digest Authentication
- HTTP Signatures
- Attribute-Based Access Control (ABAC) Authorization
- JWT Provider
- Header Assertion
- Google Login Authentication
- OpenID Connect
- IDCS Role Mapping

You can use one of three approaches to implement security in your Helidon application:

- A builder pattern where you manually provide configuration
- A configuration pattern where you provide configuration via a configuration file
- A hybrid of the builder and configuration patterns

So, let's get started learning about the Security component!

Signature

The **Security** interface has the signature as shown in Listing 9-1.

Listing 9-1. The **Security** interface signature

```
public interface Security
```

Create Method

You can use the **create()** method to create a new instance of **Security** based on configuration values. There is one defined **create()** method:

- **create(Config config)** returns a static instance of the **Security** interface based on the configuration values.

Builder Pattern

The **Security.Builder** class provides a convenient way to create an instance of **Security**. As you progress through this chapter, you will learn how all of this works.

Configuration

Configuration for security is similar to that of configuration for the WebServer or WebClient component, but things get a little more complex. Listing 9-2 shows the **security** node in a typical **application.yaml** file.

Listing 9-2. A typical **application.yaml** file for security configuration

```yaml
server:
  features:
    security:
      # Configuration of security integration with web server
      defaults:
        authenticate: true
      paths:
        - path: "/noRoles"
          methods: [ "get" ]
        - path: "/user[/{*}]"
          methods: [ "get" ]
          roles-allowed: [ "user" ]
        - path: "/admin"
          methods: [ "get" ]
          roles-allowed: [ "admin" ]
        - path: "/deny"
          methods: [ "get" ]
          roles-allowed: [ "deny" ]
          audit: true
        - path: "/noAuthn"
          roles-allowed: [ "admin" ]
          authentication-optional: true
          audit: true
        - path: "/static[/{*}]"
          roles-allowed: "user"

security:
  config:
    # Configuration of secured config (encryption of passwords in property files)
    # Set to true for production - if set to true, clear text passwords will cause failure
    require-encryption: false
  providers:
```

```
- http-basic-auth:
    realm: "helidon"
    users: ❶
      - login: "mike"
        password: "${CLEAR=password}"
        roles: [ "user", "admin" ] ❷
      - login: "rowena"
        password: "${CLEAR=password}"
        roles: [ "user" ]
      - login: "ian"
        password: "${CLEAR=password}"
        roles: [ ] ❸
```

❶ As you can see, there are three defined users: Mike, Rowena, and Ian, that have been assigned usernames: **mike**, **rowena**, and **ian**, respectively. Please note that the password for all three users is **password** in clear text. You obviously don't want to do this in a production environment!!

Let's review how to reference the users in an application defined under the **security** node of our configuration file. Consider the string that chains together the subnodes under the main **security** node as shown in Listing 9-3.

Listing 9-3. Obtaining security information for username, **mike**

`security.providers.0.http-basic-auth.users.0.login`

When the parser comes across a number in the string, it indicates there are one or more subnodes in the configuration file. In this example, the **0** right after the **providers** subnode will direct the parser to move into the first subnode, **http-basic-auth**. In this example, this is the only provider, but others can be defined here.

The **0** right after the **users** subnode will direct the parser to move into the first subnode containing the **login**, **password**, and **roles** subnodes for the username, **mike**. Therefore, the above string will return his assigned password and role information for Mike when passed into the **config.get()** method. Similarly, the password and role information for username, **rowena**, would be returned with the string as shown in Listing 9-4.

Listing 9-4. Obtaining security information for username, **rowena**

`security.providers.0.http-basic-auth.users.1.login`

> ❷ The **roles** subnode can be an array of defined roles as shown with username, **mike**.
>
> ❸ Note how the **roles** for **ian** is an empty array. In this example, Ian will be able to log in but won't have access to anything.

Putting It All Together

Now that you've learned how to secure a Helidon application, let's put it all together and build an application! You can find the full source code and relevant documentation at the **helidon-book** GitHub repository (*https://github.com/mpredli01/helidon-book*) under the **security** module. Inspiration for these examples was adapted from the Helidon examples GitHub repository (*https://github.com/helidon-io/helidon-examples/*).

To demonstrate the Helidon Security component in action, let's take a look at a small working example that shows how to add security using configuration. The application consists of the **ConfigAuthenticationApplication** class.

Dependencies

Let's start with Maven and Gradle dependencies that you would use in your application:

> **Note** The examples associated with this book use Maven as a build tool. The Gradle dependency is listed here for completeness and for the possibility of adding Gradle as a build tool in the future.

If Maven is your build tool, use the dependency as shown in Listing 9-5.

Listing 9-5. The Maven dependency for the Helidon Security component

```xml
<dependency>
    <groupId>io.helidon.security.integration</groupId>
    <artifactId>helidon-security-integration-common</artifactId>
    <version>4.1.0</version>
</dependency>
```

If Gradle is your build tool, use the dependency as shown in Listing 9-6.

Listing 9-6. The Gradle dependency for the Helidon Security component

```
implementation group: 'io.helidon.security.integration', name: 'helidon-security-integration-common', version: '4.1.0'
```

ConfigAuthenticationApplication Class

This **ConfigAuthenticationApplication** class, as shown in Listing 9-7, will rely on the configuration from the **application.yaml** file that was shown in Listing 9-2.

Listing 9-7. The ConfigAuthenticationApplication class

```java
public final class ConfigAuthenticationApplication {
    private ConfigAuthenticationApplication() {
    }
    public static void main(String[] args) {
        LogConfig.initClass();

        Config config = Config.create();

        WebServerConfig.Builder builder = WebServer.builder()
                .port(8080);
        setup(builder);
        WebServer server = builder.build();

        long nanoTime = System.nanoTime();
        server.start();
        long time = System.nanoTime() - nanoTime;
```

CHAPTER 9 HELIDON SECURITY

```
System.out.println("[APP] ---------------------------------
------");
System.out.println("[APP] Helidon Security Configuration Example");
System.out.println("[APP] ---------------------------------
------");
System.out.printf("[APP] Server started in %d ms", TimeUnit.
MILLISECONDS.convert(time, TimeUnit.NANOSECONDS));
System.out.println("\n");
System.out.println("[APP] -----------------------------------
------");
System.out.println("[APP]  Configured Users Using
Configuration File");
System.out.println("[APP] -----------------------------------
------");
System.out.println("\n");
ConfigValue<String> mike = config.get("security.providers.0.
http-basic-auth.users.0.login").asString(); ❶
ConfigValue<String> mikePassword = config.get("security.
providers.0.http-basic-auth.users.0.password").asString();
ConfigValue<List<Config>> mikeRoles = config.get("security.
providers.0.http-basic-auth.users.0.roles").asNodeList(); ❷
System.out.println("[APP] " + mike);
System.out.println("[APP] " + mikePassword);
System.out.println("[APP] " + mikeRoles);
System.out.println("\n");
ConfigValue<String> rowena = config.get("security.providers.0.http-
basic-auth.users.1.login").asString();
ConfigValue<String> rowenaPassword = config.get("security.
providers.0.http-basic-auth.users.1.password").asString();
ConfigValue<List<Config>> rowenaRoles = config.get("security.
providers.0.http-basic-auth.users.1.roles").asNodeList();
System.out.println("[APP] " + rowena);
System.out.println("[APP] " + rowenaPassword);
System.out.println("[APP] " + rowenaRoles);
System.out.println("\n");
```

CHAPTER 9 HELIDON SECURITY

```
        ConfigValue<String> ian = config.get("security.providers.0.
        http-basic-auth.users.2.login").asString();
        ConfigValue<String> ianPassword = config.get("security.
        providers.0.http-basic-auth.users.2.password").asString();
        ConfigValue<List<Config>> ianRoles = config.get("security.
        providers.0.http-basic-auth.users.2.roles").asNodeList();
        System.out.println("[APP] " + ian);
        System.out.println("[APP] " + ianPassword);
        System.out.println("[APP] " + ianRoles);
        System.out.println("\n");
        System.out.println("[APP] ---------------------");
        System.out.println("[APP]  Configured Endpoints");
        System.out.println("[APP] ---------------------");
        System.out.println("\n");
        System.out.println("[APP] No authentication: http://localhost:8080/
        public");
        System.out.println("[APP] No roles required, but authenticated:
        http://localhost:8080/noRoles");
        System.out.println("[APP] Admin role required: http://
        localhost:8080/admin");
        System.out.println("[APP] User role required: http://
        localhost:8080/user");
        System.out.println("[APP] Always forbidden (no roles defined) and
        audited: http://localhost:8080/deny");
        System.out.println("[APP] Admin role required, authenticated,
        authentication optional, audited \\");
        System.out.println("[APP] (always forbidden - challenge is not
        returned as authentication is optional): http://localhost:8080/
        noAuthn");
        System.out.println("[APP] Static content that requires a user role:
        http://localhost:8080/static/index.html");
    }

    static void setup(WebServerConfig.Builder server) { ❸
        Config config = Config.create();
```

```
server.config(config.get("server"))
        .routing(routing -> routing
                .register("/static", StaticContentService.
                create("/WEB"))
                .get("/{*}", (req, res) -> {
                    Optional<SecurityContext> securityContext
                    = req.context().get(SecurityContext.class);
                    res.headers().contentType(HttpMediaTypes.
                    PLAINTEXT_UTF_8);
                    res.send("Hello, you are: \n" + securityContext
                            .map(ctx -> ctx.user().
                            orElse(SecurityContext.ANONYMOUS)
                            .toString())
                            .orElse("Security context is null"));
                }));
    }
}
```

- ❶ Extracting Mike's username is accomplished through **config.get(String)**. You will recognize the string of nodes you examined earlier in this chapter that is passed inside the **get()** method. For a single value in the configuration file, the return type is **ConfigValue<String>**, and an additional method, **asString()**, is appended after **config.get(String)**. Extracting Mike's password is accomplished in a similar way. Just the string of subnodes is different.

- ❷ Since a user's roles is stored in an array, extracting Mike's roles is a bit different. The return type is **ConfigValue<List<Config>>**, and the method appended to **config.get(String)** is **asNodeList()**.

- ❷ The **setup()** method to start the web server and register the endpoints as you learned in Chapter 5.

Build and Execute the Application

From the command line, you can build and execute the application with Maven as shown in Listing 9-8.

Listing 9-8. Build and execute the application with Maven.

```
~ » mvn clean compile exec:java
```

Notice the **exec:java** at the end of the command line. Normally, the **-Dexec.mainClass=<fully-qualified-class-name>** flag would be required right after the **exec:java**. However, adding the Exec Maven Plugin (*https://www.mojohaus.org/exec-maven-plugin/*) to your **pom.xml** file eliminates the need to add the **-Dexec.mainClass** flag. Simply add the Maven plug-in as shown in Listing 9-9.

Listing 9-9. The Exec Maven Plugin

```
<build>
    <plugins>
        <plugin>
            <groupId>org.codehaus.mojo</groupId>
            <artifactId>exec-maven-plugin</artifactId>
            <version>3.4.1</version>
            <configuration>
                <mainClass>${mainClass}</mainClass> ❶
            </configuration>
        </plugin>
    </plugins>
</build>
```

❶ The **${mainClass}** corresponds to the fully qualified class name for this application, namely, **org.redlich.security.ConfigAuthenticationApplication**.

Exercising the Application

After a successful build and execution of the application, you will see the output in your terminal window as shown in Listing 9-10.

Listing 9-10. The terminal output from executing the application on the command line

```
[APP] ---------------------------------------
[APP] Helidon Security Configuration Example
[APP] ---------------------------------------
[APP] Server started in 50 ms

[APP] ------------------------------------------
[APP]  Configured Users Using Configuration File
[APP] ------------------------------------------

[APP] security.providers.0.http-basic-auth.users.0.login: mike
[APP] security.providers.0.http-basic-auth.users.0.password: password
[APP] security.providers.0.http-basic-auth.users.0.roles: [[security.
providers.0.http-basic-auth.users.0.roles.0] VALUE 'user', [security.
providers.0.http-basic-auth.users.0.roles.1] VALUE 'admin']

[APP] security.providers.0.http-basic-auth.users.1.login: rowena
[APP] security.providers.0.http-basic-auth.users.1.password: password
[APP] security.providers.0.http-basic-auth.users.1.roles: [[security.
providers.0.http-basic-auth.users.1.roles.0] VALUE 'user']

[APP] security.providers.0.http-basic-auth.users.2.login: ian
[APP] security.providers.0.http-basic-auth.users.2.password: password
[APP] security.providers.0.http-basic-auth.users.2.roles: []

[APP] --------------------
[APP]  Configured Endpoints
[APP] --------------------

[APP] No authentication: http://localhost:8080/public
[APP] No roles required, but authenticated: http://localhost:8080/noRoles
[APP] Admin role required: http://localhost:8080/admin
```

[APP] User role required: http://localhost:8080/user
[APP] Always forbidden (no roles defined) and audited: http://localhost:8080/deny
[APP] Admin role required, authenticated, authentication optional, audited \
[APP] (always forbidden - challenge is not returned as authentication is optional): http://localhost:8080/noAuthn
[APP] Static content that requires a user role: http://localhost:8080/static/index.html

Notice all the endpoints. All of them will work in your browser. Let's start with the main URL by navigating to **http://localhost:8080/static/index.html**. Once there, you will be challenged with authentication as shown in Figure 9-1.

Figure 9-1. *The login dialog box for the Helidon Security application*

Let's enter Mike's username, **mike**, and password, **password**, since he has administrative access. Now that Mike has been authenticated, the main content will be displayed as shown in Figure 9-2.

Hello, this is a static resource loaded from classpath.

The following endpoints are available on this server:

- Public endpoint, no authentication required
- No roles required, just authenticated user
- user role required
- admin role required
- This endpoint is always denied
- admin, authentication optional - will be denied, as it does not return a basic auth challenge

The following users are configured:

- mike/password: authenticated and authorized for the user and admin roles
- rowena/password: authenticated and authorized for the user role
- ian/password: authenticated, but not authorized for any roles

Figure 9-2. *The HTML page after a successful login*

Since Mike has full access to the application, he will be able to successfully click on any of these links except for the link in which the endpoint is always denied.

Now let's focus on the browser responses from these configured endpoints.

Listing 9-11 displays the browser response from both the **/public** and **/noRoles** endpoints.

Listing 9-11. The browser response from the **/public** and **/noRoles** endpoints

```
Hello, you are:
Subject:
    Principal: Principal{properties=BasicAttributes{registry={anonymo
    us=true, name=<ANONYMOUS>, id=<ANONYMOUS>}}, name='<ANONYMOUS>',
    id='<ANONYMOUS>'}
```

With Mike logged into the application, Listing 9-12 displays the browser response from the **/admin** and **/user** endpoints.

Listing 9-12. The browser response from the **/admin** and **/user** endpoints for username, **mike**

```
Hello, you are:
Subject:
```

```
    Principal: Principal{properties=BasicAttributes{registry={name=mike,
    id=mike}}, name='mike', id='mike'}
    Principal: role:user
    Principal: role:admin
    Private Credential: io.helidon.security.providers.httpauth.HttpBasicA
    uthProvider$BasicPrivateCredentials@7f1a5fc6
```

With Rowena now logged into the application, Listing 9-13 displays the browser response from the **/user** endpoint.

Listing 9-13. The browser response from the **/user** endpoint for username, **rowena**

```
Hello, you are:
Subject:
    Principal: Principal{properties=BasicAttributes{registry={name=rowe
    na, id=rowena}}, name='rowena', id='rowena'}
    Principal: role:user
    Private Credential: io.helidon.security.providers.httpauth.HttpBasicA
    uthProvider$BasicPrivateCredentials@4a04cf6a
```

Summary

In this chapter, you were introduced to the Security component featuring the **Security** interface, how to secure your application via configuration, and how to parse the list of nodes in the **application.yaml** file. Additionally, you learned how to exercise the application.

This chapter concludes Part II of this book on Helidon SE. Part III will introduce you to Helidon MP along with Helidon Metrics (Chapter 11), Helidon Fault Tolerance (Chapter 12), and Helidon Health Checks (Chapter 13).

PART III

Helidon MP

CHAPTER 10

Creating a Small Working Project with Helidon MP

Helidon MP is a MicroProfile runtime that allows Java developers to build portable Jakarta EE microservices applications. It is designed for ease of use and provides a Spring Boot–like development experience with significant use of dependency injection and annotations.

Helidon MP supports Jakarta EE specifications, but unlike Helidon SE, it does not require an application server. Helidon MP applications are stand-alone Java applications running in their own JVM powered by the new Helidon web server built on virtual threads.

Please refer to Chapters 2 and 3 for a refresher on the MicroProfile and Jakarta EE specifications, respectively.

You can easily get started with Project Helidon in three ways: the Quickstarts, the command-line utility, and the Helidon Project Starter. In this chapter, you will learn how to use all three of these.

Prerequisites

Throughout this book, you will be extensively using a terminal window and commands such as **mvn**, **curl**, and **json_pp** to generate, build, and execute the example applications. If you're not familiar with any of these commands, don't worry, you will learn all about them!

Before you do anything, however, let's ensure that you have the minimal versions of the JDK and other build tools:

- JDK 21
- Maven 3.8.0
- Docker 18.09
- Kubernetes 1.16.5

Note Details on the use of Docker and Kubernetes are beyond the scope of this book. For more information, please visit the Helidon website.

You can easily check for the versions installed on your computer workstation by executing the commands as shown in Listing 10-1.

Listing 10-1. The commands to check for versions of Java, Maven, Docker, and Kubernetes

```
$ » java -version
openjdk version "21" 2023-09-19
OpenJDK Runtime Environment (build 21+35-2513)
OpenJDK 64-Bit Server VM (build 21+35-2513, mixed mode, sharing)

$ » mvn -version
Apache Maven 3.9.9 (8e8579a9e76f7d015ee5ec7bfcdc97d260186937)
Maven home: /Users/mpredli01/.sdkman/candidates/maven/current
Java version: 21, vendor: Oracle Corporation, runtime: /Library/Java/JavaVirtualMachines/jdk-21.jdk/Contents/Home
Default locale: en_US, platform encoding: UTF-8
OS name: "mac os x", version: "10.15.7", arch: "x86_64", family: "mac"

$ » docker --version

$ » kubectl version
```

Quickstarts

The Quickstarts for Helidon SE and Helidon MP have been available to the Java community since the initial release of Project Helidon in 2018. As Helidon has evolved, so too have the Quickstarts.

You can initiate a Quickstart example through Maven by using **archetype:generate** and its corresponding attributes. This will download and generate the example that is complete with **/greet** and **/simple-greet** endpoints and displays a default greeting of "*Hello World!*".

So without further ado, let's get started!

Generate the Application

In your terminal window, execute the Maven command as shown in Listing 10-2.

Listing 10-2. The Maven command to download and generate the Quickstarts application

```
$ » mvn -U archetype:generate -DinteractiveMode=false \
    -DarchetypeGroupId=io.helidon.archetypes \
    -DarchetypeArtifactId=helidon-quickstart-mp \
    -DarchetypeVersion=4.1.0 \
    -DgroupId=io.helidon.examples \
    -DartifactId=helidon-quickstart-mp \
    -Dpackage=io.helidon.examples.quickstart.mp
```

This will download and create the application in a directory named **helidon-quickstart-mp**, using all of the parameters in the command for the directory structure and resulting **pom.xml** file as specified in the Maven command. The directory structure is shown in Listing 10-3.

Listing 10-3. The directory structure generated using the Maven build tool

```
.
├── Dockerfile
├── Dockerfile.jlink
├── Dockerfile.native
```

CHAPTER 10   CREATING A SMALL WORKING PROJECT WITH HELIDON MP

```
├── README.md
├── app.yaml
├── pom.xml
└── src
    ├── main
    │   ├── java
    │   │   └── io
    │   │       └── helidon
    │   │           └── examples
    │   │               └── quickstart
    │   │                   └── mp
    │   │                       ├── GreetResource.java
    │   │                       ├── GreetingProvider.java
    │   │                       ├── Message.java
    │   │                       ├── SimpleGreetResource.java
    │   │                       └── package-info.java
    │   └── resources
    │       ├── META-INF
    │       │   ├── beans.xml
    │       │   ├── microprofile-config.properties
    │       │   └── native-image
    │       │       └── io
    │       │           └── helidon
    │       │               └── examples
    │       │                   └── helidon-quickstart-mp
    │       │                       └── native-image.properties
    │       └── logging.properties
    └── test
        └── java
            └── io
                └── helidon
                    └── examples
                        └── quickstart
                            └── mp
                                └── MainTest.java
```

156

```
        └── resources
            ├── META-INF
            │   └── microprofile-config.properties
            └── application-test.yaml
```

24 directories, 18 files

Let's break down this directory tree.

First, the **README.md** file contains a wealth of information on how to build and execute the application including details on using Docker and Kubernetes for containerizing and orchestrating, respectively.

Three Docker files – **Dockerfile**, **Dockerfile.jlink**, and **Dockerfile.native** – provide all the commands to build and execute the application from Docker. The **Docker.jlink** file uses the **jlink** tool to create a custom Java runtime image, resulting in a smaller and more efficient Docker image. The **Docker.native** file builds a container image that runs a native executable that is commonly used with GraalVM Native Image.

The **app.yml** file contains the required configuration for container orchestration with Kubernetes.

The **microprofile-config.properties** file, located in the **src/main/resources/META-INF** folder, contains configuration for the server and the application as shown in Listing 10-4.

Listing 10-4. The contents of the **microprofile-config.properties** file used for configuration

```
# Microprofile server properties
server.port=8080
server.host=0.0.0.0

# Change the following to true to enable the optional MicroProfile Metrics
REST.request metrics
metrics.rest-request.enabled=false

# Application properties. This is the default greeting
app.greeting=Hello
```

Four Java files located in the **src/main/java/io/helidon/examples/quickstart.mp** folder – **GreetingProvider.java, GreetResource.java, Meeting.java**, and **SimpleGreetResource.java** – make up the application.

> **Note** The Java source files generated by the Helidon MP Maven command are different from the Helidon SE version.

The **GreetingProvider** class stores an instance of a message of type **AtomicReference<String>** that is obtained through the constructor via the **@ConfigProperty(name="app.greeting")** annotation. The default message of *"Hello"* is stored in the **microprofile-config.properties** file.

The **GreetResource** class defines the application endpoints: **/greet**, **/greet/{name}**, and **/greeting**. The first two are used in HTTP **GET** operations, and the **/greeting** endpoint is used for an HTTP **PUT** operation for changing the salutation from *"Hello"* to something like *"Hola"* or *"Guten Tag"*.

The **Message** class is a Java POJO that encapsulates a **message** and a **greeting** along with their setter and getter methods for the application.

The **SimpleGreetResource** class defines the application endpoints, **/simple-greet** and **/simple-greet/{name}**, and also adds custom metrics that are logged when the built-in **/metrics** endpoint is accessed. You will learn more about Helidon Metrics in Chapter 11.

Build the Application

Now, change directory to **helidon-quickstart-mp** where the application resides and execute the Maven command as shown in Listing 10-5.

Listing 10-5. The commands to change directory into the root of the application and build the application

```
~ » cd helidon-quickstart-mp
helidon-quickstart-mp » mvn clean package
```

> **Note** On this initial build, you don't have to include the **clean** parameter, but this is a good practice to ensure a fresh application is built.

Upon successful compilation, a JAR file named **helidon-quickstart-mp.jar** is generated, and from here, you can initiate the application via the command line or the browser.

Initiate the Application

In your terminal window, execute the **java** command to initiate the application as shown in Listing 10-6 along with the resulting response.

Listing 10-6. Initiating the application and the resulting output

```
$ helidon-quickstart-mp » java -jar target/helidon-quickstart-mp.jar
2024.08.27 19:03:46.625 Logging at runtime configured using classpath:
/logging.properties
2024.08.27 19:03:47.458 Helidon SE 4.1.0 features: [Config, Encoding,
Health, Media, Metrics, Observe, WebServer]
2024.08.27 19:03:47.485 [0x04e2fa50] http://0.0.0.0:8080 bound for socket
'@default'
2024.08.27 19:03:47.497 Started all channels in 44 milliseconds. 1164
milliseconds since JVM startup. Java 21+35-2513
WEB server is up! http://localhost:8080/simple-greet
```

Notice the last line in which the application provides the URL that you will use to exercise the application.

The Client URL and JSON Pretty Printer Utilities

The **curl** command, a portmanteau for Client URL, is a popular built-in command-line tool in the UNIX/Linux environments that enables data transfer over various network protocols. It communicates with a web or application server by specifying a relevant URL and the data that need to be sent or received.

Note The **curl** command is highly configurable with many options. Therefore, the most basic use of **curl** will be demonstrated throughout this book.

The **json_pp** command, an acronym for JSON Pretty Printer (*https://github.com/deftek/json_pp/blob/master/README.md*), prints JSON data in legible, indented format in the terminal window.

Exercise the Application via the Command Line

First, you will need to open a new terminal window since the first one is occupied running the server.

Let's start with the **/simple-greet** endpoint. The application defined this endpoint to be simple, unconfigurable, with a response that doesn't support JSON.

As shown in Listing 10-7, you can execute the **curl** command and you should see the resulting response.

Listing 10-7. Executing the **curl** command with the **/simple-greet** endpoint and corresponding response

```
~ » curl http://localhost:8080/simple-greet
Hello World!
```

Now, let's use the **/greet** endpoint that has many options.

As shown in Listing 10-8, you can execute the **curl** and **json_pp** commands, and you should see the resulting response in JSON format.

Listing 10-8. Executing the **curl** command with the **/greet** endpoint and corresponding response

```
~ » curl -s http://localhost:8080/greet/ | json_pp
{
   "message" : "Hello World!"
}
```

The application was built to accept a named parameter after the **/greet** endpoint. This allows you to personalize the greeting. The endpoint and its named parameter are in the form of **/greet/{name}**. Let's experiment with this by passing in "*Mike*" as the named parameter as shown in Listing 10-9.

Listing 10-9. Executing the **curl** command with the **/greet/Mike** endpoint and resulting response

```
~ » curl -s http://localhost:8080/greet/Mike | json_pp
{
   "message" : "Hello Mike!"
}
```

But wait, there is more! You can change the salutation from "*Hello*" to "*Guten Tag*" by executing a more complex version of the **curl** command as shown in Listing 10-10.

Listing 10-10. Executing a more complex curl command to change the greeting from "Hello" to "Guten Tag"

```
~ » curl -X PUT -H "Content-Type: application/json" -d '{"greeting" : "Guten Tag"}' http://localhost:8080/greet/greeting
```

Note that there is no response when you execute this command.
Now let's use "*Dieter*" as the named parameter as shown in Listing 10-11.

Listing 10-11. Executing the curl command with the **/greet/Dieter** endpoint and resulting response

```
~ » curl -s GET http://localhost:8080/greet/Dieter | json_pp
{
   "message" : "Guten Tag Dieter!"
}
```

Exercise the Application via the Browser

If you would prefer not to type all of those commands on the command line, you can simply use the browser! To exercise the application in the browser, simply add the URL in the address bar as shown in Listing 10-12.

Listing 10-12. Executing the application in the browser

```
http://localhost:8080/greet/Dieter
```

The resulting JSON response may be formatted differently depending on whether you have a JSON parser utility installed on your browser.

Server Shutdown

To shut down the server, return to your first terminal window and simply use **CTRL-C** and you will be returned to your command-line prompt.

Command-Line Interface

Introduced in Helidon 2.0, you can now create, build, and run Helidon applications via the Helidon Command-Line Interface (CLI) tool. A separate download and installation is required to use the CLI tool.

Installation

You can install the Helidon CLI from the usual operating system environments.

In macOS, you can use the **curl** command, as shown in Listing 10-13, to install the Helidon CLI utility, set the appropriate permissions, and move the executable to the **/usr/local/bin** directory.

Listing 10-13. Install the Helidon CLI utility on macOS.

```
~ » curl -L -O https://helidon.io/cli/latest/darwin/helidon
chmod +x ./helidon
sudo mv ./helidon /usr/local/bin/
```

Similarly in Linux, you can use the **curl** command, as shown in Listing 10-14, to install the Helidon CLI utility, set the appropriate permissions, and move the executable to the **/usr/local/bin** directory. Note that the URL is slightly different from that of the macOS installation.

Listing 10-14. Install the Helidon CLI utility on Linux.

```
~ » curl -L -O https://helidon.io/cli/latest/linux/helidon
chmod +x ./helidon
sudo mv ./helidon /usr/local/bin/
```

CHAPTER 10   CREATING A SMALL WORKING PROJECT WITH HELIDON MP

For those of you using the Windows environment, you can use the PowerShell command, as shown in Listing 10-15, to install the Helidon CLI utility.

Listing 10-15. Install the Helidon CLI utility on Windows.

```
C:> PowerShell -Command Invoke-WebRequest -Uri "https://helidon.io/cli/
latest/windows/helidon.exe" -OutFile "C:\Windows\system32\helidon.exe"

PowerShell -Command Invoke-WebRequest -Uri "https://helidon.io/cli/latest/
windows/helidon.exe" -OutFile "C:\Windows\system32\helidon.exe"
```

You will now have a new **helidon** command installed on your computer workstation to generate a Helidon application. Now that you have the CLI installed, let's start using it!

Upon executing the **helidon** command by itself, you will be provided with a simple help screen as shown in Listing 10-16.

Listing 10-16. Executing the **helidon** command

```
~ » helidon
Helidon command line tool

Usage: helidon [OPTIONS] COMMAND

Options

  -D<name>=<value>   Define a system property
  --verbose          Produce verbose output
  --debug            Produce debug output
  --error            Print error stack traces
  --plain            Do not use color or styles in output
  --args-file        Path to a file with arguments for Helidon CLI tool
  --props-file       Path to a properties file with user inputs for
                     Helidon CLI tool
Commands
  build              Build the application
  dev                Continuous application development
  info               Print project information
```

163

CHAPTER 10   CREATING A SMALL WORKING PROJECT WITH HELIDON MP

```
init               Generate a new project
version            Print version information
```

Run helidon COMMAND --help for more information on a command.

Now let's explore the **init** option to generate a Helidon application. As you will see, this is configurable for your application needs, and there are options that weren't available in the Quickstarts. For now, let's just invoke the default values.

In Listing 10-17, you are presented with the latest versions in the Helidon 4.0, Helidon 3.0, and Helidon 2.0 release trains.

Listing 10-17. The list of available Helidon versions

```
/usr/local/apps/helidon-apps » helidon init
Looking up default Helidon version
Helidon versions
   (1) 4.1.0
   (2) 3.2.8
   (3) 2.6.7
   (4) Show all versions
Enter selection (default: 1):
```

In Listing 10-18, you have a choice to generate a Helidon SE or Helidon MP application. In the Quickstarts section, you generated a Helidon SE application using the appropriate Maven command. Generating the Helidon SE equivalent is essentially the same, but you already learned those details in Chapter 4.

Listing 10-18. The list of available Helidon flavors

```
Helidon version: 4.1.0

| Helidon Flavor

Select a Flavor
   (1) se | Helidon SE
   (2) mp | Helidon MP
Enter selection (default: 1):
```

You should select **2** here since this is a Helidon MP application.

As you will see in Listing 10-19, here is where things look different from the Quickstarts. As you can see, a Quickstart example is still an available option, but you can also generate Database and Custom applications. Let's continue to focus on building Quickstart for now and discuss the Database and Custom examples when you learn about the Helidon components.

Listing 10-19. The list of available application types

```
| Application Type

Select an Application Type
  (1) quickstart  | Quickstart
  (2) database    | Database
  (3) custom      | Custom
Enter selection (default: 1):
```

Now select your preferred media support type as shown in Listing 10-20. The default is the Jakarta JSON Processing library, also known as JSON-P.

Listing 10-20. The list of available media types

```
| Media Support

Select a JSON library
  (1) jsonp    | JSON-P
  (2) jackson  | Jackson
  (3) jsonb    | JSON-B
Enter selection (default: 1):
```

And, finally, you can customize your project with your preferred **groupId**, **artifactId**, version number, and package name as shown in Listing 10-21.

Listing 10-21. The list of custom options for your Helidon project

```
| Customize Project

Project groupId (default: me.mpredli01-helidon):
Project artifactId (default: quickstart-mp):
Project version (default: 1.0-SNAPSHOT):
```

CHAPTER 10   CREATING A SMALL WORKING PROJECT WITH HELIDON MP

Java package name (default: me.mpredli01.mp.quickstart):

Switch directory to /usr/local/apps/helidon-apps/quickstart-mp to use CLI

Start development loop? (default: n):

You can provide your own **groupId**, **artifactId**, **version**, and **package name** if you'd like. For example, I normally use **org.redlich** as the **groupId** and the name of the project as the **artifactId**. Let's continue to use the default values.

Start development loop? (default: n):

The development loop is similar to the hot reloading provided by Quarkus (**quarkus:dev**). This monitors your source files for changes and automatically triggers a restart of the application.

When you choose the default value of **n**, the example application will be downloaded and generated in the same manner as the Quickstarts and you will be returned to the command prompt. Otherwise, you will do the same, but then automatically build and execute the application for you.

Listing 10-22 displays the resulting directory structure. Other than some of the directory names, this looks familiar, right?

Listing 10-22. The resulting directory structure after executing the **helidon init** command

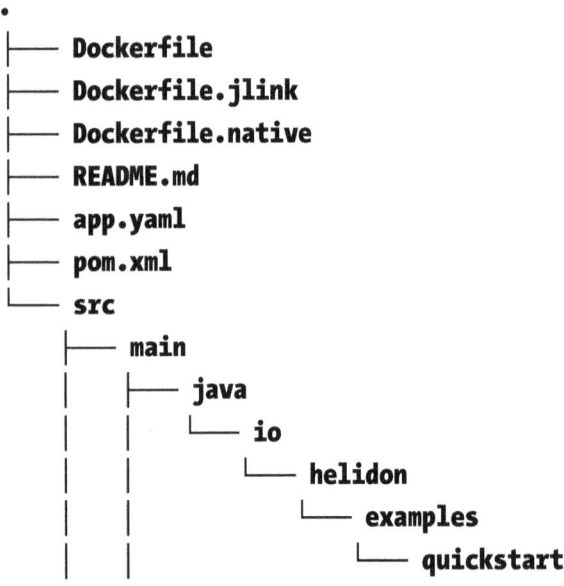

166

CHAPTER 10 CREATING A SMALL WORKING PROJECT WITH HELIDON MP

```
|   |           └── mp
|   |               ├── GreetResource.java
|   |               ├── GreetingProvider.java
|   |               ├── Message.java
|   |               ├── SimpleGreetResource.java
|   |               └── package-info.java
|   └── resources
|       ├── META-INF
|       |   ├── beans.xml
|       |   ├── microprofile-config.properties
|       |   └── native-image
|       |       └── io
|       |           └── helidon
|       |               └── examples
|       |                   └── helidon-quickstart-mp
|       |                       └── native-image.properties
|       └── logging.properties
└── test
    ├── java
    |   └── io
    |       └── helidon
    |           └── examples
    |               └── quickstart
    |                   └── mp
    |                       └── MainTest.java
    └── resources
        ├── META-INF
        |   └── microprofile-config.properties
        └── application-test.yaml
```

24 directories, 18 files

Now, let's build the application using the **build** option as shown in Listing 10-23. But first, you should change the directory to where the application resides, that is, the **quickstart-mp** directory.

167

Listing 10-23. Executing the **helidon build** command

/usr/local/apps/helidon-apps » cd quickstart-mp
/usr/local/apps/helidon-apps/quickstart-mp » helidon build

$ helidon build

At this point, you can exercise the application in the same manner as with the Quickstarts.

Now that you have completed exploring the Helidon CLI, let's make our way over to the Helidon Project Starter.

Project Starter

Introduced in Helidon 3.0, Project Starter (*https://helidon.io/starter/*) is a web-based application for generating Helidon applications. This is essentially an online GUI version of the Helidon CLI.

Let's go through each of the sections and, once again, select the default values as shown in Figures 10-1 through 10-4.

CHAPTER 10 CREATING A SMALL WORKING PROJECT WITH HELIDON MP

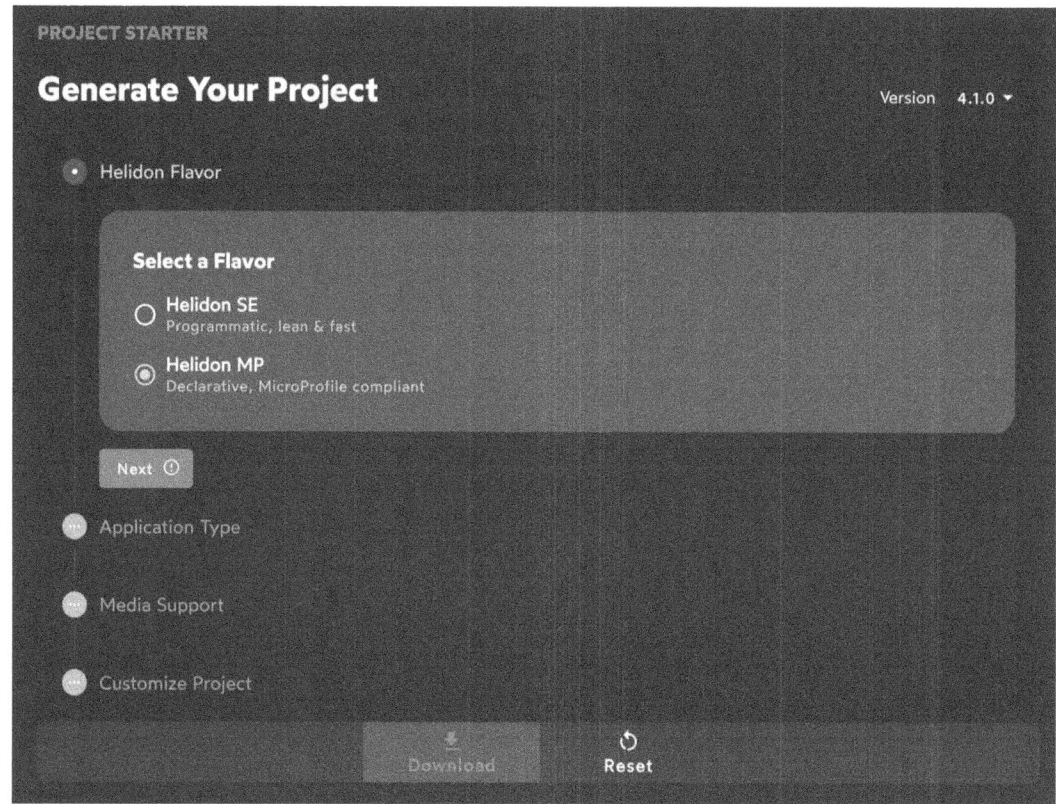

Figure 10-1. *The Helidon flavor section of the Helidon Starter page*

Click "*Next*".

CHAPTER 10   CREATING A SMALL WORKING PROJECT WITH HELIDON MP

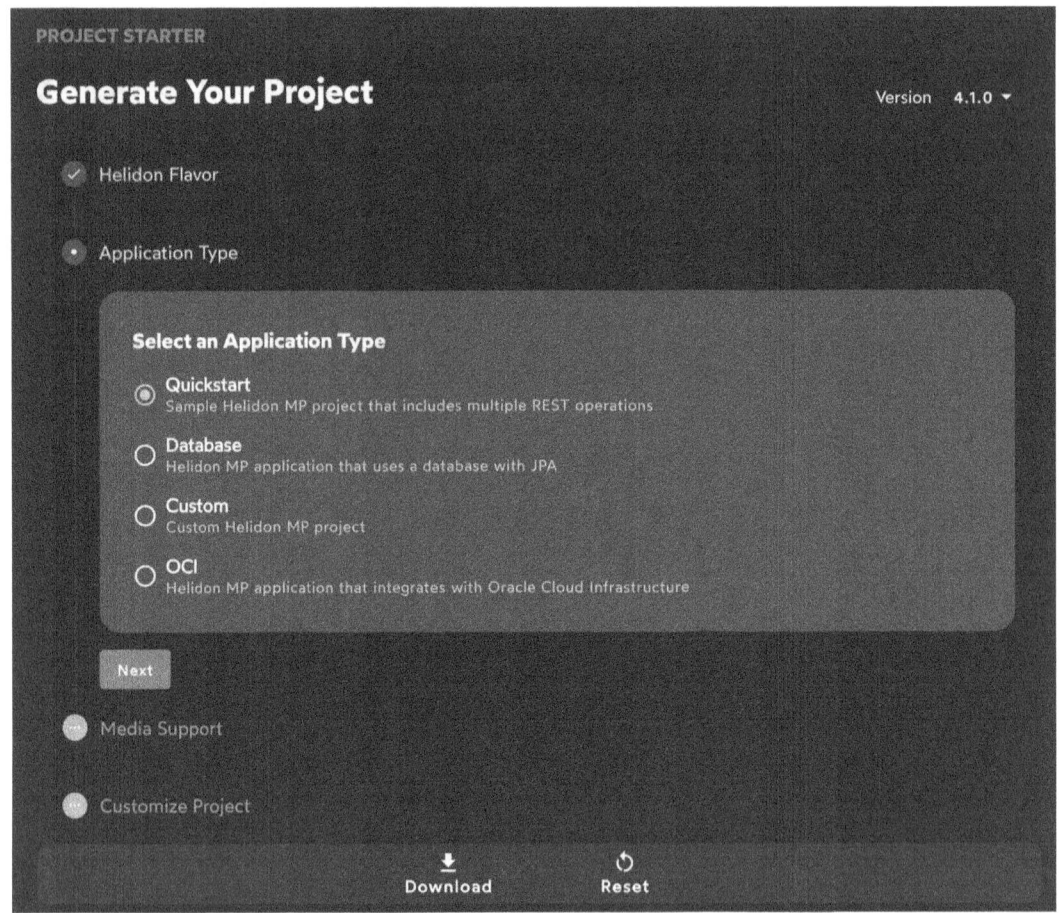

Figure 10-2. *The application type section of the Helidon Starter page*

Click "*Next*".

CHAPTER 10   CREATING A SMALL WORKING PROJECT WITH HELIDON MP

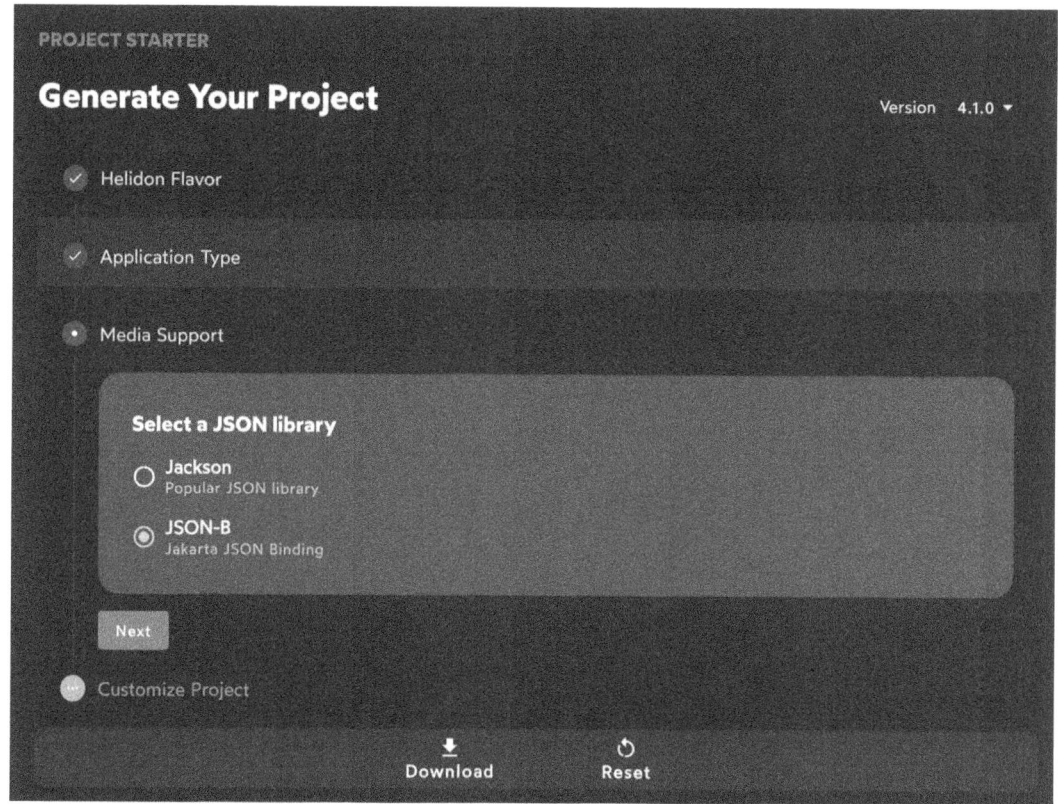

Figure 10-3. *The media support section of the Helidon Starter page*

Click "*Next*".

CHAPTER 10   CREATING A SMALL WORKING PROJECT WITH HELIDON MP

Figure 10-4. *The customize project section of the Helidon Starter page*

You can now click the "Download" button. You will be provided with a **myproject.zip** file in your default downloads directory. Once you extract the ZIP file, a **myproject** folder will be created and you will see the resulting directory structure as shown in Listing 10-24.

Listing 10-24. The resulting directory structure from unzipping the myproject.zip file

```
.
├── Dockerfile
├── Dockerfile.jlink
├── Dockerfile.native
```

172

CHAPTER 10　CREATING A SMALL WORKING PROJECT WITH HELIDON MP

```
├── README.md
├── app.yaml
├── pom.xml
└── src
    ├── main
    │   ├── java
    │   │   └── io
    │   │       └── helidon
    │   │           └── examples
    │   │               └── quickstart
    │   │                   └── mp
    │   │                       ├── GreetResource.java
    │   │                       ├── GreetingProvider.java
    │   │                       ├── Message.java
    │   │                       ├── SimpleGreetResource.java
    │   │                       └── package-info.java
    │   └── resources
    │       ├── META-INF
    │       │   ├── beans.xml
    │       │   ├── microprofile-config.properties
    │       │   └── native-image
    │       │       └── io
    │       │           └── helidon
    │       │               └── examples
    │       │                   └── helidon-quickstart-mp
    │       │                       └── native-image.properties
    │       └── logging.properties
    └── test
        └── java
            └── io
                └── helidon
                    └── examples
                        └── quickstart
                            └── mp
                                └── MainTest.java
```

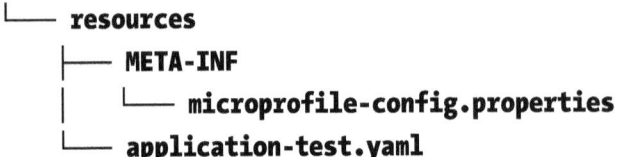

```
24 directories, 18 files
```

This, too, looks familiar, right? As with the Quickstarts, you can build the application with Maven and initiate the project using the **java** command as shown in Listing 10-25.

Listing 10-25. Initiate and execute the application.

```
myproject » mvn clean package
myproject » java -jar target/myproject.jar
```

Summary

In this chapter, you learned how to get started with Helidon MP by working with a small example that can be generated with your choice of Quickstarts, the Command-Line Interface, or Helidon Project Starter.

The next three chapters in Part III will cover Helidon MP components: Metrics, Fault Tolerance, and Health Checks.

CHAPTER 11

Helidon Metrics

Helidon Metrics in Helidon MP is a compatible implementation of the MicroProfile Metrics specification. Helidon Metrics is just one of the observability features available for your Helidon applications. This chapter will cover Helidon Metrics in detail and provide a working example application. You will be introduced to other observability features, that is, Helidon Fault Tolerance and Helidon Health Checks in Chapters 12 and 13, respectively.

Instrumenting Your Application

By default, any MicroProfile-compliant application automatically generates metrics-related endpoints that provide default metrics. You can add your own custom metrics using the available annotations in Helidon Metrics.

There are three methods for adding metrics to your application:

- Use annotations on bean methods which typically have a defined REST endpoint.

- Explicitly invoke the Metrics API to register, retrieve, and update metrics and their values.

- Enable the built-in simple `REST.request` metrics.

Helidon automatically registers and maintains these metrics for all REST endpoints. Annotated methods are updated when they are injected using the `@Inject` annotation from the Jakarta Contexts and Dependency Injection (CDI) specification.

Helidon Metrics Scopes and Corresponding REST Endpoints

The MicroProfile Metrics specification defines scopes, or metric types, for different use cases. Table 11-1 lists these built-in scopes and their respective use cases and endpoints.

Table 11-1. *The Helidon Metrics scopes, use cases, and corresponding endpoints*

Scope	Use Case	REST Endpoint
base	Operating system or Java runtime measurements.	**/metrics/base**
vendor	Implemented by vendors that include metrics under **REST.request** and other key performance indicator measurements.	**/metrics/vendor**
application	Declared through the Helidon Metrics annotations or programmatically registered by your application.	**/metrics/application**

Note By default, registering your own custom metrics is found in the **application** scope.

Base Metrics

Base metrics is an optional list of metrics that vendors may implement. As described in Table 11-1, these metrics are exposed under **/metrics/base** endpoint. Table 11-2 lists these base metrics (*https://github.com/eclipse/microprofile-metrics/blob/main/spec/src/main/asciidoc/base-metrics.adoc*) along with their respective meter, unit of measure, and description.

Table 11-2. *The list of base metrics from the Base Metrics section of the MicroProfile specification*

Name	Meter	Unit	Description
`memory.usedHeap`	Gauge	Bytes	Displays the amount of used heap memory.
`memory.committedHeap`	Gauge	Bytes	Displays the amount of memory that is committed and guaranteed for the Java virtual machine to use.
`memory.maxHeap`	Gauge	Bytes	Displays the maximum amount of heap memory that can be used for memory management. A value of -1 is displayed if the maximum heap memory size is undefined.
`gc.total`	Counter	None	Displays the total number of collections that have occurred. A value of -1 is displayed if the count is undefined for this metric.
`gc.time`	Counter	Seconds	Displays the approximate accumulated elapsed collection time. A value of -1 is displayed if the elapsed time is undefined for this metric.
`jvm.uptime`	Gauge	Seconds	Displays the time elapsed since the start of the Java virtual machine.
`thread.count`	Gauge	None	Displays the current number of live threads. This includes both daemon and non-daemon threads.
`thread.daemon.count`	Gauge	None	Displays the current number of live daemon threads.
`thread.max.count`	Gauge	None	Displays the peak live thread count since the Java virtual machine started or peak was reset. This includes both daemon and non-daemon threads.
`threadpool.activeThreads`	Gauge	None	Number of active threads that belong to a specific thread pool.

(*continued*)

Table 11-2. (*continued*)

Name	Meter	Unit	Description
threadpool.size	Gauge	None	The size of a specific thread pool.
classloader.loadedClasses.count	Gauge	None	Displays the number of classes that are currently loaded in the Java virtual machine.
classloader.loadedClasses.total	Counter	None	Displays the total number of classes that have been loaded since execution of the Java virtual machine has started.
classloader.unloadedClasses.total	Counter	None	Displays the total number of classes unloaded since execution of the Java virtual machine has started.
cpu.availableProcessors	Gauge	None	Displays the number of processors available to the Java virtual machine. This value may change during a particular invocation of the virtual machine.
cpu.systemLoadAverage	Gauge	None	Displays the system load average for the last minute. The system load average is calculated as • The sum of the number of runnable entities queued to the available processors • The number of runnable entities running on the available processors averaged over a period of time The way in which the load average is calculated is specific to the operating system but is typically a damped time-dependent average. A negative value is displayed if the load average is not available.
cpu.processCpuLoad	Gauge	Percent	Displays the recent CPU usage for the Java virtual machine process.
cpu.processCpuTime	Gauge	Seconds	Displays the CPU time used by the process on which the Java virtual machine is running.

Metric Registries and the MetricRegistry API

A metric registry, also referred to as MetricRegistry, collects and stores your registered metrics and related metadata for a specified scope. Helidon supports one metric registry for each scope. The metric registry provides methods to register, create, and retrieve metrics. As you programmatically create a metric, your source code locates the appropriate metric registry and then registers that metric.

The MetricRegistry API, defined in the MicroProfile Metrics specification and implemented in Helidon, programmatically registers or looks up metrics. Your application code uses an instance of the **MetricRegistry** interface for the scope of interest, which is **base**, **vendor**, and **application**, as described in Table 11-1, or a custom scope.

You can use one of the following techniques to obtain a **MetricRegistry** reference. Remember that injection works only if the class is a Java bean so that CDI can inject into it.

- Inject an instance of the **MetricRegistry** with the Jakarta CDI **@Inject** annotation optionally using the **@RegistryScope** annotation to indicate the scope of the registry.

- Obtain an instance of the **RegistryFactory** class and invoke its **getRegistry()** method.

Helidon Metrics Annotations

You can add metrics in your application using the built-in annotations provided by Helidon. These metrics are then registered in the **application** scope. Table 11-3 lists these annotations and their respective use cases.

Table 11-3. The Helidon Metrics annotations and their use cases

Annotation	Use Cases
@Counted	A measure of an increasing count of events.
@Gauge	A measure of a value managed by code in your application.
@Timed	A measure of the frequency of invocations and the corresponding distribution of time.

@Counted Annotation

The **@Counted** annotation marks a method, constructor, or class as counted. This metric will be registered in MetricRegistry declared in your application.

When you use this annotation with at least one of its parameters, as shown in Listing 11-1, a counter with the *fully qualified class name* + **countedName** will be created, and for each time the **countedName(String)** method is invoked, the counter will be marked. Similarly, the same applies for a constructor annotated with **@Counted**.

Listing 11-1. Using the **@Counted** annotation with a parameter

```
@Counted(name = "countedName")
public String countedName(String name) {
    return "I am a counter named: " + name;
}
```

When you use this annotation without specifying any of its parameters, as shown in Listing 11-2, a counter for the defining class will be created for each of the constructors and methods. Each time the constructor or method is invoked, the respective counter will be marked. The counter value will only monotonically increase. This annotation will throw an **IllegalStateException** if the constructor and/or method is invoked, but the metric no longer exists in the metric registry.

Listing 11-2. Using the **@Counted** annotation without a parameter

```
@Counted
public class CounterBean {
    public void countMethod1() {}
    public void countMethod2() {}
}
```

@Gauge Annotation

The **@Gauge** annotation marks a method or field as a gauge. This metric will be registered in the MetricRegistry declared in your application.

When you use this annotation with at least one of its parameters, as shown in Listing 11-3, a gauge with the *fully qualified class name* + **gaugeName** will be created, which uses the annotated method's return value as its value. The annotated method and field must be of a numeric type.

Listing 11-3. Using the **@Gauge** annotation

```
@Gauge(name = "gaugeName")
public int getQueueSize() {
    return queue.size;
}
```

@Timed Annotation

The **@Timed** annotation marks a method, constructor, or class as timed. This metric will be registered in the MetricRegistry declared in your application. The underlying timer metric aggregates timing durations and provides duration statistics.

When you use this annotation with at least one of the parameters, as shown in Listing 11-4, a timer with the *fully qualified class name* + **timedName** will be created, and each time the **timedName(String)** method is invoked, the method's execution will be timed.

Listing 11-4. Using the **@Timed** annotation with a parameter

```
@Timed(name = "timedName")
public String timedName(String name) {
    return "I am a timer named: " + name;
}
```

When you use this annotation without specifying any of its parameters, as shown in Listing 11-5, a timer for the defining class will be created for each of the constructors and methods. Each time a constructor or method is invoked, the execution will be timed with the respective timer. This annotation will throw an **IllegalStateException** if the constructor and/or method is invoked, but the metric no longer exists in the metric registry.

Listing 11-5. Using the **@Timed** annotation without a parameter

```
@Timed
public class TimedBean {
    public void timedMethod1() {}
    public void timedMethod2() {}
}
```

Annotation Parameters

For all three of these annotations, the parameters for each one are listed, along with their respective return types and descriptions, in Table 11-4.

Table 11-4. *The annotation parameters for the **@Counted**, **@Gauge**, and **@Timed** annotations*

Return Type	Parameter	Description
boolean	absolute	Denotes whether to use the absolute name or use the default given name relative to the annotated class.
String	description	The description of the gauge.
String	name	The name of the gauge.
String	scope	The scope to which this gauge belongs.
String[]	tags	The tags of the gauge.
String	unit	The unit of the counter.

Putting It All Together

Now that you've learned how to instrument your application with metrics, let's put it all together and build an application! You can find the full source code and relevant documentation at the **helidon-book** GitHub repository (*https://github.com/mpredli01/helidon-book*) under the **metrics** module. Inspiration for these examples was adapted from the Helidon examples GitHub repository (*https://github.com/helidon-io/helidon-examples/*).

CHAPTER 11 HELIDON METRICS

To demonstrate Helidon Metrics in action, let's take a look at a small working example that demonstrates the metric types, the **MetricRegistry** API, and annotations such as **@Counted**, **@Timed**, and **@Gauge**. You will even see how to add a histogram metric. The application consists of five classes: **Message**, **SimpleGreetResource**, **GaugeMetric**, **HttpStatusMetricFilter**, and **TemperatureHistogramFilter**. The **Message** class is a standard Plain Old Java Object (POJO) containing getters and setters for two strings: **message** and **greeting**. The **SimpleGreetResource** class defines endpoints, **/simple-greeting** and **/simple-greeting/{name}**, that you already know from the Quickstart examples. So, that leaves the remaining classes that are the main focus of this example application.

Dependencies

Let's start with Maven and Gradle dependencies that you would use in your application.

> **Note** The examples associated with this book use Maven as a build tool. The Gradle dependency is listed here for completeness and for the possibility of adding Gradle as a build tool in the future.

If Maven is your build tool, use the dependency as shown in Listing 11-6.

Listing 11-6. The Maven dependency for Helidon Metrics

```xml
<dependency>
    <groupId>io.helidon.microprofile.metrics</groupId>
    <artifactId>helidon-microprofile-metrics</artifactId>
    <version>4.1.0</version>
</dependency>
```

If Gradle is your build tool, use the dependency as shown in Listing 11-7.

Listing 11-7. The Gradle dependency for Helidon Metrics

```
implementation group: 'io.helidon.microprofile.metrics', name: 'helidon-microprofile-metrics', version: '4.1.0'
```

CHAPTER 11 HELIDON METRICS

Using the @Counted and @Timed Annotations

First, let's start with a modified version of the **SimpleGreetResource** class to include some basic metrics as shown in Listing 11-8.

Listing 11-8. A modified version of the **SimpleGreetResource** class to include base metrics

```
@Path("/simple-greet")
public class SimpleGreetResource {
    private static final String PERSONALIZED_GETS_COUNTER_NAME
    = "personalizedGetCounter";
    private static final String PERSONALIZED_GETS_COUNTER_DESCRIPTION
    = "Counts the number of personalized GET operations using the
    /simple-greet/{name} endpoint";
    private static final String GETS_TIMER_NAME = "personalizedGetTimer";
    private static final String GETS_TIMER_DESCRIPTION = "Tracks the time
    for the personalized GET operations using the /simple-greet/{name}
    endpoint";
    private final String message;

    @Inject
    public SimpleGreetResource(@ConfigProperty(name = "app.greeting")
    String message) {
        this.message = message;
    }

    @GET
    @Produces(MediaType.APPLICATION_JSON)
    public Message getDefaultMessage() {
        String msg = String.format("%s %s!", message, "World");
        Message message = new Message();
        message.setMessage(msg);
        return message;
        }

    @Path("/{name}")
    @GET
```

```
@Produces(MediaType.APPLICATION_JSON)
@Counted(name = PERSONALIZED_GETS_COUNTER_NAME, absolute = true,
description = PERSONALIZED_GETS_COUNTER_DESCRIPTION) ❶
@Timed(name = GETS_TIMER_NAME, absolute = true, description
= GETS_TIMER_DESCRIPTION, unit = MetricUnits.SECONDS) ❷
public Message getMessage(@PathParam("name") String name) {
    String message = String.format("Hello %s", name);
    return new Message(message);
    }
}
```

❶ Using the **@Counted** annotation to mark the **getMessage()** method as counted

❷ Using the **@Timed** annotation to mark the same **getMessage()** method as timed

Histogram Metric

Now let's take a look at the **TemperatureHistogramFilter** class, as shown in Listing 11-9, that takes the values of the July 2024 daily high temperatures, as measured at the Trenton-Mercer Airport in Ewing, New Jersey, and creates a histogram that will be displayed in the metrics response.

Listing 11-9. The **TemperatureHistrogramFilter** class

```
@ConstrainedTo(RuntimeType.SERVER) ❶
@Provider ❷
public class TemperatureHistogramFilter implements
ContainerResponseFilter { ❸

    static final int[] RECENT_TRENTON_TEMPERATURES = { 80,83,84,91,95,9
    6,92,94,93,93,88,82,90,90,96,97,94,83,84,82,87,82,83,80,83,83,85,87,8
    6,87,91 };

    static final String TEMPERATURE_HISTOGRAM_NAME = "temperatureHis
    togram";
```

```java
    static final String TEMPERATURE_HISTOGRAM_DESCRIPTION = "A histogram of
    temperatures in Trenton, New Jersey for the month of July 2024";

    @Inject
    private MetricRegistry metricRegistry; ❹

    @Inject
    @Metric(name = "temperatures", description = TEMPERATURE_HISTOGRAM_
    DESCRIPTION) ❺
    private Histogram histogram;

    @PostConstruct ❻
    public void init() {
        Metadata metadata = new MetadataBuilder() ❼
                .withName(TEMPERATURE_HISTOGRAM_NAME)
                .withDescription(TEMPERATURE_HISTOGRAM_DESCRIPTION)
                .withUnit(MetricUnits.NONE)
                .build();
        histogram = metricRegistry.histogram(metadata, new Tag("unit",
        "°F")); ❽
    }

    @Override
    public void filter(ContainerRequestContext containerRequestContext,
ContainerResponseContext containerResponseContext) ❾
            throws IOException {
        updateHistogram();
    }

    private void updateHistogram() { ❿
        for(int temp : RECENT_TRENTON_TEMPERATURES) {
            histogram.update(temp);
        }
    }
}
```

❶ The **@ConstrainedTo** annotation restricts an implementation of the **ContainerResponseFilter** provider interface, which is the **TemperatureHistogramFilter** class, to run only as part of a Jakarta RESTful Web Services server runtime.

❷ The **@Provider** annotation marks an implementation of an extension interface that should be discoverable by Jakarta RESTful Web Services runtime during the provider scanning phase.

❸ The **ContainerResponseFilter** is an extension interface implemented by container response filters.

Note The **@ConstrainedTo** and **@Provider** annotations and the **ContainerResponseFilter** interface are defined in the Jakarta RESTful Web Services specification.

---

❹ Injecting an instance of the **MetricRegistry** interface into the application.

❺ The **@Metric** annotation that requests that a metric be injected or registered. The metric will be registered in the application's metric registry.

❻ The **@PostConstruct** annotation, defined in the Jakarta Annotations specification, is used on a method that needs to be executed after dependency injection to perform any initialization.

❼ Building the histogram metadata with the **MetadataBuilder** class.

❽ The **histogram()** method that returns a histogram registered under the metric ID with the defined histogram name with the provided tags.

❾ Implementing the **filter(ContainerRequest Context, ContainerResponseContext)** method, declared in the **ContainerResponseFilter** interface, to call the **updateHistogram()** method.

❿ The **updateHistogram()** method iterates through the list of daily high temperatures, defined in the **RECENT_TRENTON_ TEMPERATURES** integer array, and updates the histogram via the **for** loop.

Using a Gauge

While the **@Counted** and **@Timed** annotations are similar, the **@Gauge** annotation is slightly different. Let's take a look at the **GaugeMetric** class as shown in Listing 11-10.

Listing 11-10. The **GaugeMetric** class

```
@ApplicationScoped
public class GaugeMetric {

    private AtomicLong startTime = new AtomicLong(0);

    public void onStartUp(@Observes @Initialized(ApplicationScoped.class)
    Object init) { ❶❷
        startTime = new AtomicLong(System.currentTimeMillis());
    }

    @Gauge(unit = MetricUnits.SECONDS) ❸
    public long applicationUpTime() { ❹
        return Duration.ofMillis(System.currentTimeMillis() - startTime.
        get()).getSeconds();
    }
}
```

❶ The **@Initialized** annotation is a qualifier to trigger an event with this qualifier when a context is initialized, that is, ready for use.

❷ The **@Observes** annotation identifies an event parameter of an observer method or a parameter of that method of a bean class or extension.

❸ Using the **@Gauge** annotation on the **applicationUpTime()** method to define the required **unit** parameter of **MetricUnits.SECONDS**.

❹ The **applicationUpTime()** method calculates the time the application has been up and running.

Prometheus Format

Before we build and exercise the application, you need to know a little about Prometheus format, which is the default response from the metrics endpoints.

Prometheus (*https://prometheus.io/*) is an open source systems monitoring and alerting toolkit introduced in 2012. Prometheus collects and stores its metrics as time series data alongside labels that are optional key-value pairs.

As per the Prometheus documentation, lines that start with a hashtag or pound symbol (**#**) as the first non-whitespace character are classified as comments. These are ignored unless the first token after the hashtag is either **HELP** or **TYPE**. Those lines are treated as follows:

- If the token is **HELP**, at least one more token is expected, which is the metric name. All remaining tokens are classified as a document string for that metric name. Only one **HELP** line may exist for any given metric name.

- If the token is **TYPE**, exactly two more tokens are expected. The first is the metric name, and the second is either *counter*, *gauge*, *histogram*, *summary*, or *untyped*, which defines the type for the metric of that name. Only one **TYPE** line may exist for a given metric name. The **TYPE** line for a metric name must appear before the first sample is reported for that metric name. If there is no **TYPE** line for a metric name, the type is set to *untyped*.

Now that everything has been covered, let's build, execute, and exercise the application!

Build and Execute the Application

From the command line, you can build and package the application as a JAR file with Maven as shown in Listing 11-11.

Listing 11-11. Build and package the application as a JAR file with Maven.

```
~ » mvn clean package
```

Now you can invoke the JAR file using the **java** command as shown in Listing 11-12. Note the last part of the response that displays the URL and JVM startup time.

Listing 11-12. Invoke the application with the **java** command.

```
~ » java -jar target/metrics.jar
2024.08.11 08:48:34 INFO io.helidon.microprofile.server.ServerCdiExtension
Thread[#1,main,5,main]: Server started on http://localhost:8080 (and all
other host addresses) in 3183 milliseconds (since JVM startup).
2024.08.11 08:48:34 INFO io.helidon.common.features.HelidonFeatures
Thread[#51,features-thread,5,main]: Helidon MP 4.1.0 features: [CDI,
Config, Fault Tolerance, Health, Metrics, Server]
```

Exercising the Application

Using the defined endpoints, **/metrics/base** and **/metrics/application**, let's exercise the application with each one and examine their respective responses in Prometheus format.

Listing 11-13 demonstrates how to exercise the **/metrics/base** endpoint.

Listing 11-13. Exercising the **/metrics/base** endpoint

```
~ » curl localhost:8080/metrics/base
# HELP classloader_loadedClasses_count Displays the number of classes that
are currently loaded in the Java virtual machine.
# TYPE classloader_loadedClasses_count gauge
classloader_loadedClasses_count{mp_scope="base",} 7398.0
# HELP classloader_unloadedClasses_total Displays the total number of
classes unloaded since the Java virtual machine has started execution.
```

```
# TYPE classloader_unloadedClasses_total counter
classloader_unloadedClasses_total{mp_scope="base",} 0.0
# HELP memory_maxHeap_bytes Displays the maximum amount of heap memory in
bytes that can be used for memory management. This attribute displays -1
if the maximum heap memory size is undefined. This amount of memory is not
guaranteed to be available for memory management if it is greater than the
amount of committed memory. The Java virtual machine may fail to allocate
memory even if the amount of used memory does not exceed this maximum size.
# TYPE memory_maxHeap_bytes gauge
memory_maxHeap_bytes{mp_scope="base",} 2.147483648E9
# HELP cpu_availableProcessors Displays the number of processors available
to the Java virtual machine. This value may change during a particular
invocation of the virtual machine.
# TYPE cpu_availableProcessors gauge
cpu_availableProcessors{mp_scope="base",} 8.0
# HELP thread_count Displays the current number of live threads including
both daemon and nondaemon threads
# TYPE thread_count gauge
thread_count{mp_scope="base",} 17.0
# HELP jvm_uptime_seconds Displays the start time of the Java virtual
machine in seconds. This attribute displays the approximate time when the
Java virtual machine started.
# TYPE jvm_uptime_seconds gauge
jvm_uptime_seconds{mp_scope="base",} 1016.519
# HELP thread_daemon_count Displays the current number of live daemon
threads.
# TYPE thread_daemon_count gauge
thread_daemon_count{mp_scope="base",} 15.0
# HELP thread_max_count Displays the peak live thread count since the Java
virtual machine started or peak was reset. This includes daemon and
non-daemon threads.
# TYPE thread_max_count gauge
thread_max_count{mp_scope="base",} 28.0
# HELP memory_usedHeap_bytes Displays the amount of used heap memory
in bytes.
```

```
# TYPE memory_usedHeap_bytes gauge
memory_usedHeap_bytes{mp_scope="base",} 1.9936312E7
# HELP cpu_systemLoadAverage Displays the system load average for the
last minute. The system load average is the sum of the number of runnable
entities queued to the available processors and the number of runnable
entities running on the available processors averaged over a period of
time. The way in which the load average is calculated is operating system
specific but is typically a damped timedependent average. If the load
average is not available, a negative value is displayed. This attribute
is designed to provide a hint about the system load and may be queried
frequently. The load average may be unavailable on some platforms where it
is expensive to implement this method.
# TYPE cpu_systemLoadAverage gauge
cpu_systemLoadAverage{mp_scope="base",} 1.78076171875
# HELP classloader_loadedClasses_total Displays the total number of classes
that have been loaded since the Java virtual machine has started execution.
# TYPE classloader_loadedClasses_total counter
classloader_loadedClasses_total{mp_scope="base",} 7398.0
# HELP gc_time_seconds_total Displays the approximate accumulated
collection elapsed time in seconds. This attribute displays -1 if the
collection elapsed time is undefined for this collector. The Java virtual
machine implementation may use a high resolution timer to measure the
elapsed time. This attribute may display the same value even if the
collection count has been incremented if the collection elapsed time is
very short.
# TYPE gc_time_seconds_total counter
gc_time_seconds_total{mp_scope="base",name="G1 Old Generation",} 0.0
gc_time_seconds_total{mp_scope="base",name="G1 Concurrent GC",} 0.0
gc_time_seconds_total{mp_scope="base",name="G1 Young Generation",} 0.0
# HELP gc_total Displays the total number of collections that have
occurred. This attribute lists -1 if the collection count is undefined for
this collector.
# TYPE gc_total counter
gc_total{mp_scope="base",name="G1 Old Generation",} 0.0
gc_total{mp_scope="base",name="G1 Concurrent GC",} 2.0
```

```
gc_total{mp_scope="base",name="G1 Young Generation",} 4.0
# HELP memory_committedHeap_bytes Displays the amount of memory in bytes
that is committed for the Java virtual machine to use. This amount of
memory is guaranteed for the Java virtual machine to use.
# TYPE memory_committedHeap_bytes gauge
memory_committedHeap_bytes{mp_scope="base",} 4.6137344E7
```

Base metrics report operating system or Java runtime measurements. For example, the **classloader.loadedClasses.count** measurement is represented in the response as shown in Listing 11-14.

Listing 11-14. The listing and corresponding value of the **classloader.loadedClasses.count** measurement

```
# TYPE classloader_loadedClasses_count gauge
classloader_loadedClasses_count{mp_scope="base",} 7398.0
```

Notice how the dot notation in the metric name is replaced with an underscore character. Also, the base scope is explicitly displayed as **{mp_scope="base}**.

Now, let's execute the **/metrics/application** endpoint as shown in Listing 11-15.

Listing 11-15. Exercising the **/metrics/application** endpoint

```
~ » curl localhost:8080/metrics/application
# HELP org_redlich_metrics_TemperatureHistogramFilter_temperatures_max A
histogram of temperatures in Trenton, New Jersey for the month of July 2024
# TYPE org_redlich_metrics_TemperatureHistogramFilter_temperatures_max gauge
org_redlich_metrics_TemperatureHistogramFilter_temperatures_max
{mp_scope="application",} 0.0
# HELP org_redlich_metrics_TemperatureHistogramFilter_temperatures A
histogram of temperatures in Trenton, New Jersey for the month of July 2024
# TYPE org_redlich_metrics_TemperatureHistogramFilter_temperatures summary
org_redlich_metrics_TemperatureHistogramFilter_temperatures{mp_scope=
"application",quantile="0.5",} 0.0
org_redlich_metrics_TemperatureHistogramFilter_temperatures{mp_scope=
"application",quantile="0.75",} 0.0
org_redlich_metrics_TemperatureHistogramFilter_temperatures{mp_scope=
"application",quantile="0.95",} 0.0
```

CHAPTER 11   HELIDON METRICS

```
org_redlich_metrics_TemperatureHistogramFilter_temperatures{mp_scope=
"application",quantile="0.98",} 0.0
org_redlich_metrics_TemperatureHistogramFilter_temperatures{mp_scope=
"application",quantile="0.99",} 0.0
org_redlich_metrics_TemperatureHistogramFilter_temperatures{mp_scope=
"application",quantile="0.999",} 0.0
org_redlich_metrics_TemperatureHistogramFilter_temperatures_count
{mp_scope="application",} 0.0
org_redlich_metrics_TemperatureHistogramFilter_temperatures_sum
{mp_scope="application",} 0.0
# HELP org_redlich_metrics_GaugeMetric_applicationUpTime_seconds
# TYPE org_redlich_metrics_GaugeMetric_applicationUpTime_seconds gauge
org_redlich_metrics_GaugeMetric_applicationUpTime_seconds
{mp_scope="application",} 4.0
# HELP temperatureHistogram_max A histogram of temperatures in Trenton,
New Jersey for the month of July 2024
# TYPE temperatureHistogram_max gauge
temperatureHistogram_max{mp_scope="application",unit="°F",} 97.0
# HELP temperatureHistogram A histogram of temperatures in Trenton,
New Jersey for the month of July 2024
# TYPE temperatureHistogram summary
temperatureHistogram{mp_scope="application",unit="°F",quantile="0.5",} 87.0
temperatureHistogram{mp_scope="application",unit="°F",quanti
le="0.75",} 93.0
temperatureHistogram{mp_scope="application",unit="°F",quanti
le="0.95",} 96.0
temperatureHistogram{mp_scope="application",unit="°F",quanti
le="0.98",} 97.0
temperatureHistogram{mp_scope="application",unit="°F",quanti
le="0.99",} 97.0
temperatureHistogram{mp_scope="application",unit="°F",quanti
le="0.999",} 97.0
temperatureHistogram_count{mp_scope="application",unit="°F",} 31.0
temperatureHistogram_sum{mp_scope="application",unit="°F",} 2721.0
# HELP httpStatus_total Counts the number of HTTP responses in each status
category (1xx, 2xx, etc.)
```

```
# TYPE httpStatus_total counter
httpStatus_total{mp_scope="application",range="4xx",} 1.0
httpStatus_total{mp_scope="application",range="3xx",} 0.0
httpStatus_total{mp_scope="application",range="5xx",} 0.0
httpStatus_total{mp_scope="application",range="2xx",} 0.0
httpStatus_total{mp_scope="application",range="1xx",} 0.0
# HELP personalizedGetTimer_seconds_max Tracks the time for the
personalized GET operations using the /simple-greet/{name} endpoint
# TYPE personalizedGetTimer_seconds_max gauge
personalizedGetTimer_seconds_max{mp_scope="application",} 0.0
# HELP personalizedGetTimer_seconds Tracks the time for the personalized
GET operations using the /simple-greet/{name} endpoint
# TYPE personalizedGetTimer_seconds summary
personalizedGetTimer_seconds{mp_scope="application",quantile="0.5",} 0.0
personalizedGetTimer_seconds{mp_scope="application",quantile="0.75",} 0.0
personalizedGetTimer_seconds{mp_scope="application",quantile="0.95",} 0.0
personalizedGetTimer_seconds{mp_scope="application",quantile="0.98",} 0.0
personalizedGetTimer_seconds{mp_scope="application",quantile="0.99",} 0.0
personalizedGetTimer_seconds{mp_scope="application",quantile="0.999",} 0.0
personalizedGetTimer_seconds_count{mp_scope="application",} 0.0
personalizedGetTimer_seconds_sum{mp_scope="application",} 0.0
# HELP personalizedGetCounter_total Counts the number of personalized GET
operations using the /simple-greet/{name} endpoint
# TYPE personalizedGetCounter_total counter
personalizedGetCounter_total{mp_scope="application",} 0.0
```

Application metrics are declared via annotations or programmatically registered by your application code.

For our modified **SimpleGreetResource** class, the **personalizedGetCounter** metric increments the count at each execution of the **/simple-greet/{name}** endpoint. This is represented as shown in Listing 11-16.

Listing 11-16. The listing and value of the **personalizedGetCounter** metric

```
# TYPE personalizedGetCounter_total counter
personalizedGetCounter_total{mp_scope="application",} 0.0
```

The counter is currently at **0.0** since the **/simple-greet/{name}** endpoint hasn't yet been executed.

As shown in Listing 11-17, let's execute the **/simple-greet/{name}** endpoint using *Mike* as the name.

Listing 11-17. Executing the **/simple-greet/Mike** endpoint

```
~ » curl -s localhost:8080/simple-greet/Mike | json_pp
{
   "message" : "Hello Mike"
}
```

Upon refreshing the **/metrics/application** endpoint, the **personalizedGetCounter** metric will now be displayed with an updated counter at **1.0** as shown in Listing 11-18.

Listing 11-18. The listing and updated value of the **personalizedGetCounter** metric

```
# TYPE personalizedGetCounter_total counter
personalizedGetCounter_total{mp_scope="application",} 1.0
```

For the **TemperatureHistogramFilter** class, the response is shown in Listing 11-19.

Listing 11-19. The listing and corresponding values of the **temperatureHistogram** metric

```
# HELP org_redlich_metrics_TemperatureHistogramFilter_temperatures_max A
histogram of temperatures in Trenton, New Jersey for the month of July 2024
# TYPE org_redlich_metrics_TemperatureHistogramFilter_temperatures_max gauge
org_redlich_metrics_TemperatureHistogramFilter_temperatures_max
{mp_scope="application",} 0.0
# HELP org_redlich_metrics_TemperatureHistogramFilter_temperatures A
histogram of temperatures in Trenton, New Jersey for the month of July 2024
# TYPE org_redlich_metrics_TemperatureHistogramFilter_temperatures summary
org_redlich_metrics_TemperatureHistogramFilter_temperatures{mp_scope=
"application",quantile="0.5",} 0.0
org_redlich_metrics_TemperatureHistogramFilter_temperatures{mp_scope=
"application",quantile="0.75",} 0.0
```

```
org_redlich_metrics_TemperatureHistogramFilter_temperatures{mp_scope
="application",quantile="0.95",} 0.0
org_redlich_metrics_TemperatureHistogramFilter_temperatures{mp_scope
="application",quantile="0.98",} 0.0
org_redlich_metrics_TemperatureHistogramFilter_temperatures{mp_scope
="application",quantile="0.99",} 0.0
org_redlich_metrics_TemperatureHistogramFilter_temperatures{mp_scope
="application",quantile="0.999",} 0.0
org_redlich_metrics_TemperatureHistogramFilter_temperatures_count
{mp_scope="application",} 0.0
org_redlich_metrics_TemperatureHistogramFilter_temperatures_sum
{mp_scope="application",} 0.0

# HELP temperatureHistogram_max A histogram of temperatures in Trenton,
New Jersey for the month of July 2024
# TYPE temperatureHistogram_max gauge
temperatureHistogram_max{mp_scope="application",unit="°F",} 97.0
# HELP temperatureHistogram A histogram of temperatures in Trenton,
New Jersey for the month of July 2024
# TYPE temperatureHistogram summary
temperatureHistogram{mp_scope="application",unit="°F",quantile="0.5",} 87.0
temperatureHistogram{mp_scope="application",unit="°F",quanti
le="0.75",} 93.0
temperatureHistogram{mp_scope="application",unit="°F",quantile="0.95",} 96.0
temperatureHistogram{mp_scope="application",unit="°F",quantile="0.98",} 97.0
temperatureHistogram{mp_scope="application",unit="°F",quantile="0.99",} 97.0
temperatureHistogram{mp_scope="application",unit="°F",quantile="0.999",} 97.0
temperatureHistogram_count{mp_scope="application",unit="°F",} 31.0
temperatureHistogram_sum{mp_scope="application",unit="°F",} 2721.0
```

The resulting histogram is displayed along with all of the defined metadata. Notice the fully qualified class name, **org.redlich.metrics.TemperatureHistogramFilter**, and metric name are concatenated together, separated by the underscore character as shown in Listing 11-20.

Listing 11-20. The fully qualified class name for the **TemperatureHistogramFilter** class

`org_redlich_metrics_TemperatureHistogramFilter_temperatures`

And finally, for our **GaugeMetric** class, the response is shown in Listing 11-21.

Listing 11-21. The listing and corresponding value of the **applicationUpTime** metric

```
# HELP org_redlich_metrics_GaugeMetric_applicationUpTime_seconds
# TYPE org_redlich_metrics_GaugeMetric_applicationUpTime_seconds gauge
org_redlich_metrics_GaugeMetric_applicationUpTime_seconds
{mp_scope="application",} 318.0
```

Also, the application scope is explicitly displayed as **{mp_scope="application"}**.

Summary

In this chapter, you were introduced to the Helidon Metrics, an implementation of the MicroProfile Metrics specification, featuring the MetricRegistry API, metrics scopes and their corresponding endpoints, a comprehensive look at base metrics, the Prometheus format, and annotations such as **@Counted**, **@Timed**, and **@Gauge**, and how to add a histogram meter.

In the next chapter, you will be introduced to the Helidon Fault Tolerance, an implementation of the MicroProfile Fault Tolerance specification.

> # CHAPTER 12

Helidon Fault Tolerance

Helidon Fault Tolerance in Helidon MP is a compatible implementation of the MicroProfile Fault Tolerance specification. Helidon Fault Tolerance is just one of the observability features available for your Helidon applications. This chapter will cover the Helidon Fault Tolerance in detail and provide a working example application. For other observability features, you learned about Helidon Metrics in Chapter 11, and you will be introduced to the Helidon Health Checks in Chapter 13.

Helidon Fault Tolerance Annotations

Helidon Fault Tolerance defines annotations that improve application robustness with the ability to conveniently handle error conditions, or faults, that may occur in real-world applications. Examples of this include service restarts, network delays, and temporal infrastructure instabilities.

The annotations in Helidon Fault Tolerance (*https://helidon.io/docs/v4/mp/fault-tolerance#_api*) along with a brief description are listed in Table 12-1.

Table 12-1. The Helidon Fault Tolerance annotations and short descriptions

Annotation	Short Description
`@Retry`	Retries the execution of a method in the event of a failure.
`@Timeout`	Defines an upper bound on a method's execution time.
`@CircuitBreaker`	Defines a policy to avoid repeated execution of logic that is likely to fail.
`@Bulkhead`	Defines a policy to limit the number of concurrent executions allowed over some application logic.
`@Fallback`	Establishes a handler to be executed in the event of an invocation failure.
`@Asynchronous`	Asynchronously executes an invocation without blocking the calling thread.

You will learn all about these annotations in more detail including their respective parameters and default values.

Note For the annotations listed in Table 12-1, their corresponding parameters, as you will see in Tables 12-2 through 12-6, will list a default value of **ChronoUnit .MILLIS**. The Java SE **ChronoUnit** is an **enum** class that defines a standard set of date period units, such as **MILLIS** (representing milliseconds), **DECADES**, and **CENTURIES**. This set of units provides unit-based access to manipulate a date, time, or date-time.

@Retry

The **@Retry** annotation, as shown in Listing 12-1, retries the execution of a method in the event of a failure. The annotation attributes may be used to control the number of retries, delay between retries, and the exceptions upon which to retry or abort.

Listing 12-1. The **@Retry** annotation and its parameter list

```
@Retry(
    maxRetries=3,
    delay=0,
    delayUnit=ChronoUnit.MILLIS,
    maxDuration=180000,
    durationUnit=ChronoUnit.MILLIS,
    jitter=200,
    jitterDelayUnit=ChronoUnit.MILLIS,
    retryOn={Exception.class},
    abortOn={}
)
```

Let's take a detailed look at all of these parameters as described in Table 12-2.

Table 12-2. The @Retry annotation parameters, descriptions, and default values

Parameter	Description	Default Value
`int maxRetries()`	The maximum number of the retries. A value of -1 means to retry forever. The value must be greater than or equal to -1.	3
`long delay()`	The delay between retries. The value must be greater than or equal to 0.	0
`ChronoUnit delayUnit()`	The specified delay unit for the `delay()` parameter.	`ChronoUnit.MILLIS`
`long maxDuration()`	The maximum duration to perform retries. The maximum duration must be greater than the delay duration if set. A value of 0 means that the maximum duration is not set.	180000 ms
`ChronoUnit durationUnit()`	The duration unit for the `maxDuration()` parameter.	`ChronoUnit.MILLIS`
`long jitter()`	Sets the jitter to randomly vary retry delays. The value must be greater than or equal to 0. A value of 0 means that the jitter is not set. The effective delay is calculated as • `[delay - jitter, delay + jitter]` • Should always be greater than or equal to 0 Negative delays will be set to 0. For example, a jitter of 200 milliseconds will randomly add between -200 and 200 milliseconds to each retry delay.	200 ms

(*continued*)

Table 12-2. (*continued*)

Parameter	Description	Default Value
ChronoUnit jitterDelayUnit()	The delay unit for the **jitter()** parameter.	**ChronoUnit.MILLIS**
Class<? extends Throwable>[] retryOn()	The list of exception types that should trigger a retry.	**{Exception.class}**
Class<? extends Throwable>[]abortOn()	The list of exception types that should **not** trigger a retry.	{}

@Timeout

The **@Timeout** annotation, as shown in Listing 12-2, defines an upper bound on a method's execution time.

Listing 12-2. The **@Timeout** annotation and its parameters

```
@Timeout(
    value=1000,
    unit=ChronoUnit.MILLIS
)
```

Let's take a detailed look at all of these parameters as described in Table 12-3.

Table 12-3. The **@Timeout** annotation parameters, descriptions, and default values

Parameter	Description	Default Value
long value()	The timeout value. The value must be greater than or equal to 0. A value of 0 means no timeout has been configured. Otherwise, a **FaultToleranceDefinitionException** will be thrown.	1000 ms
ChronoUnit unit()	The timeout unit.	**ChronoUnit.MILLIS**

@CircuitBreaker

The **@CircuitBreaker** annotation, as shown in Listing 12-3, defines a policy to avoid repeated execution of logic that is likely to fail. A circuit breaker has states defined as *closed*, *open*, or *half-open*. In the *closed* state, a circuit breaker will execute logic normally. In the *open* state, a circuit breaker will prevent execution of logic that has been determined to fail. And in the *half-open* state, a circuit breaker will allow trial executions in an attempt to switch its internal state back to *closed*. The other annotation parameters are used to control how these state transitions are triggered.

Listing 12-3. The **@CircuitBreaker** annotation and its parameter list

```
@CircuitBreaker(
    failOn={Throwable.class},
    skipOn={},
    delay=5000,
    delayUnit=ChronoUnit.MILLIS,
    requestVolumeThreshold=20,
    failureRatio=.50,
    successThreshold=1
)
```

Let's take a detailed look at all of these parameters as described in Table 12-4.

Table 12-4. The **@CircuitBreaker** annotation parameters, descriptions, and default values

Parameter	Description	Default Value
Class<? extends Throwable>[] failOn()	The list of exception types which should be considered failures.	**{Throwable.class}**
Class<? extends Throwable>[] skipOn()	The list of exception types which should **not** be considered failures. This list takes priority over the types listed in the **failOn()** parameter.	**{}**

(*continued*)

Table 12-4. (*continued*)

Parameter	Description	Default Value
long delay()	The delay after which an open circuit will transition to a half-open state. The amount of delay is taken from this delay value and the value returned by the **delayUnit()** parameter. The value must be greater than or equal to 0. A value of 0 means there is no delay.	5000 ms
long delayUnit()	The delay unit after which an open circuit will transition to a half-open state.	**ChronoUnit.MILLIS**
int requestVolume Threshold()	The number of consecutive requests in a rolling window. The circuit breaker will trip if the number of failures exceeds the value returned from the **failureRatio()** parameter within the rolling window of consecutive requests. The value must be greater than or equal to 1.	20
double failureRatio()	The ratio of failures within the rolling window that will trip the circuit to an open state. The circuit breaker will trip if the number of failures exceeds the **failureRatio()** within the rolling window of consecutive requests. For example, if the value returned by the **requestVolumeThreshold()** parameter is 20 and the value returned by the **failureRatio()** parameter is 0.50, then ten or more failures in 20 consecutive requests will trigger the circuit to an open state. The value must be between 0 and 1 inclusive.	0.5

(*continued*)

Table 12-4. (*continued*)

Parameter	Description	Default Value
int successThreshold()	The number of successful executions, before a half-open circuit is closed again. A half-open circuit will be closed once **successThreshold()** executions were made without failures. If a failure occurs while in a half-open state, the circuit is immediately opened again. The value must be greater than or equal to 1.	1

@Bulkhead

The **@Bulkhead** annotation, as shown in Listing 12-4, defines a policy to limit the number of concurrent executions allowed over some application logic. A queue is used to park tasks awaiting execution after a defined limit has been reached. A queue is only active when invocations are annotated with **@Asynchronous**.

Listing 12-4. The **@Bulkhead** annotation and its parameter list

```
@Bulkhead(
    value=10,
    waitingTaskQueue=10
)
```

Let's take a detailed look at all of these parameters as described in Table 12-5.

*Table 12-5. The **@Bulkhead** annotation parameters, descriptions, and default values*

Parameter	Description	Default Value
`int value()`	Specifies the maximum number of concurrent calls to an instance. The value must be greater than 0. Otherwise, a `FaultToleranceDefinitionException` will be thrown.	10
`int waitingTaskQueue()`	Specifies the waiting task queue. This setting only takes effect on asynchronous invocation, achieved by using the **@Asynchronous** annotation. The value must be greater than 0. Otherwise, a `FaultToleranceDefinitionException` will be thrown.	10

@Fallback

The **@Fallback** annotation, as shown in Listing 12-5, establishes a handler to be executed in the event of an invocation failure. A handler is either a class that implements the `FallbackHandler<T>` interface or just a simple method within the same class. Additional properties are used to control the conditions under which these handlers are called.

Listing 12-5. The **@Fallback** annotation and its parameter list

```
@Fallback(
    value=DEFAULT.class,
    fallbackMethod="",
    applyOn={Throwable.class},
    skipOn={}
)
```

Let's take a detailed look at all of these parameters as described in Table 12-6.

*Table 12-6. The **@Fallback** annotation parameters, descriptions, and default values*

Parameter	Description	Default Value
Class<? extends FallbackHandler<?>> value()	Specifies the fallback class to be used. A new instance of the **Fallback<T>** interface is returned, but the instance is unmanaged. The type parameter **<T>** of the **Fallback<T>** interface must be assignable to the return type of the annotated method. Otherwise, a **FaultToleranceDefinition Exception** is thrown.	**DEFAULT.class**
String fallbackMethod()	Specifies the method name on which to fall back. This method belongs to the same class as the method to fall back. The method must have the exact same arguments as the method being annotated. The method return type must be assignable to the return type of the method for the fallback. Otherwise, a **FaultToleranceDefinition Exception** is thrown.	" "
Class<? extends Throwable>[] applyOn()	The list of exception types which should trigger a fallback.	**{Throwable.class}**
Class<? extends Throwable>[] skipOn()	The list of exception types which should **not** trigger a fallback. This list takes priority over the types listed in the **applyOn()** parameter.	{}

@Asynchronous

The **@Asynchronous** annotation asynchronously executes an invocation without blocking the calling thread. The annotated method must return type **Future** or **CompletionStage**. This annotation is typically used to avoid blocking the calling thread on I/O or on a long-running computation. There are no parameters for this annotation.

Putting It All Together

Now that you've learned how to handle application faults, let's put it all together and build an application! You can find the full source code and relevant documentation at the **helidon-book** GitHub repository (*https://github.com/mpredli01/helidon-book*) under the **faulttolerance** module. Inspiration for these examples was adapted from the Helidon examples GitHub repository (*https://github.com/helidon-io/helidon-examples/*).

To demonstrate Helidon Fault Tolerance in action, let's take a look at a small working example that simulates faults and how they are resolved. The application consists of three main classes: **Message**, **SimpleGreetResource**, and **FaultToleranceResource**. The **Message** class is a standard Plain Old Java Object (POJO) containing getters and setters for two strings: **message** and **greeting**. The **SimpleGreetResource** class defines endpoints, **/simple-greeting** and **/simple-greeting/{name}**, that you already know from the Quickstart examples. So, that leaves the **FaultToleranceResource** class as the main focus of this example application.

Dependencies

Let's start with Maven and Gradle dependencies that you would use in your application.

Note The examples associated with this book use Maven as a build tool. The Gradle dependency is listed here for completeness and for the possibility of adding Gradle as a build tool in the future.

If Maven is your build tool, use the dependency as shown in Listing 12-6.

Listing 12-6. The Maven dependency for Helidon Fault Tolerance

```
<dependency>
    <groupId>io.helidon.microprofile</groupId>
    <artifactId>helidon-microprofile-fault-tolerance</artifactId>
    <version>4.1.0</version>
</dependency>
```

If Gradle is your build tool, use the dependency as shown in Listing 12-7.

Listing 12-7. The Gradle dependency for Helidon Fault Tolerance

```
implementation group: 'io.helidon.microprofile', name: 'helidon-microprofile-fault-tolerance', version: '4.1.0'
```

Fallback

The first method in the **FaultToleranceResource** class, **fallbackHandler()**, as shown in Listing 12-8, defines an endpoint and the fallback handler as assigned in the **@Fallback** annotation.

Listing 12-8. The **fallbackHandler()** method defined in the **FaultToleranceResource** class

```
@Fallback(fallbackMethod = "fallbackMethod") ❶
@Path("/fallback/{success}") ❷
@GET
public Response fallbackHandler(@PathParam("success") String success) { ❸
    if (!Boolean.parseBoolean(success)) { ❹
        terminate(); ❺
    }
    return reactive(); ❻
}
```

> ❶ The **@Fallback** annotation defines the fallback method, **"fallbackMethod"**, as a string that maps to the **fallbackMethod()**, as shown in Listing 12-9, defined later in the **FaultToleranceResource** class.

Listing 12-9. The **fallbackMethod()** method defined in the **FaultToleranceResource** class

```
private Response fallbackMethod(String success) {
    return Response.ok("Fallback endpoint reached").build();
}
```

- ❷ The Jakarta RESTful Web Services **@Path** annotation to define the endpoint, **/fallback/{success}**, that we will use when we exercise the application.

- ❸ The method, **fallbackHandler()**, that accepts a string, **success**, annotated with the Jakarta RESTful Web Services **@PathParam**. The value of **success** maps to the **/fallback/{success}** endpoint. This method returns an appropriate Jakarta RESTful Web Services **Response**, depending on the flow of control from the **if** statement.

- ❹ The **parseBoolean()** method, defined in the Java **Boolean** class, parses the string argument as a boolean and returns **true** if the string value is **true** and **false** for anything else.

- ❺ The **terminate()** method, as shown in Listing 12-10, simply throws a **RuntimeException**, and flow of the application moves to the **fallbackMethod()** method.

Listing 12-10. The **terminate()** method defined in the **FaultToleranceResource** class

```
private void terminate() {
    throw new RuntimeException("failure");
}
```

- ❻ The **reactive()** method calls the **blocking()** method, as shown in Listings 12-11 and 12-12, respectively, that will pause the application for five seconds and returns the string, *"Blocked for 5 seconds".*

Listing 12-11. The **reactive()** method defined in the **FaultToleranceResource** class

```
private Response reactive() {
    return Response.ok(blocking()).build();
}
```

Listing 12-12. The **blocking()** method defined in the **FaultToleranceResource** class

```
private String blocking() {
    try {
        Thread.sleep(5000);
    }
    catch (InterruptedException ignored) {
    }
    return "Blocked for 5 seconds";
}
```

Retry

The second method in the **FaultToleranceResource** class, **retryHandler()**, as shown in Listing 12-13, defines an endpoint and the maximum number of retries as assigned in the **@Retry** annotation.

Listing 12-13. The **retryHandler()** method defined in the **FaultToleranceResource** class

```
private static int retry;   ❶

@Retry(maxRetries = 2)   ❷
@Path("/retry")   ❸
@GET
public Response retryHandler() {   ❹
    if (++retry < 2) {   ❺
        terminate();
    }
    String response = String.format("Number of failures: %s", retry);   ❻
```

211

```
retry = 0;
return Response.ok(response).build();
}
```

- ❶ The **retry** variable is defined at the beginning of the **FaultToleranceResource** class.

- ❷ The **@Retry** annotation defines the maximum number of retries before "giving up," as it were.

- ❸ The Jakarta RESTful Web Services **@Path** annotation to define the endpoint, **/retry**, that we will use when we exercise the application.

- ❹ The **retryHandler()** method that returns an appropriate Jakarta RESTful Web Services **Response** depending on the flow of control from the **if** statement.

- ❺ The value of the **retry** variable is incremented and checked for the maximum number of retries. If the value is less than **2**, the aforementioned **terminate()** method is called, and the control of flow is resumed in the **if** statement.

- ❻ Once the value of **2** has been reached, then the string, "*Number of failures: 2*" will be the response.

Now that everything has been covered, let's build, execute, and exercise the application!

Build and Execute the Application

From the command line, you can build and package the application as a JAR file with Maven as shown in Listing 12-14.

Listing 12-14. Build and package the application as a JAR file with Maven.

```
~ » mvn clean package
```

Now you can invoke the JAR file using the **java** command as shown in Listing 12-15. Note the last part of the response that displays the URL and JVM startup time.

Listing 12-15. Invoke the application with the **java** command.

```
~ » java -jar target/faultolerance.jar
2024.08.11 08:48:34 INFO io.helidon.microprofile.server.ServerCdiExtension
Thread[#1,main,5,main]: Server started on http://localhost:8080 (and all
other host addresses) in 3183 milliseconds (since JVM startup).
2024.08.11 08:48:34 INFO io.helidon.common.features.HelidonFeatures
Thread[#51,features-thread,5,main]: Helidon MP 4.1.0 features: [CDI,
Config, Fault Tolerance, Health, Metrics, Server]
```

Exercising the Application

Now, let's exercise the **@Fallback** annotation, as shown in Listing 12-16, using **true** for the value of **{success}** in the endpoint. Note the response.

Listing 12-16. Exercising the **/ft/fallback/true** endpoint

```
~ » curl http://localhost:8080/ft/fallback/true
Blocked for 5 seconds
```

Conversely, let's exercise the **@Fallback** annotation, as shown in Listing 12-17, using **false** for the value of **{success}** in the endpoint. Note the response.

Listing 12-17. Exercising the **/ft/fallback/false** endpoint

```
~ » curl http://localhost:8080/ft/fallback/false
Fallback endpoint reached
```

Now, let's exercise the **@Retry** annotation as shown in Listing 12-18. Note the response.

Listing 12-18. Exercising the **/ft/retry** endpoint

```
~ » curl http://localhost:8080/ft/retry
Number of failures: 2
```

And, as usual, you can use these URLs in your favorite browser.

Summary

In this chapter, you were introduced to the Helidon Fault Tolerance, an implementation of the MicroProfile Fault Tolerance specification, featuring a set of annotations – **@Retry**, **@Timeout**, **@CircuitBreaker**, **@Bulkhead**, **@Fallback**, and **@Asynchronous** – to handle faults in your application to make it more robust.

In the next chapter, you will be introduced to the Helidon Health Checks, an implementation of the MicroProfile Health specification.

CHAPTER 13

Helidon Health Checks

Helidon Health Checks in Helidon MP is a compatible implementation of the MicroProfile Health Checks specification. Helidon Health Checks is just one of the observability features available for your Helidon applications. This chapter will cover the Helidon Health Checks in detail and provide a working example application. You learned about the other observability features, that is, Helidon Metrics and Helidon Fault Tolerance in Chapters 11 and 12, respectively.

By default, a MicroProfile-compliant application automatically generates health-related endpoints that provide default health checks. You can add your own custom health checks using the annotations available in Helidon Health Checks.

Helidon Health Checks Types and REST Endpoints

Web applications running in browsers (or using the **curl** command) retrieve health checks supported by Helidon using the REST endpoints as shown in Table 13-1.

Table 13-1. *The Helidon Health Checks types and corresponding endpoints*

Type	Description	Endpoint
Liveness	Reports if the runtime environment is sufficient for a microservice to perform its task at that snapshot in time. If a microservice instance reports a liveness check of **DOWN**, it should never report **UP** later. It will need to be stopped and require a replacement instance.	**/health/live**
Readiness	Reports if the microservice is capable of performing its task at that snapshot in time. A service that reports **DOWN** cannot perform its task but may be able to do so at some future point without requiring a restart.	**/health/ready**
Startup	Reports if the microservice has started to the point where the liveness and readiness checks are relevant. A service reporting a startup check of **DOWN** for a is most likely still initializing and will soon report a startup check of **UP** assuming it is able to successfully start.	**/health/started**

Responses from these endpoints report **HTTP 200** (OK), **HTTP 204** (No Content), or **HTTP 503** (Service Unavailable) depending on the outcome of executing those health checks. HTTP **GET** responses include JSON content that displays the detailed results of all health checks that the server executed after receiving the request. HTTP **HEAD** requests return only the status with no payload.

Annotations that support the three types of health checks are listed in Table 13-2.

Table 13-2. *The Helidon Health Checks annotations*

Annotation	Short Description
`@Liveness`	Indicates that the class is a liveness health check procedure.
`@Readiness`	Indicates that the class is a readiness health check procedure.
`@Startup`	Indicates that the class is a startup health check procedure.

HealthCheck Interface

The **HealthCheck** interface defines methods – **call()**, **name()**, **path()**, and **type()** – for building custom health checks by implementing this interface. You will learn how to do this.

Putting It All Together

Now that you've learned how to implement health checks, let's put it all together and build an application! You can find the full source code and relevant documentation at the **helidon-book** GitHub repository (*https://github.com/mpredli01/helidon-book*) under the **health** module. Inspiration for these examples was adapted from the Helidon examples GitHub repository (*https://github.com/helidon-io/helidon-examples/*).

To demonstrate Helidon Health Checks in action, let's take a look at a small working example that shows how to use the liveness, readiness, and startup types. The application consists of seven main classes: **Message**, **SimpleGreetResource**, **SystemResource**, **SimpleHealthCheck**, **SystemLivenessCheck**, **SystemReadinessCheck**, and **SystemStartupCheck**. The **Message** class is a standard Plain Old Java Object (POJO) containing getters and setters for two strings: **message** and **greeting**. The **SimpleGreetResource** class defines endpoints, **/simple-greeting** and **/simple-greeting/{name}**, that you already know from the Quickstarts. So, that leaves the other classes as the main focus of this example application to investigate.

Dependencies

Let's start with Maven and Gradle dependencies that you would use in your application.

> **Note** The examples associated with this book use Maven as a build tool. The Gradle dependency is listed here for completeness and for the possibility of adding Gradle as a build tool in the future.

If Maven is your build tool, use the dependency as shown in Listing 13-1.

Listing 13-1. The Maven dependency for Helidon Health Checks

```xml
<dependency>
    <groupId>io.helidon.microprofile.health</groupId>
    <artifactId>helidon-microprofile-health</artifactId>
    <version>4.1.0</version>
</dependency>
```

If Gradle is your build tool, use the dependency as shown in Listing 13-2.

Listing 13-2. The Gradle dependency for Helidon Health Checks

```
implementation group: 'io.helidon.microprofile.health', name: 'helidon-microprofile-health', version: '4.1.0'
```

System Resources

The **SystemResource** class, as shown in Listing 13-3, defines an endpoint, **/properties**, that returns the full set of properties from your computer workstation.

Listing 13-3. The **SystemResource** class

```java
@RequestScoped
@Path("properties")
public class SystemResource {

    @GET
    @Produces(MediaType.APPLICATION_JSON)
    public Response getProperties() {
        return Response.ok(System.getProperties()).build(); ❶
    }
}
```

❶ The **getProperties()** method, defined in the Java **System** class, that returns the system properties on your computer workstation

System Liveness

The **SystemLivenessCheck** class, as shown in Listing 13-4, checks the heap memory usage and compares it to the available system memory.

Listing 13-4. The **SystemLivenessCheck** class

```
@Liveness  ❶
@ApplicationScoped
public class SystemLivenessCheck implements HealthCheck {  ❷

    @Override
    public HealthCheckResponse call() {  ❸
        MemoryMXBean memoryBean = ManagementFactory.getMemoryMXBean();
        long memoryUsed = memoryBean.getHeapMemoryUsage().getUsed();
        long memoryMax = memoryBean.getHeapMemoryUsage().getMax();

        return HealthCheckResponse  ❹
                .named(name())
                .withData("resource", SystemResource.class.getSimpleName())
                .withData("type", type().toString())
                .withData("memory bean", memoryBean.toString())
                .withData("memory used", memoryUsed)
                .withData("memory max", memoryMax)
                .status(memoryUsed < memoryMax * 0.9)
                .build();
    }

    public String name() {  ❺
        return "System Liveness Check";
    }

    public HealthCheckType type() {  ❻
        return HealthCheckType.LIVENESS;
    }
}
```

① The required **@Liveness** annotation that indicates that the **SystemLivenessCheck** class is a liveness health check procedure.

② The **SystemLivenessCheck** class that implements the **HealthCheck** interface.

③ The **call()** method is used to return the health status of this service that checks the memory of the system. If current memory usage is less than 90% of the maximum amount of memory, the service will return a status of **UP**. Otherwise, it will return a status of **DOWN**.

④ This builds an instance of the **HealthCheckResponse** interface using methods **named()**, **withData()**, and **status()** along with the **build()** terminating method.

⑤ The **name()** method that defines the name of the health check.

⑥ The **type()** method that defines the type of health check.

System Readiness

The **SystemReadinessCheck** class, as shown in Listing 13-5, compares the value of the system property, **java.vm.name**, with the value passed into the string comparison method, **equals()**.

Listing 13-5. The **SystemReadinessCheck** class

```
@Readiness ①
@ApplicationScoped
public class SystemReadinessCheck implements HealthCheck { ②

    private static final String READINESS_CHECK = SystemResource.class
    .getSimpleName() + " Readiness Check";

    @Override
    public HealthCheckResponse call() { ③
        if (!System.getProperty("java.vm.name").equals("OpenJDK 64-Bit
        Server VM")) {
```

```
            return HealthCheckResponse
                    .down(READINESS_CHECK);
        }
        return HealthCheckResponse
                .up(READINESS_CHECK);
    }
}
```

- ❶ The required **@Readiness** annotation that indicates that the **SystemReadinessCheck** class is a readiness health check procedure.

- ❷ The **SystemReadinessCheck** class that implements the **HealthCheck** interface.

- ❸ The **call()** method is used to return the health status of this service that compares the value of the property, **java.vm.name**, with the value passed into the string comparison method, **equals()**. If the values match, the service will return a status of **UP** via the **up()** method. Otherwise, it will return a status of **DOWN** via the **down()** method.

System Startup

The **SystemStartupCheck** class, as shown in Listing 13-6, checks the CPU usage. If more than 95% of the CPU is being used, a status of **DOWN** is returned.

Listing 13-6. The **SystemStartupCheck** class

```
@Startup ❶
@ApplicationScoped
public class SystemStartupCheck implements HealthCheck { ❷

    @Override
    public HealthCheckResponse call() { ❸
        OperatingSystemMXBean bean = (com.sun.management.Operating
        SystemMXBean)ManagementFactory.getOperatingSystemMXBean();
        double cpuUsed = bean.getCpuLoad();
```

```java
        String cpuUsage = String.valueOf(cpuUsed);
        return HealthCheckResponse    ❹
                .named(name())
                .withData("resource", SystemResource.class.getSimpleName())
                .withData("type", type().toString())
                .withData("bean", bean.toString())
                .withData("cpu usage", cpuUsage)
                .status(cpuUsed < 0.95)
                .build();
    }
    public String name() {    ❺
        return "System Startup Check";
    }
    public HealthCheckType type() {    ❻
        return HealthCheckType.STARTUP;
    }
}
```

> ❶ The required **@Startup** annotation that indicates that the **SystemStartupCheck** class is a startup health check procedure.
>
> ❷ The **SystemStartupCheck** class that implements the **HealthCheck** interface.
>
> ❸ The **call()** method is used to return the health status of this service that checks the CPU usage of the system. If current CPU usage is less than 95%, the service will return a status of **UP**. Otherwise, it will return a status of **DOWN**.
>
> ❹ This builds an instance of the **HealthCheckResponse** interface using methods **named()**, **withData()**, and **status()** along with the **build()** terminating method.
>
> ❺ The **name()** method that defines the name of the health check.
>
> ❻ The **type()** method that defines the type of health check.

Did you notice that there are two different ways to communicate whether a service is **UP** or **DOWN**? In the liveness and startup class, the **status(boolean)** method was used. In the readiness class, the **up()** and **down()** methods were used.

Build and Execute the Application

From the command line, you can build and package the application as a JAR file with Maven as shown in Listing 13-7.

Listing 13-7. Build and package the application as a JAR file with Maven.

```
~ » mvn clean package
```

Now you can invoke the JAR file using the **java** command as shown in Listing 13-8. Note the last part of the response that displays the URL and JVM startup time.

Listing 13-8. Invoke the application with the **java** command.

```
~ » java -jar target/health.jar
2024.08.11 08:48:34 INFO io.helidon.microprofile.server.ServerCdiExtension
Thread[#1,main,5,main]: Server started on http://localhost:8080 (and all
other host addresses) in 3183 milliseconds (since JVM startup).
2024.08.11 08:48:34 INFO io.helidon.common.features.HelidonFeatures
Thread[#51,features-thread,5,main]: Helidon MP 4.1.0 features: [CDI,
Config, Fault Tolerance, Health, Metrics, Server]
```

Exercising the Application

Before exercising the application, let's take a look at the default JSON health check response, as shown in Listing 13-9, from an application that doesn't define custom health checks.

Listing 13-9. Exercising the default **/health** endpoint and corresponding JSON response

```
~ » curl -s http://localhost:8080/health | json_pp
{
   "checks" : [],
   "status" : "UP"
}
```

As you can see, the list of checks is empty, and the only useful information is that the system is up and running.

Now that the application server is running, let's exercise the main **/health** endpoint and see the resulting JSON response as shown in Listing 13-10.

Listing 13-10. Exercising the **/health** endpoint with custom health checks and corresponding JSON response

```
~ » curl -s http://localhost:8080/health | json_pp
{
   "status" : "UP",
   "checks" : [
      {
         "name" : "Simple Health Check",
         "status" : "UP"
      },
      {
         "status" : "UP",
         "name" : "System Liveness Check",
         "data" : {
            "resource" : "SystemResource",
            "memory used" : 31880440,
            "type" : "LIVENESS",
            "memory max" : 2147483648,
            "memory bean" : "sun.management.MemoryImpl@e044b4a"
         }
      },
      {
```

```
      "data" : {
         "user" : "Barry",
         "admin" : "Mike"
      },
      "name" : "Health Check with Data",
      "status" : "UP"
   },
   {
      "status" : "UP",
      "name" : "SystemResource Readiness Check"
   },
   {
      "status" : "UP",
      "name" : "System Startup Check",
      "data" : {
         "bean" : "com.sun.management.internal.OperatingSystemImpl
         @1f651cd8",
         "resource" : "SystemResource",
         "type" : "STARTUP",
         "cpu usage" : "0.07406470881682645"
      }
   }
 ]
}
```

Now let's exercise the **/health/live** endpoint and see the resulting JSON response as shown in Listing 13-11.

Listing 13-11. Exercising the **/health/live** endpoint and corresponding JSON response

```
~ » curl -s http://localhost:8080/health/live | json_pp
{
   "status" : "UP",
   "checks" : [
      {
         "status" : "UP",
```

```
            "name" : "Simple Health Check"
        },
        {
            "data" : {
                "resource" : "SystemResource",
                "memory bean" : "sun.management.MemoryImpl@e044b4a",
                "type" : "LIVENESS",
                "memory max" : 2147483648,
                "memory used" : 32929016
            },
            "name" : "System Liveness Check",
            "status" : "UP"
        },
        {
            "data" : {
                "admin" : "Mike",
                "user" : "Barry"
            },
            "name" : "Health Check with Data",
            "status" : "UP"
        }
    ]
}
```

Now let's exercise the **/health/ready** endpoint and see the resulting JSON response as shown in Listing 13-12.

Listing 13-12. Exercising the **/health/ready** endpoint and corresponding JSON response

```
~ » curl -s http://localhost:8080/health/ready | json_pp
{
    "status" : "UP",
    "checks" : [
        {
            "status" : "UP",
            "name" : "SystemResource Readiness Check"
```

          }
     ]
}

Now let's exercise the **/health/started** endpoint and see the resulting JSON response as shown in Listing 13-13.

Listing 13-13. Exercising the **/health/started** endpoint and corresponding JSON response

```
~ » curl -s http://localhost:8080/health/started | json_pp
{
   "status" : "UP",
   "checks" : [
      {
         "data" : {
            "bean" : "com.sun.management.internal.OperatingSystemImpl
            @1f651cd8",
            "type" : "STARTUP",
            "cpu usage" : "0.03344554240416983",
            "resource" : "SystemResource"
         },
         "status" : "UP",
         "name" : "System Startup Check"
      }
   ]
}
```

And finally, just for fun, let's exercise the **/properties** endpoint, as shown in Listing 13-14, that was defined and see the resulting JSON response.

Listing 13-14. Exercising the **/properties** endpoint and corresponding JSON response

```
~ » curl -s http://localhost:8080/properties | json_pp
{
   "java.vm.version" : "21+35-2513",
```

```
"java.library.path" : "/Users/mpredli01/Library/Java/Extensions:
/Library/Java/Extensions:/Network/Library/Java/Extensions:/System/
Library/Java/Extensions:/usr/lib/java:.",
"jersey.config.allowSystemPropertiesProvider" : "true",
"java.vendor" : "Oracle Corporation",
"java.vendor.url.bug" : "https://bugreport.java.com/bugreport/",
"sun.cpu.endian" : "little",
"sun.java.command" : "target/health.jar",
"jersey.config.client.ignoreExceptionResponse" : "true",
"line.separator" : "\n",
"user.home" : "/Users/mpredli01",
"user.name" : "mpredli01",
"path.separator" : ":",
"java.class.path" : "target/health.jar",
"stdout.encoding" : "UTF-8",
"java.vm.name" : "OpenJDK 64-Bit Server VM",
"java.vendor.url" : "https://java.oracle.com/",
"os.version" : "10.15.7",
"java.class.version" : "65.0",
"java.vm.info" : "mixed mode, sharing",
"user.timezone" : "America/New_York",
"os.name" : "Mac OS X",
"java.vm.specification.vendor" : "Oracle Corporation",
"java.home" : "/Library/Java/JavaVirtualMachines/jdk-21.jdk
/Contents/Home",
"native.encoding" : "UTF-8",
"sun.io.unicode.encoding" : "UnicodeBig",
"user.language" : "en",
"user.country" : "US",
"file.encoding" : "UTF-8",
"java.vm.vendor" : "Oracle Corporation",
"apple.awt.application.name" : "Main",
"sun.jnu.encoding" : "UTF-8",
"sun.management.compiler" : "HotSpot 64-Bit Tiered Compilers",
"java.runtime.name" : "OpenJDK Runtime Environment",
```

```
    "java.runtime.version" : "21+35-2513",
    "file.separator" : "/",
    "stderr.encoding" : "UTF-8",
    "java.io.tmpdir" : "/var/folders/tt/7lxy2q7d55jbvvv1pnjj05cm0000gn/T/",
    "socksNonProxyHosts" : "local|*.local|169.254/16|*.169.254/16",
    "sun.java.launcher" : "SUN_STANDARD",
    "java.specification.name" : "Java Platform API Specification",
    "java.version.date" : "2023-09-19",
    "java.specification.version" : "21",
    "java.vm.specification.name" : "Java Virtual Machine Specification",
    "ftp.nonProxyHosts" : "local|*.local|169.254/16|*.169.254/16",
    "java.vm.specification.version" : "21",
    "http.nonProxyHosts" : "local|*.local|169.254/16|*.169.254/16",
    "os.arch" : "x86_64",
    "jdk.debug" : "release",
    "user.dir" : "/usr/local/publications/helidon-book/health",
    "java.vm.compressedOopsMode" : "Zero based",
    "java.version" : "21",
    "sun.boot.library.path" : "/Library/Java/JavaVirtualMachines/jdk-21.jdk/Contents/Home/lib",
    "java.specification.vendor" : "Oracle Corporation",
    "sun.arch.data.model" : "64"
}
```

Summary

In this chapter, you were introduced to the Helidon Health Checks, an implementation of the MicroProfile Health specification, featuring a set of annotations – **@Liveness**, **@Readiness**, and **@Startup** – to build custom health checks in your application to make it more robust.

Conclusion

You have reached the end of this Helidon Revealed book. Hopefully, you enjoyed reading it, learned some things about Helidon, and had a chance to explore the GitHub repository (*https://github.com/mpredli01/helidon-book*). Feedback is always welcome, and it would be much appreciated to improve the quality for a potential second edition of this book and the example applications.

Thank you very much for your time!

APPENDIX A

MicroProfile Release History

This appendix serves to complement Chapter 2. The intent is to give you an appreciation on how MicroProfile has evolved since 2016. For each MicroProfile release, there is a brief overview complete with a diagram of the specifications and the compatible implementations.

To guide you through all of the new specifications and respective updates within each release, just follow the color code as shown in Figure A-1.

Figure A-1. *Color code for the MicroProfile specifications*

Now let's check out each of the MicroProfile releases!

MicroProfile 1.0

The release of MicroProfile 1.0, announced on September 19, 2016, at JavaOne 2016, consisted of three JSR-based APIs from Java EE 7 that were considered minimal for creating microservices applications:

- JSR-346: Contexts and Dependency Injection (CDI) 1.1
- JSR-353: Java API for JSON Processing (JSON-P) 1.0
- JSR-339: Java API for RESTful Web Services (JAX-RS) 2.0

Specification Diagram

These new specifications are shown in Figure A-2.

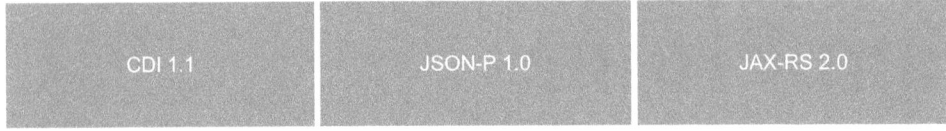

Figure A-2. *The MicroProfile 1.0 specifications*

Compatible Implementations

Compatible implementations for this release are shown in Table A-1.

Table A-1. *The compatible implementations for MicroProfile 1.0*

• WildFly Swarm 2016.8.1	• TomEE 7.1.0
• WebSphere Liberty 16.0.0.3	• KumuluzEE 2.1.0

MicroProfile 1.1

Released on August 8, 2017, MicroProfile 1.1 introduced one new specification, namely:

- **Config**, a specification for specifying configuration data, external from an application, to avoid having to repackage the application. Configuration can be specified from multiple sources, such as system properties, environmental variables, and text files.

Specification Diagram

The updated specification diagram is shown in Figure A-3.

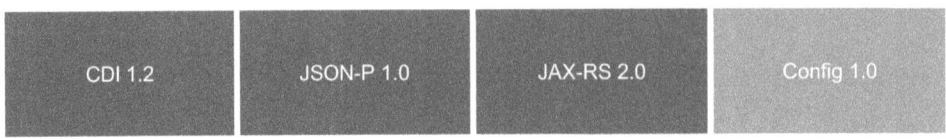

Figure A-3. *The MicroProfile 1.1 specifications*

APPENDIX A   MICROPROFILE RELEASE HISTORY

Compatible Implementations

Compatible implementations for this release are shown in Table A-2.

Table A-2. *The compatible implementations for MicroProfile 1.1*

- Fujitsu Launcher 1.0
- Hammock 2.0
- Payara Server 5.174
- Payara Micro 5.174
- Helidon 0.9.4 ❶
- KumuluzEE 2.5.2

❶ This is the first release in which Helidon is introduced as a compatible implementation.

MicroProfile 1.2

Released in September 2017, MicroProfile 1.2 provided an update to the Config specification and introduced four new specifications, namely:

- **Fault Tolerance**, a specification that handles application faults using strategies, such as retries, fallback methods, and circuit breakers

- **Metrics**, a specification that provides a unified service to catalog built-in or custom metrics for an application

- **JWT Propagation**, a specification that provides processing of security tokens in JSON Web Token (JWT) format

- **Health Check**, a specification that provides the health of an application and determines if a service needs to be shut down and replaced by a different instance of that service

Specification Diagram

The updated specification diagram is shown in Figure A-4.

APPENDIX A   MICROPROFILE RELEASE HISTORY

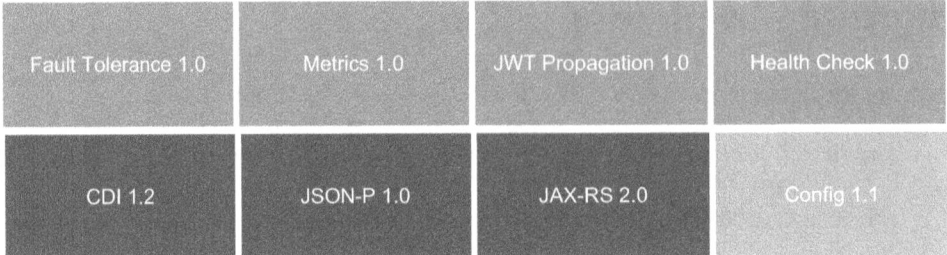

Figure A-4. *The MicroProfile 1.2 specifications*

Compatible Implementations

Compatible implementations for this release are shown in Table A-3.

Table A-3. *The compatible implementations for MicroProfile 1.2*

- Open Liberty 17.0.0.3
- WebSphere Liberty 17.0.0.3
- WildFly Swarm 2017.12.1
- Red Hat OpenShift Application Runtimes 1.0
- Payara Server 5.181
- Payara Micro 5.181
- KumuluzEE 3.0.0
- Helidon 1.0

MicroProfile 1.3

Released on March 16, 2018, MicroProfile 1.3 delivered updates to the Config and Metrics specifications and introduced three new specifications, namely:

- **Open Tracing**, a specification that follows the Open Tracing (*https://opentracing.io/*) standard for adding observability to an application

- **Open API**, a specification that follows the Open API standard for exposing documentation for an application

- **Rest Client**, a specification that provides a type-safe approach to invoke RESTful web services over HTTP

APPENDIX A   MICROPROFILE RELEASE HISTORY

Specification Diagram

The updated specification diagram is shown in Figure A-5.

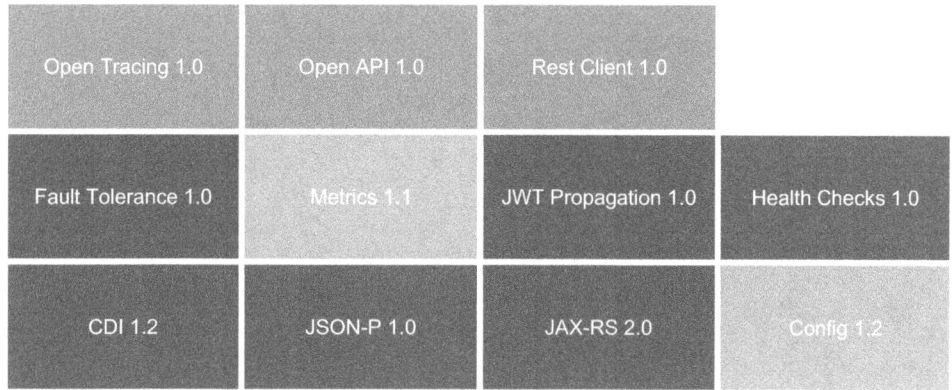

Figure A-5. *The MicroProfile 1.3 specifications*

In less than 18 months since the release of MicroProfile 1.0, a total of seven community-based specifications, complementing the original three Java EE 7 JSR-based specifications, were created for building more robust microservices-based applications.

Compatible Implementations

Compatible implementations for this release are shown in Table A-4.

Table A-4. *The compatible implementations for MicroProfile 1.3*

- Helidon 1.2.0
- Open Liberty 18.0.0.1
- WebSphere Liberty 18.0.0.1
- Payara Server 5.182
- Payara Micro 5.182
- Thorntail 2.1.0.Final
- TomEE 8.0.0-M1
- KumuluzEE 3.2.0

MicroProfile 1.4

Released on June 29, 2018, MicroProfile 1.4 delivered updates to the Config, Fault Tolerance, JWT Propagation, Open Tracing, and Rest Client specifications.

APPENDIX A   MICROPROFILE RELEASE HISTORY

Specification Diagram

The updated specification diagram is shown in Figure A-6.

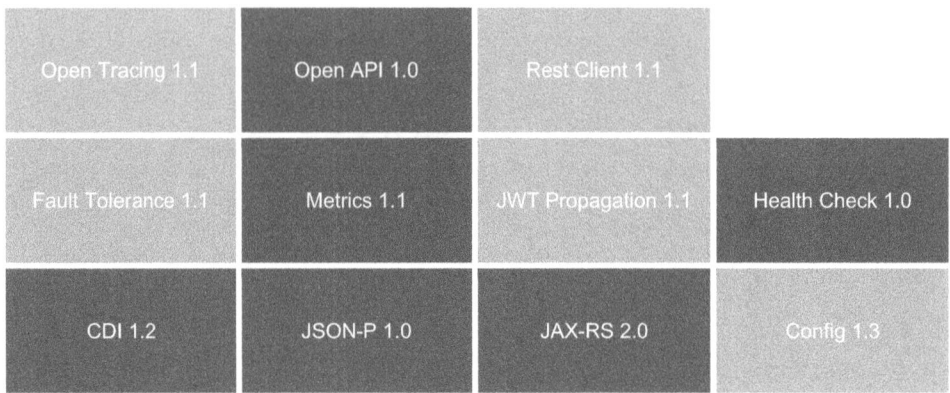

Figure A-6. *The MicroProfile 1.4 specifications*

The original three specifications were still based on Java EE 7, but this has changed as you will read in the next section describing MicroProfile 2.0, concurrently released with version 1.4.

Compatible Implementations

Compatible implementations for this release are shown in Table A-5.

Table A-5. *The compatible implementations for MicroProfile 1.4*

• Helidon 1.2.0	• Open Liberty 18.0.0.3
• Payara Server 5.183	• WebSphere Liberty 18.0.0.3
• Payara Micro 5.183	• KumuluzEE 3.2.0

MicroProfile 2.0

Also released on June 29, 2018, MicroProfile 2.0, built upon MicroProfile 1.4, delivered updates to the three original JSR-based specifications and introduced one new specification, namely:

- **Java API for JSON Binding** (JSON-B), a specification that provides the binding layer for converting Java objects to/from JSON messages

APPENDIX A   MICROPROFILE RELEASE HISTORY

Specification Diagram

The updated specification diagram is shown in Figure A-7.

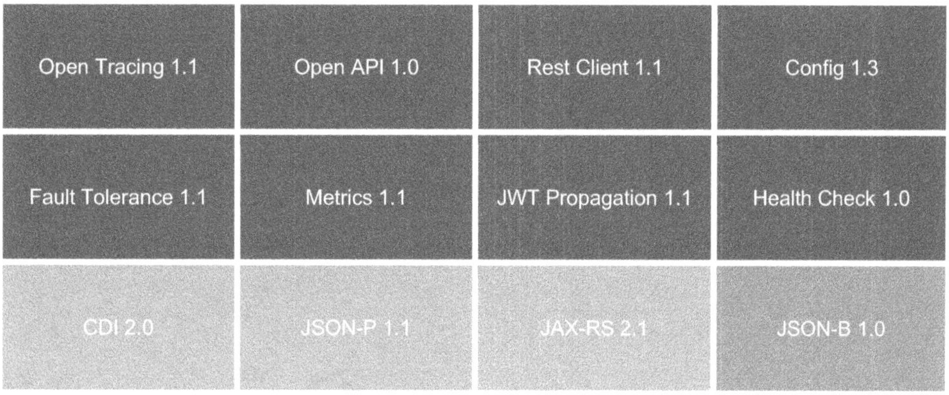

Open Tracing 1.1	Open API 1.0	Rest Client 1.1	Config 1.3
Fault Tolerance 1.1	Metrics 1.1	JWT Propagation 1.1	Health Check 1.0
CDI 2.0	JSON-P 1.1	JAX-RS 2.1	JSON-B 1.0

Figure A-7. *The MicroProfile 2.0 specifications*

The original three specifications and the new JSON-B specification were based on Java EE 8:

- JSR 365: Contexts and Dependency Injection (CDI) 2.0
- JSR 374: Java API for JSON Processing (JSON-P) 1.1
- JSR 370: Java API for RESTful Web Services (JAX-RS) 2.1
- JSR 367: Java API for JSON Binding (JSON-B) 1.0

With the concurrent releases of MicroProfile 1.4 and 2.0, developers had a choice to remain on Java EE 7 or migrate to Java EE 8, respectively.

Compatible Implementations

Compatible implementations for this release are shown in Table A-6.

Table A-6. *The compatible implementations for MicroProfile 2.0*

- Helidon 1.2.0
- Payara Server 5.183
- Payara Micro 5.183
- Open Liberty 18.0.0.3
- WebSphere Liberty 18.0.0.3
- TomEE 8.0.0-M2
- KumuluzEE 3.2.0

APPENDIX A   MICROPROFILE RELEASE HISTORY

MicroProfile 2.1

Released on October 19, 2018, MicroProfile 2.1 delivered updates to the Open Tracing specification.

Specification Diagram

The updated specification diagram is shown in Figure A-8.

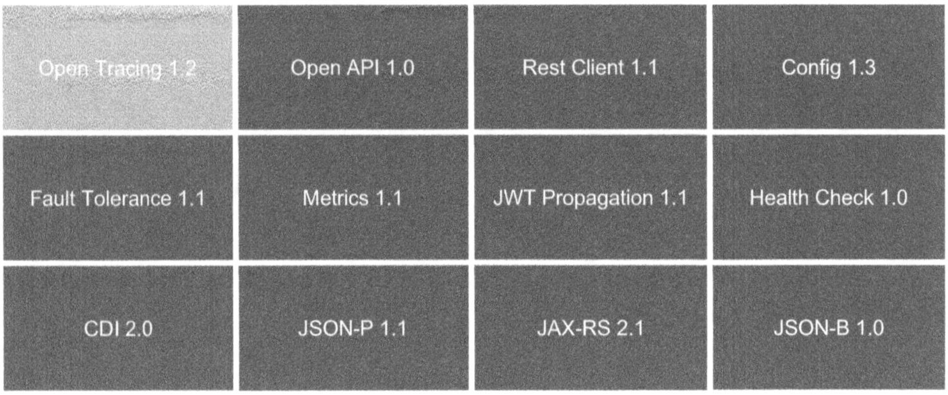

Open Tracing 1.2	Open API 1.0	Rest Client 1.1	Config 1.3
Fault Tolerance 1.1	Metrics 1.1	JWT Propagation 1.1	Health Check 1.0
CDI 2.0	JSON-P 1.1	JAX-RS 2.1	JSON-B 1.0

Figure A-8. *The MicroProfile 2.1 specifications*

Compatible Implementations

Compatible implementations for this release are shown in Table A-7.

Table A-7. *The compatible implementations for MicroProfile 2.1*

- Helidon 1.2.0
- Open Liberty 18.0.0.4
- WebSphere Liberty 18.0.0.4
- Thorntail 2.3.0.Final
- Payara Server 5.191
- Payara Micro 5.191
- TomEE 8.0.0-M3
- KumuluzEE 3.2.0

APPENDIX A   MICROPROFILE RELEASE HISTORY

MicroProfile 2.2

Released on February 10, 2019, MicroProfile 2.2 delivered updates to the Fault Tolerance, Open Tracing, Open API, and Rest Client specifications.

Specification Diagram

The updated specification diagram is shown in Figure A-9.

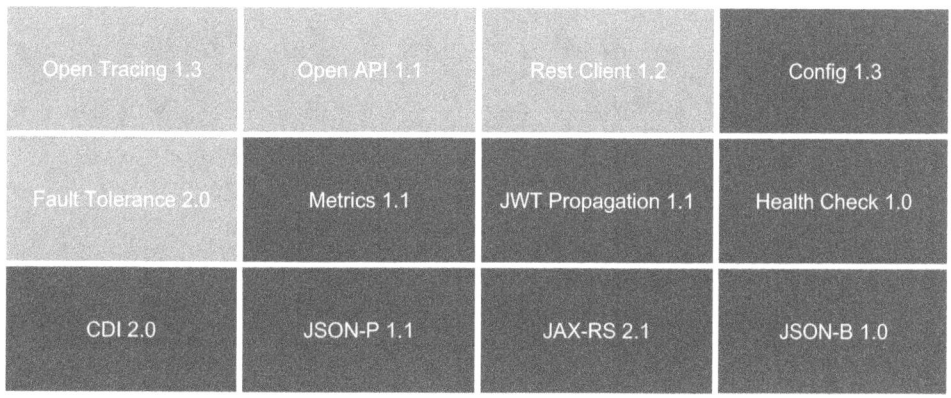

Figure A-9. *The MicroProfile 2.2 specifications*

Compatible Implementations

Compatible implementations for this release are shown in Table A-8.

Table A-8. *The compatible implementations for MicroProfile 2.2*

- Helidon 1.2.0
- Thorntail 2.4.0.Final
- Open Liberty 19.0.0.3
- WebSphere Liberty 19.0.0.3
- Payara Server 5.192
- Payara Micro 5.192
- KumuluzEE 3.5.0

APPENDIX A   MICROPROFILE RELEASE HISTORY

MicroProfile 3.0

Released on June 11, 2019, MicroProfile 3.0 delivered updates to the Metrics, Health Check, and Rest Client specifications.

Specification Diagram

The updated specification diagram is shown in Figure A-10.

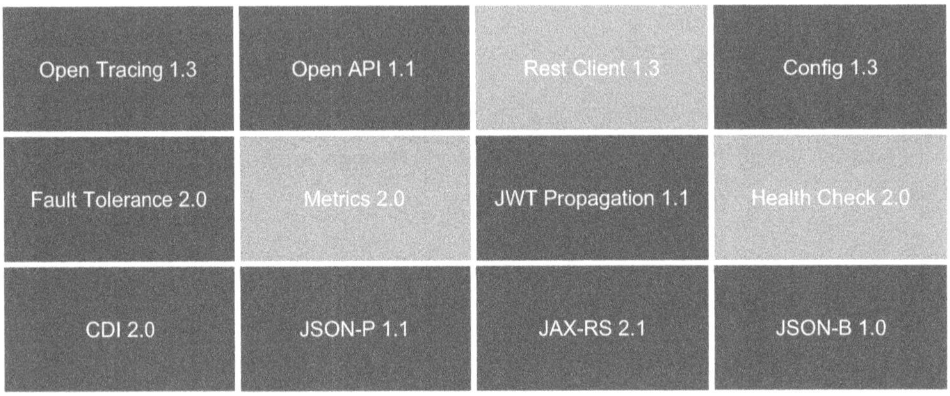

Open Tracing 1.3	Open API 1.1	Rest Client 1.3	Config 1.3
Fault Tolerance 2.0	Metrics 2.0	JWT Propagation 1.1	Health Check 2.0
CDI 2.0	JSON-P 1.1	JAX-RS 2.1	JSON-B 1.0

Figure A-10. *The MicroProfile 3.0 specifications*

Compatible Implementations

Compatible implementations for this release are shown in Table A-9.

Table A-9. *The compatible implementations for MicroProfile 3.0*

- Helidon 1.3.0
- WebSphere Liberty 19.0.0.7
- Thorntail 2.5.0.Final
- KumuluzEE 3.6.0
- Open Liberty 19.0.0.7
- Fujitsu Launcher 2.0

MicroProfile 3.1

Released on October 13, 2019, MicroProfile 3.1 delivered updates to the Metrics and Health Check specifications.

APPENDIX A   MICROPROFILE RELEASE HISTORY

Specification Diagram

The updated specification diagram is shown in Figure A-11.

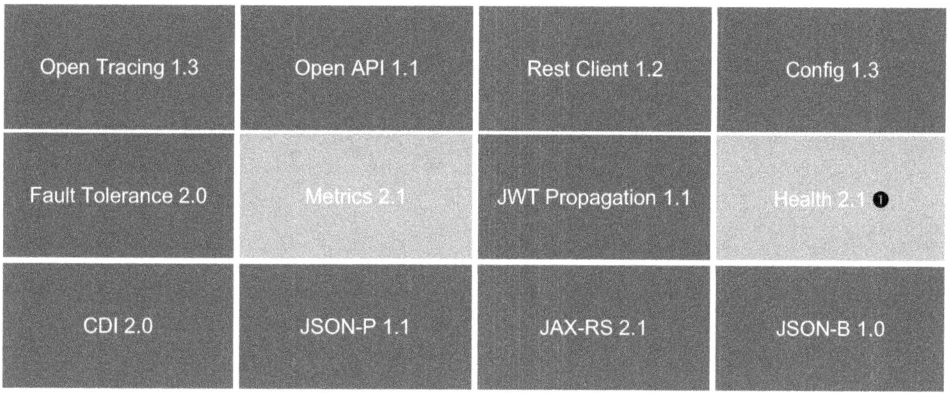

Open Tracing 1.3	Open API 1.1	Rest Client 1.2	Config 1.3
Fault Tolerance 2.0	Metrics 2.1	JWT Propagation 1.1	Health 2.1 ❶
CDI 2.0	JSON-P 1.1	JAX-RS 2.1	JSON-B 1.0

Figure A-11. *The MicroProfile 3.1 specifications*

❶ The Health Check specification had been renamed to **Health**.

Compatible Implementations

There were no compatible implementations for this release.

MicroProfile 3.2

Released on November 11, 2019, less than a month after MicroProfile 3.1 was released, MicroProfile 3.2 delivered updates to the Metrics and Health specifications.

Specification Diagram

The updated specification diagram is shown in Figure A-12.

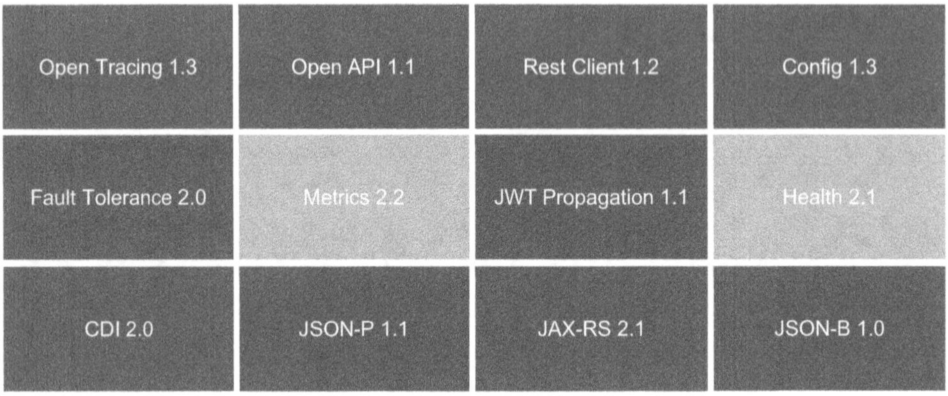

APPENDIX A   MICROPROFILE RELEASE HISTORY

Open Tracing 1.3	Open API 1.1	Rest Client 1.2	Config 1.3
Fault Tolerance 2.0	Metrics 2.2	JWT Propagation 1.1	Health 2.1
CDI 2.0	JSON-P 1.1	JAX-RS 2.1	JSON-B 1.0

Figure A-12. The MicroProfile 3.2 specifications

Compatible Implementations

Compatible implementations for this release are shown in Table A-10.

Table A-10. The compatible implementations for MicroProfile 3.2

- Quarkus 1.1.0.Final
- Helidon 2.0.2
- Payara Server 5.194
- Payara Micro 5.194
- Thorntail 2.6.0.Final
- Open Liberty 19.0.0.12
- WebSphere Liberty 19.0.0.12
- KumuluzEE 3.7.0
- WildFly 19.0.0.Beta1

MicroProfile 3.3

Released on February 17, 2020, MicroProfile 3.3 delivered updates to the Config, Metrics, Fault Tolerance, Health, and Rest Client specifications.

Specification Diagram

The updated specification diagram is shown in Figure A-13.

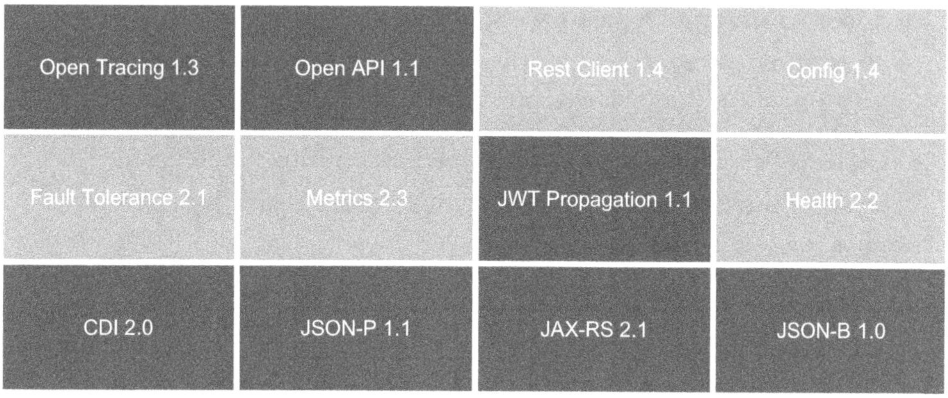

APPENDIX A MICROPROFILE RELEASE HISTORY

Open Tracing 1.3	Open API 1.1	Rest Client 1.4	Config 1.4
Fault Tolerance 2.1	Metrics 2.3	JWT Propagation 1.1	Health 2.2
CDI 2.0	JSON-P 1.1	JAX-RS 2.1	JSON-B 1.0

Figure A-13. The MicroProfile 3.3 specifications

Compatible Implementations

Compatible implementations for this release are shown in Table A-11.

Table A-11. *The compatible implementations for MicroProfile 3.3*

- WildFly 19
- KumuluzEE 3.9.0
- Open Liberty 20.0.0.4
- WebSphere Liberty 20.0.0.4
- Thorntail 2.7.0.Final
- Payara Server 5.2020.2
- Payara Micro 5.2020.2
- JBoss EAP XP 1.0.0
- Helidon 2.1.0

MicroProfile 4.0

Originally scheduled for a June 2020 release, MicroProfile 4.0 was delayed so that the MicroProfile Working Group could be established as mandated by the Eclipse Foundation. Released on December 23, 2020, this was the first release of the newly established MicroProfile Working Group featuring updates to all 12 core specifications and alignment with Jakarta EE 8 and introduced four new specifications, namely:

- **Reactive Messaging**, a specification that provides asynchronous messaging based on the Reactive Streams Operators specification

- **Reactive Streams Operators**, a specification that allows two different asynchronous streaming libraries to more easily stream data to/from each other
- **Context Propagation**, a specification that provides the ability for CompletableFutures, backed by managed threads, to capture context from these threads
- **GraphQL**, a specification that follows the GraphQL (https://graphql.org/) standard, a data query and manipulation language, to prevent the under-fetching and over-fetching of data that is inherent in REST endpoints

These specifications, characterized as *stand-alone*, because it was decided that vendors weren't required to implement these specifications, were in development over the previous year, but not listed on the specification diagrams until MicroProfile 4.0.

Specification Diagram

The updated specification diagram is shown in Figure A-14.

Figure A-14. *The MicroProfile 4.0 core and stand-alone specifications*

Most of these specification updates contained breaking changes.

Compatible Implementations

Compatible implementations for this release are shown in Table A-12.

Table A-12. *The compatible implementations for MicroProfile 4.0*

- Payara Micro 5.2021.1
- WildFly 23
- Open Liberty 21.0.0.3
- WebSphere Liberty 21.0.0.3

MicroProfile 4.1

Released on July 20, 2021, MicroProfile 4.1 delivered updates to the Config, Health, Open Tracing, Open API, Rest Client, Reactive Messaging, Reactive Streams Operators, Context Propagation, and GraphQL specifications and introduced two new specifications, namely:

- Support for the **Jakarta Annotations**, a Jakarta EE specification that defines a collection of annotations representing common semantic concepts to enable a declarative style of programming that may apply across Java SE and Jakarta EE specifications
- **Long-Running Actions**, a specification that allows for loosely coupled services to coordinate long-running activities to guarantee a globally consistent outcome without the need to take locks on data

Specification Diagram

The updated specification diagram is shown in Figure A-15.

APPENDIX A   MICROPROFILE RELEASE HISTORY

Figure A-15. *The MicroProfile 4.1 core and stand-alone specifications*

Compatible Implementations

Compatible implementations for this release are shown in Table A-13.

Table A-13. *The compatible implementations for MicroProfile 4.1*

- Open Liberty 21.0.0.9 (JDK 8 and JDK 11)
- Quarkus 2.7.2.Final (JDK 11)
- Payara Enterprise 5.37.0 (JDK 8)
- Payara Enterprise (Web Profile) 5.37.0 (JDK 8)
- Payara Community 5.2022.2 (JDK 8)
- Payara Community (Web Profile) 5.2022.2 (JDK 8)
- WildFly 26.1.2.Final (JDK 8, JDK 11, JDK 17)
- WildFly 26.1.3.Final (JDK 8, JDK 11, JDK 17)
- AISWare Flying Server MP 3.5.0 (JDK 8)

MicroProfile 5.0

Released on December 7, 2021, MicroProfile 5.0 delivered updates to all 12 core specifications and the Context Propagation specification and alignment with Jakarta EE 9.1.

Specification Diagram

The updated specification diagram is shown in Figure A-16.

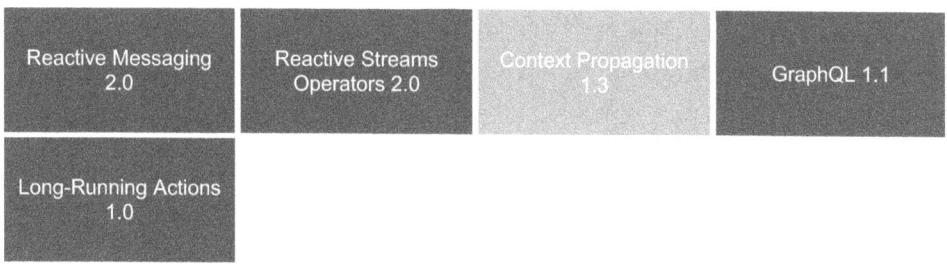

Figure A-16. *The MicroProfile 5.0 core and stand-alone specifications*

Compatible Implementations

Compatible implementations for this release are shown in Table A-14.

Table A-14. The compatible implementations for MicroProfile 5.0

- Open Liberty 22.0.0.1 (JDK 11, JDK 17)
- Fujitsu Launcher 4.0 (JDK 11)
- WildFly 26.0.0.Final (JDK 8, JDK 11, JDK 17)
- WildFly 27.0.0.Final (JDK 8, JDK 11, JDK 17)
- Apache TomEE 9.0.0.RC1 (JDK 11+)
- Payara Server Community 6.2022.2 (JDK 11+)
- Payara Server Community (Web Profile) 6.2022.2 (JDK 11+)
- Helidon 3.1 (JDK 17)

MicroProfile 6.0

Released in January 2023, MicroProfile 6.0 delivered updates to the Metrics, JWT Authentication, and Open API specifications and introduced one new specification, namely:

- **Telemetry**, a specification that follows the OpenTelemetry (*https://opentelemetry.io/*) standard, which provides telemetry data such as tracing, metrics, logging, and baggage

The OpenTelemetry standard, formed in April 2019, was a merger between the Open Tracing (*https://opentracing.io/*) and OpenCensus (*https://opencensus.io/*) standards designed to create one unified telemetry standard.

Specification Diagram

The updated specification diagram is shown in Figure A-17.

APPENDIX A   MICROPROFILE RELEASE HISTORY

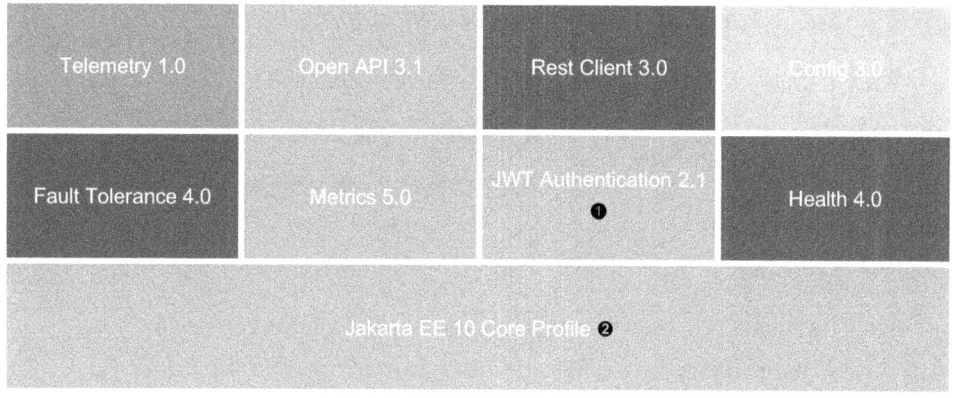
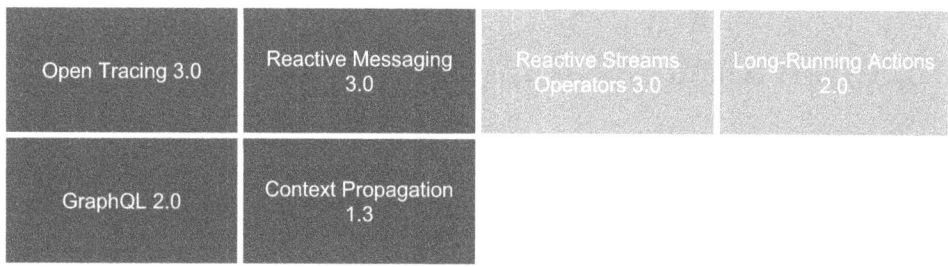

Figure A-17. *The MicroProfile 6.0 core and stand-alone specifications*

❶ The JWT Propagation specification had been renamed to **JWT Authentication**.

❷ The Jakarta EE Core Profile, introduced with the release of Jakarta EE 10 in September 2022, defines a subset of the Jakarta EE Platform specifications focused on providing a minimal basis for cloud-native runtimes, including runtimes that support build time applications. These include the updated versions of the original three JSR-related specifications from back in 2016. Table A-15 lists these specifications.

Table A-15. *The Jakarta EE Core Profile specifications*

- Jakarta RESTful Web Services 3.1
- Jakarta JSON Processing 2.1
- Jakarta JSON Binding 3.0
- Jakarta Annotations 2.1 ❸
- Jakarta Interceptors 2.1
- Jakarta Dependency Injection 2.0
- Jakarta Contexts and Dependency Injection 4.0

❸ The Jakarta Annotations specification, having been listed in the MicroProfile core specification diagram for versions 4.1 and 5.0, is now part of the Jakarta EE Core Profile.

Compatible Implementations

Compatible implementations for this release are shown in Table A-16.

Table A-16. *The compatible implementations for MicroProfile 6.0*

- Open Liberty 22.0.0.13-beta (JDK 11, JDK 17)
- Open Liberty 23.0.0.3 (JDK 11, JDK 17)
- Payara Server Enterprise 6.0.0 (JDK 11+)
- Fujitsu Launcher 5.0 (JDK 17)
- Helidon 4.0 (JDK 21+)

MicroProfile 6.1

Released on October 16, 2023, MicroProfile 6.1 delivered updates to the Config, Metrics, and Telemetry specifications.

Specification Diagram

The updated specification diagram is shown in Figure A-18.

APPENDIX A   MICROPROFILE RELEASE HISTORY

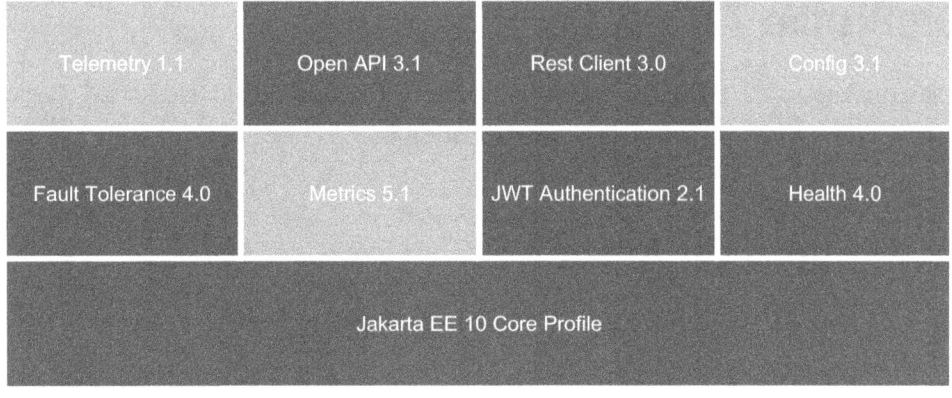
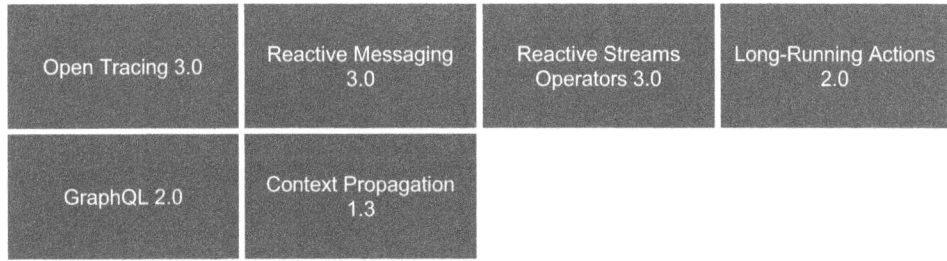

Figure A-18. *The MicroProfile 6.1 core and stand-alone specifications*

Compatible Implementations

Compatible implementations for this release are shown in Table A-17.

Table A-17. *The compatible implementations for MicroProfile 6.1*

- Open Liberty 23.0.0.10-beta (JDK 11, JDK 17)
- Open Liberty 23.0.0.12 (JDK 11, JDK 17)
- IBM WebSphere Liberty 23.0.0.12 (JDK 11, JDK 17)
- Payara Server Enterprise 6.12.0 (JDK 11)
- Payara Server Community 6.2024.3 (JDK 11)
- Payara Server Community (Web Profile) 6.2024.3 (JDK 11)
- Payara Server Enterprise (Web Profile) 6.12.0 (JDK 11)

251

APPENDIX A   MICROPROFILE RELEASE HISTORY

MicroProfile 7.0

Released on August 22, 2024, MicroProfile 7.0 delivered updates to the Fault Tolerance, Telemetry, Open API, and Rest Client specifications.

Specification Diagram

The updated specification diagram is shown in Figure A-19.

Figure A-19. *The MicroProfile 7.0 core and stand-alone specifications*

- ❶ The Metrics specification was moved from the core set of specifications to the stand-alone specifications. This was done for two reasons:
    - The addition of more comprehensive metrics in the OpenTelemetry standard and, therefore, the Telemetry 2.0 specification.
    - Some vendors have chosen not to implement the original Metrics specification.

Compatible Implementations

Compatible implementations for this release are shown in Table A-18.

Table A-18. *The compatible implementations for MicroProfile 7.0*

- Open Liberty - 24.0.0.9-beta (JDK 11, JDK 17, and JDK 21)

Summary

In this appendix, you were introduced to a comprehensive listing of the MicroProfile release history from version 1.0 in September 2016 to the latest version 7.0 release, as of this writing) in August 2024.

In Appendix B, you will learn about all 42 of the Jakarta EE specifications. Chapter 3 only introduced the specifications that targeted Jakarta EE 11, the latest release as of this writing.

APPENDIX B

The Jakarta EE Specifications

This appendix serves to complement Chapter 3. The intent is to give you an appreciation and background information for all 42 of the specifications. In Chapter 3, you were only introduced to the specifications that targeted Jakarta EE 11, the latest release as of this writing.

First, let's review the concept of compatible implementations and the Jakarta EE profiles.

Compatible Implementations

A compatible implementation is a process for an organization to certify that their implementation of the Jakarta EE specifications (or any Java-related specifications for that matter) has passed a series of tests known as the Technology Compatibility Kit (TCK). These tests check for correctness and consistency of all Jakarta EE specifications. Once these tests have passed, the organization may submit a Compatibility Certification Request (CCR) to the Jakarta EE Working Group for approval.

Jakarta EE Profiles

There are three Jakarta EE profiles: **Platform**, **Web Profile**, and the new **Core Profile** that was introduced with the release of Jakarta EE 10. What follows is a brief introduction to each profile and a list of the specifications contained within it.

Platform

The Jakarta EE Platform defines a standard platform for hosting all Jakarta EE applications. It is designed for developers who require the full set of Jakarta EE specifications for developing enterprise applications. The following 30 specifications, as shown in Figure B-1, are included in the Platform.

APPENDIX B   MICROPROFILE RELEASE HISTORY

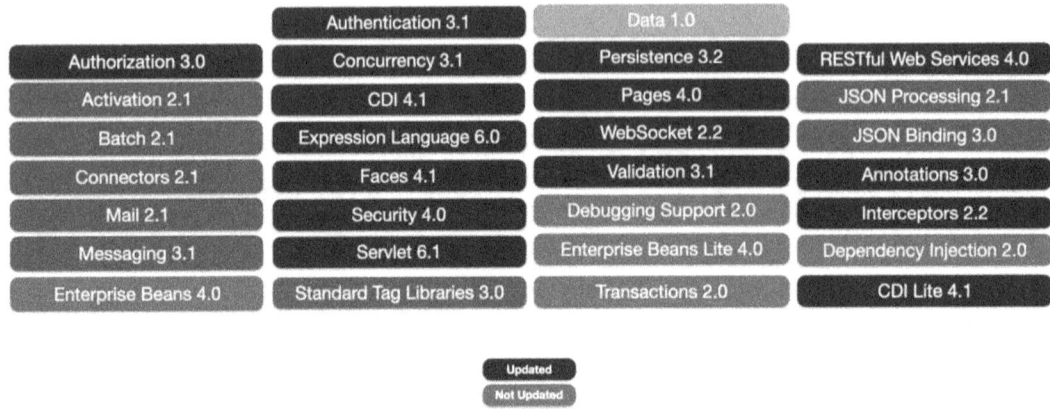

Figure B-1. The specifications included in the Jakarta EE Platform (image courtesy of the Eclipse Foundation)

Web Profile

The Web Profile defines a subset of the Jakarta EE Platform that contains web technologies specifically targeted for developing web applications. The 23 specifications, as shown in Figure B-2, are included in the Web Profile.

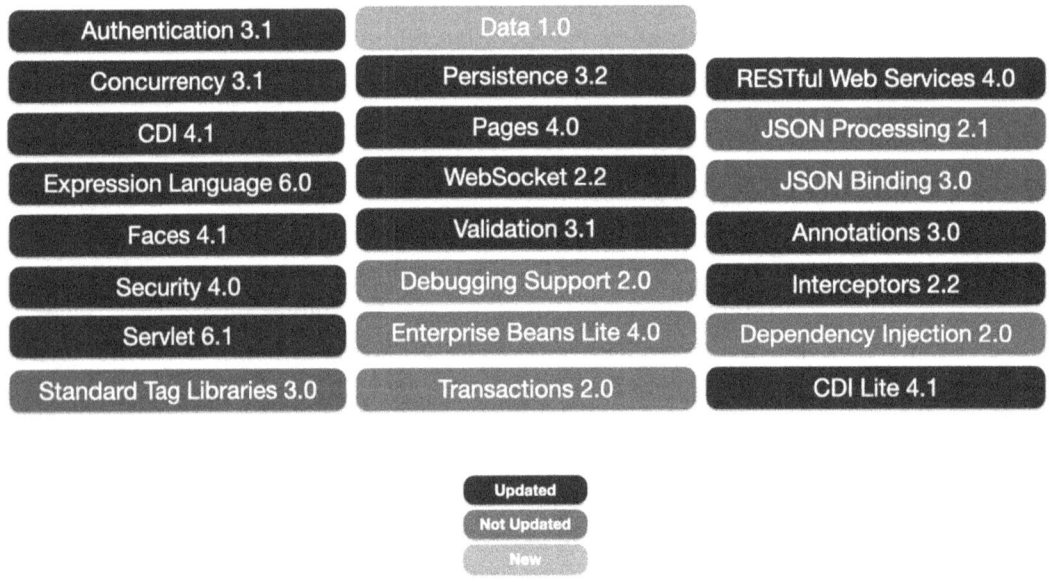

Figure B-2. The specifications included in the Jakarta EE Web Profile (image courtesy of the Eclipse Foundation)

256

APPENDIX B   MICROPROFILE RELEASE HISTORY

Core Profile

The new Core Profile, available with the release of Jakarta EE 10, defines a subset of the Jakarta EE Platform specifications focused on providing a minimal basis for cloud-native runtimes, including runtimes that support build time applications.

It contains a set of Jakarta EE specifications targeting smaller runtimes suitable for microservices and Ahead-of-Time compilation. The eight specifications, as shown in Figure B-3, are included in the Core Profile.

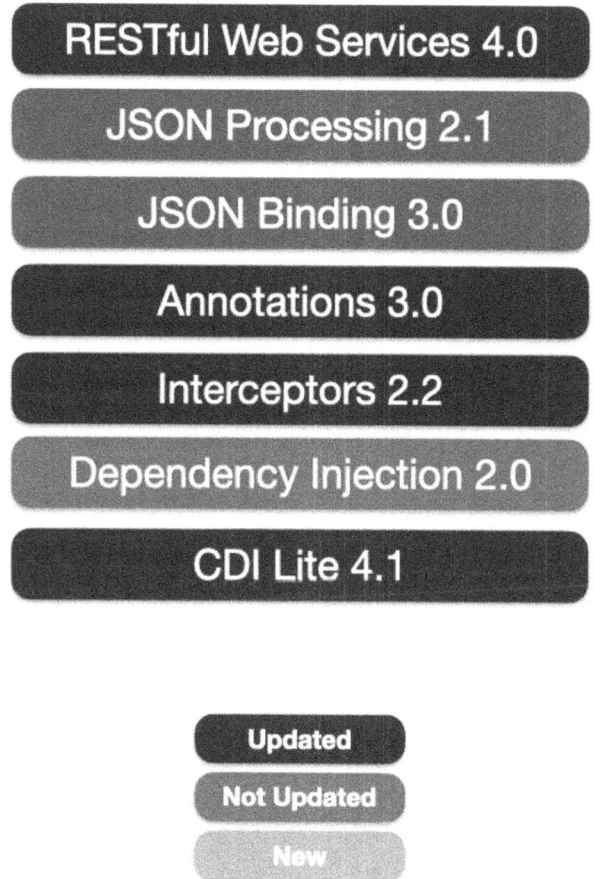

Figure B-3. The specifications included in the Jakarta EE Core Profile (image courtesy of the Eclipse Foundation)

APPENDIX B   MICROPROFILE RELEASE HISTORY

Meet the Jakarta EE Specifications

There are 42 Jakarta EE specifications, but only 30 of them are part of the Jakarta EE Platform. Some specifications haven't been updated since Jakarta EE 8 or Jakarta EE 9. The remainder of this appendix is dedicated to providing you with a brief introduction of each specification, the current version, and their corresponding compatible implementations.

Note The descriptions for these specifications in this appendix have been adapted from the Jakarta EE specifications website (https://jakarta.ee/specifications/).

Now let's check out each of the Jakarta EE specifications!

Jakarta Activation

The **Jakarta Activation** specification (https://jakarta.ee/specifications/activation/), currently at version 2.1 for Jakarta EE 10, defines a set of standard services to determine the MIME type of an arbitrary piece of data; encapsulate access to it; discover the operations available on it; and instantiate the appropriate bean to perform the operation(s).

The compatible implementation for this specification is **Eclipse Angus/Activation 2.0.2**.

Jakarta Annotations

The **Jakarta Annotations** specification (https://jakarta.ee/specifications/annotations/), currently at version 3.0 for Jakarta EE 11, defines a collection of annotations representing common semantic concepts that enable a declarative style of programming that applies across a variety of Java technologies.

The compatible implementation for this specification is **Eclipse GlassFish 8.0.0-M3**.

Jakarta Authentication

The **Jakarta Authentication** specification (*https://jakarta.ee/specifications/authentication/*), currently at version 3.1 for Jakarta EE 11, defines a general low-level SPI for authentication mechanisms, which are controllers that interact with a caller and a container's environment to obtain the caller's credentials, validate these, and pass an authenticated identity (such as name and groups) to the container.

The compatible implementations for this specification are **Eclipse Epicyro 3.1.0** and **Eclipse GlassFish 8.0.0-M6**.

Jakarta Authorization

The **Jakarta Authorization** specification (*https://jakarta.ee/specifications/authorization/*), currently at version 3.0 for Jakarta EE 11, defines a low-level SPI for authorization modules, which are repositories of permissions facilitating subject-based security by determining whether a given subject has a given permission, and algorithms to transform security constraints for specific containers (such as Jakarta Servlet or Jakarta Enterprise Beans) into these permissions.

The compatible implementations for this specification are **Eclipse Exousia 3.0.0-M3** and **Eclipse GlassFish 8.0.0-M5**.

Jakarta Batch

The **Jakarta Batch** specification (*https://jakarta.ee/specifications/batch/*), currently at version 2.1 for Jakarta EE 10, specifies a Java API plus an XML-based job specification language (JSL), which lets you compose batch jobs in XML from reusable Java application artifacts and conveniently parameterize different executions of a single job.

The compatible implementation for this specification is **JBatch 2.1.0-M2**.

APPENDIX B   MICROPROFILE RELEASE HISTORY

Jakarta Concurrency

The **Jakarta Concurrency** specification (*https://jakarta.ee/specifications/concurrency/*), currently at version 3.1 for Jakarta EE 11, provides a specification for using concurrency from application components without compromising container integrity while still preserving the Jakarta EE Platform's fundamental benefits.

The compatible implementation for this specification is **Open Liberty 22.0.0.6-beta**.

Jakarta Config

The **Jakarta Config** specification (*https://jakarta.ee/specifications/config/*), currently under development, defines a core framework for the Jakarta EE Platform allowing applications and other Jakarta EE components to read configuration data from different environment-aware sources in a portable way.

There is no compatible implementation at this time.

Jakarta Connectors

The **Jakarta Connectors** specification (*https://jakarta.ee/specifications/connectors/*), currently at version 2.1 for Jakarta EE 10, defines a standard architecture for Jakarta EE application components to connect to Enterprise Information Systems.

The compatible implementation for this specification is **Eclipse GlassFish 7.0.0-M4**.

Jakarta Contexts and Dependency Injection

The **Jakarta Contexts and Dependency Injection** specification (*https://jakarta.ee/specifications/cdi/*), currently at version 4.1 for Jakarta EE 11, defines a powerful set of complementary services that help to improve the structure of application code.

The compatible implementation for this specification is **Weld 6.0.0.Beta1**.

Jakarta Data

The **Jakarta Data** specification (*https://jakarta.ee/specifications/data/*), at version 1.0 for Jakarta EE 11, defines core APIs for the Jakarta EE Platform allowing applications and other Jakarta EE components to explore the benefits of easy access to data technologies, such as relational and nonrelational databases and cloud-based data services.

The compatible implementations for this specification are **Hibernate ORM 6.6.0** and **Open Liberty 24.0.0.6**.

Jakarta Debugging Support for Other Languages

The **Jakarta Debugging Support for Other Languages** specification (*https://jakarta.ee/specifications/debugging/*), currently at version 2.0 for Jakarta EE 9, provides a mechanism by which programs executed under the Java virtual machine but written in languages other than the Java programming language can be debugged with references to the original source (e.g., source file and line number references).

The compatible implementation for this specification is **Eclipse GlassFish 6.0.0**.

Jakarta Dependency Injection

The **Jakarta Dependency Injection** specification (*https://jakarta.ee/specifications/dependency-injection/*), currently at version 2.0 for Jakarta EE 9, specifies a means for obtaining objects in such a way as to maximize reusability, testability, and maintainability compared to traditional approaches such as constructors, factories, and service locators such as JNDI.

The compatible implementations for this specification are **Weld 4.0.3.Final** and **Weld 5.0.0.SP2**.

Jakarta Deployment

The **Jakarta Deployment** specification (*https://jakarta.ee/specifications/deployment/*), currently at version 1.7 for Jakarta EE 8, defines standard APIs that will enable any deployment tool that uses the deployment APIs to deploy any assembled application onto a Jakarta EE-compatible platform.

The compatible implementation for this specification is **Eclipse GlassFish 5.1.0**.

Jakarta Enterprise Beans

The **Jakarta Enterprise Beans** specification (*https://jakarta.ee/specifications/enterprise-beans/*), currently at version 4.0 for Jakarta EE 9, defines an architecture for the development and deployment of component-based business applications.

The compatible implementation for this specification is **Eclipse GlassFish 6.0.0-RC2**.

Jakarta Enterprise Web Services

The **Jakarta Enterprise Web Services** specification (*https://jakarta.ee/specifications/enterprise-ws/*), currently at version 2.0 for Jakarta EE 9, provides a client and server programming model which is portable and interoperable across application servers in a scalable secure environment.

The compatible implementation for this specification is **Eclipse GlassFish 6.0.0**.

Jakarta Expression Language

The **Jakarta Expression Language** specification (*https://jakarta.ee/specifications/expression-language/*), currently at version 6.0 for Jakarta EE 11, defines a simple language to meet the needs of the presentation layer in web applications that features a simple syntax restricted to the evaluation of expressions; variables and nested properties; relational, logical, arithmetic, conditional, and empty operators; and functions implemented as static methods on Java classes.

The compatible implementation for this specification is **Tomcat 11.0.0-M18**.

Jakarta Faces

The **Jakarta Faces** specification (*https://jakarta.ee/specifications/faces/*), formerly known as *Jakarta Server Faces* and currently at version 4.1 for Jakarta EE 11, defines an MVC framework for building user interfaces for web applications, including UI components, state management, event handling, input validation, page navigation, and support for internationalization and accessibility.

The compatible implementations for this specification are **Eclipse Mojarra 4.1.0** and **Eclipse GlassFish 8.0.0-M6**.

Jakarta Interceptors

The **Jakarta Interceptors** specification (*https://jakarta.ee/specifications/interceptors/*), currently at version 2.2 for Jakarta EE 11, defines a means of interposing on business method invocations and specific events, such as lifecycle events and timeout events, that occur on instances of Jakarta EE components and other managed classes.

The compatible implementation for this specification is **Weld 6.0.0.Beta1**.

Jakarta JSON Binding

The **Jakarta JSON Binding** specification (*https://jakarta.ee/specifications/jsonb/*), currently at version 3.0 for Jakarta EE 10, defines a binding framework for converting Java objects to and from JSON documents.

The compatible implementation for this specification is **Eclipse Yasson 3.0.0-RC1**.

Jakarta JSON Processing

The **Jakarta JSON Processing** specification (*https://jakarta.ee/specifications/jsonp/*), currently at version 2.1 for Jakarta EE 10, defines a Java-based framework for parsing, generating, transforming, and querying JSON documents.

The compatible implementation for this specification is **Eclipse Parsson 1.1.2**.

Jakarta Mail

The **Jakarta Mail** specification (*https://jakarta.ee/specifications/mail/*), currently at version 2.1 for Jakarta EE 10, defines a platform-independent and protocol-independent framework to build mail and messaging applications.

The compatible implementation for this specification is **Eclipse Angus Mail 2.0.2**.

Jakarta Managed Beans

The **Jakarta Managed Beans** specification (*https://jakarta.ee/specifications/managedbeans/*), currently at version 2.0 for Jakarta EE 9, defines a set of basic services for container-managed objects with minimal requirements, otherwise known under the acronym POJOs (Plain Old Java Objects).

The compatible implementation for this specification is **Eclipse GlassFish 6.0.0**.

Jakarta Management

The **Jakarta Management** specification (*https://jakarta.ee/specifications/management/*), currently at version 1.1 for Jakarta EE 8, defines a standard management model for exposing and accessing the management information, operations, and parameters of the Jakarta EE Platform components.

The compatible implementation for this specification is **Eclipse GlassFish 5.1.0**.

Jakarta Messaging

The **Jakarta Messaging** specification (*https://jakarta.ee/specifications/messaging/*), currently at version 3.1 for Jakarta EE 10, describes a means for Java applications to create, send, and receive messages via loosely coupled, reliable asynchronous communication services.

The compatible implementation for this specification is **Eclipse OpenMQ 6.3.0-RC1**.

Jakarta MVC

The **Jakarta MVC** specification (*https://jakarta.ee/specifications/mvc/*), currently at version 3.0 and under development supporting Jakarta EE 11, defines a standard for creating web applications following the action-based Model-View-Controller (MVC) pattern.

There is no defined compatible implementation for Jakarta MVC 3.0 at this time, but it is worth noting that the compatible implementations for Jakarta MVC 2.1 supporting Jakarta EE 10 are **Eclipse Krazo for Jersey 3.0.0**, **Eclipse Krazo for RESTEasy 3.0.1**, and **Eclipse GlassFish 7.0.0-M9**.

Jakarta NoSQL

The **Jakarta NoSQL** specification (*https://jakarta.ee/specifications/nosql/*), currently at version 1.0 and under development supporting Jakarta EE 11, defines a set of APIs and provides a standard implementation for most NoSQL databases and streamlines the integration of Java applications with NoSQL databases.

The compatible implementation for this specification is **Eclipse JNoSQL 1.1.1**.

Jakarta Pages

The **Jakarta Pages** specification (*https://jakarta.ee/specifications/pages/*), formerly known as *Jakarta Server Pages* and currently at version 4.0 for Jakarta EE 11, defines a template engine for web applications that supports mixing of textual content (including HTML and XML) with custom tags, expression language, and embedded Java code, which gets compiled into a Jakarta Servlet.

The compatible implementation for this specification is **Apache Tomcat 11.0.0-M20**.

Jakarta Persistence

The **Jakarta Persistence** specification (*https://jakarta.ee/specifications/persistence/*), currently at version 3.2 for Jakarta EE 11, defines a standard for management of persistence and object/relational mapping in Java environments.

The compatible implementations for this specification are **EclipseLink 5.0.0-B02** and **Hibernate ORM 7.0.0.Alpha2**.

Jakarta RESTful Web Services

The **Jakarta RESTful Web Services** specification (*https://jakarta.ee/specifications/restful-ws/*), currently at version 4.0 for Jakarta EE 11, provides a foundational API to develop web services following the Representational State Transfer (REST) architectural pattern.

The compatible implementation for this specification is **Eclipse RESTEasy 7.0.0.Alpha1** and **Eclipse Jersey 4.0.0-M1**.

Jakarta RPC

The **Jakarta RPC** specification (*https://jakarta.ee/specifications/rpc/*), currently under development, defines a standard that allows developers to define Google Remote Procedure Call (gRPC) services and clients in the same manner as REST services and clients through annotated classes on the server and annotated interfaces on the client. This makes it easier to integrate those services with existing Jakarta EE technologies.

Since this specification has not yet been completed, there is no compatible implementation at this time.

Jakarta Security

The **Jakarta Security** specification (*https://jakarta.ee/specifications/security/*), currently at version 4.0 for Jakarta EE 11, defines a standard for creating secure Jakarta EE applications in modern application paradigms.

The compatible implementation for this specification is **Eclipse Soteria 4.0.0** and **Eclipse GlassFish 8.0.0-M6**.

Jakarta Servlet

The **Jakarta Servlet** specification (*https://jakarta.ee/specifications/servlet/*), currently at version 6.1 for Jakarta EE 11, defines a server-side API for handling HTTP requests and responses.

The compatible implementation for this specification is **Tomcat 11.0.0-M20**.

Jakarta SOAP with Attachments

The **Jakarta SOAP with Attachments** specification (*https://jakarta.ee/specifications/soap-attachments/*), currently at version 3.0 for Jakarta EE 10, defines an API enabling developers to produce and consume messages conforming to the SOAP 1.1 and SOAP 1.2 protocols and the SOAP Attachment Feature.

The compatible implementation for this specification is **Eclipse Implementation of Jakarta SOAP with Attachments 3.0.0-M2**.

Jakarta Standard Tag Library

The **Jakarta Standard Tag Library** specification (*https://jakarta.ee/specifications/tags/*), currently at version 3.0 for Jakarta EE 10, encapsulates the core functionality common to many web applications as simple tags for easier development with the Jakarta Pages specification.

The compatible implementation for this specification is the **EE4J implementation of Jakarta Standard Tag Library 3.0.0**.

Jakarta Transactions

The **Jakarta Transactions** specification (*https://jakarta.ee/specifications/transactions/*), currently at version 2.0 for Jakarta EE 9, defines a standard that allows the demarcation of transactions and the transactional coordination of XA-aware resource managers as described in the X/Open XA specification (*https://pubs.opengroup.org/onlinepubs/009680699/toc.pdf*) and mapped to the Java SE **XAResource** interface within applications.

The compatible implementation for this specification is **Eclipse GlassFish 6.0.0-SNAPSHOT-2020-10-04**.

Jakarta Validation

The **Jakarta Validation** specification (*https://jakarta.ee/specifications/bean-validation/*), formerly known as *Jakarta Bean Validation* and currently at version 3.1 for Jakarta EE 11, provides an object-level constraint declaration and validation facility as well as a constraint metadata repository and query API. It also offers method and constructor validation facilities to ensure constraints on their parameters and return values.

The compatible implementation for this specification is **Hibernate Validator 8.0.1.Final**.

Jakarta Web Services Metadata

The **Jakarta Web Services Metadata** specification (*https://jakarta.ee/ specifications/web-services-metadata/*), currently at version 3.0 for Jakarta EE 9, defines a programming model for Java web services, use of metadata, a non-normative processing model for metadata annotated web service source files, runtime requirements for a container, and annotations used for Web Services Description Language (WSDL), binding, and configuration.

The compatible implementations for this specification are **Eclipse Implementation of XML Web Services 3.0.0 and Eclipse Metro 3.0.0**.

Jakarta WebSocket

The **Jakarta WebSocket** specification (*https://jakarta.ee/specifications/ websocket/*), currently at version 2.2 for Jakarta EE 11, defines an API for client and server endpoints for the WebSocket protocol as defined by the Internet Engineering Task Force (IETF) RFC6455.

The compatible implementation for this specification is **Eclipse Tyrus 2.2.0-M1** and **Apache Tomcat 11.0.0-M20**.

Jakarta XML Binding

The **Jakarta XML Binding** specification (*https://jakarta.ee/specifications/xml-binding/*), currently at version 4.0 for Jakarta EE 10, defines an API and corresponding tools that automate mapping between XML documents and Java objects.

The compatible implementation for this specification is **Jakarta XML Binding 4.0.0-M3**.

Jakarta XML Registries

The **Jakarta XML Registries** specification (*https://jakarta.ee/specifications/xml-registries/*), currently at version 1.0 for Jakarta EE 8, defines APIs specifically designed for an open and interoperable set of registry services that enable sharing of information among interested parties. The shared information is maintained as objects in a compliant registry. Access to the content in the registry is exposed via interfaces defined for the registry services.

The compatible implementation for this specification is **Eclipse GlassFish 5.1.0**.

Jakarta XML RPC

The **Jakarta XML RPC** specification (`https://jakarta.ee/specifications/xml-rpc/`), currently at version 1.1 for Jakarta EE 8, defines consistent Java APIs for using XML-based Remote Procedure Calls (RPC) standards.

The compatible implementation for this specification is **Eclipse XML RPC 1.1.5**.

Jakarta XML Web Services

The **Jakarta XML Web Services** specification (`https://jakarta.ee/specifications/xml-web-services/`), currently at version 4.0 for Jakarta EE 10, defines a means for implementing XML-based web services based on the Jakarta SOAP with Attachments and Jakarta Web Services Metadata specifications.

The compatible implementations for this specification are **Eclipse Implementation of XML Web Services 4.0.0-M3** and **Eclipse Metro 4.0.0-M3**.

Summary

In this appendix, you were introduced to all 42 specifications. Only 30 of them are part of the Jakarta EE Platform. The remaining 12 specifications are in various stages of development, sunsetting, or deprecations.

Java User Groups are encouraged to participate in the Adopt-a-Spec program (`https://jakarta.ee/community/adopt-a-spec/`) to increase developer-level participation in the evolution of the Jakarta EE.

In Appendix C, you will learn about the original Helidon asynchronous and reactive web server that is still supported in the Helidon 2.0 and Helidon 3.0 release trains.

APPENDIX C

Helidon Reactive WebServer Component

Inspired by Node.js and other Java frameworks, Helidon's WebServer component is an asynchronous and reactive API that runs on top of Netty, an asynchronous event-driven network application framework. In this chapter, we will explore all of these.

> **Note** With the release of Helidon 4.0 in October 2023, the WebServer component was rebuilt from the ground up and is now based on virtual threads.
>
> Oracle still maintains the Helidon 2.0 and 3.0 release trains that use the reactive web server, and details may be found in this appendix.

As you can imagine, the Helidon WebServer component is the cornerstone to Helidon applications because you will always need to spin up an instance of a web server for any Helidon SE application and its related testing.

WebServer Component

The WebServer component represents an immutably configured web server. The **WebServer** interface is at the heart of this component and provides basic server lifecycle and monitoring enhanced by configuration, routing, error handling, and building metrics and health endpoints.

Signature

The WebServer interface has the signature as shown in Listing C-1.

Listing C-1. The **WebServer** interface signature

`public interface WebServer`

This interface defines a number of methods that, of course, require implementation for configuring, building, starting, and stopping a web server.

Create Method

The **WebServer** interface defines four overloaded **create()** methods to create a web server handling configuration and routing information that return a static instance of the **WebServer** interface as shown in Listing C-2.

Listing C-2. The overloaded **create()** methods

- **create(Routing routing)** creates a new instance from the provided routing and default configuration.
- **create(Routing routing, Config config)** creates a new instance from the provided routing and configuration.
- **create(Supplier<? extends Routing> routingBuilder)** creates a new instance from the provided routing and default configuration.
- **create(Supplier<Routing> routingBuilder, Config config)** creates a new instance from the provided routing and configuration.

Supplier<T> is a functional interface defined in Java SE that may be used as an assignment target for a lambda expression or method reference. Type **T** is a generic that represents the type of results supplied by this supplier.

Builder Pattern

The **WebServer.Builder** class provides a convenient way to implement an instance of the **WebServer** interface with multiple server sockets and optional multiple routings. As we progress through this chapter, you will learn how all of this works.

APPENDIX C   MICROPROFILE RELEASE HISTORY

Configuration

You can configure the web server directly or through the Helidon Config component. You will learn more about the Config component in Chapter 7, but let's take a sneak peek on how it works here.

Direct Configuration

You can take advantage of a number of methods defined in the **WebServer.Builder** class to directly configure your web server. Consider the example as shown in Listing C-3.

Listing C-3. Building the web server using direct configuration

```
WebServer server = WebServer.builder()  ❶
    .bindAddress(InetAddress.getLocalHost())  ❷
    .port(8080)  ❸
    .build();  ❹
```

❶ The **builder()** method creates a fluent API builder of the **WebServer** interface and returns a static instance of **WebServer.Builder** from which the following methods are used in this example.

❷ The **bindAddress(InetAddress bindAddress)** method configures a local address where the server listens with the server socket. In our example, the **getLocalHost()** method defined in the **InetAddress** class returns the IP address of a developer's localhost (usually 127.0.0.1). If this is not configured, then the web server listens on all local addresses.

❸ The **port(int port)** method configures a server port on which to listen with the server socket. If the port is set to **0**, then any available ephemeral port will be used.

❹ Then finally, the **build()** method builds an instance of the **WebServer** interface using this configuration by this builder and its parameters.

External Configuration

A configuration file may also be used to create your web server. In Helidon, the default configuration file is **application.yaml** located in the **src/main/resources** folder. However, you can use other commonly used file names, such as **application.properties** or **microprofile-config.properties**. A typical server configuration, defined in YAML format, is shown in Listing C-4.

Listing C-4. A typical server configuration defined in YAML format

```
server:
  port: 8080
  host: 0.0.0.0
```

Assuming you're using the default **application.yaml** file, you can load the file by creating an instance of the **Config** interface as shown in Listing C-5.

Listing C-5. Loading configuration properties from the **application.yaml** file

```
Config config = Config.create();
```

Then, to extract the contents of the **server** section, you can use either the **get(Config.Key key)** or **get(String key)** method. Let's use the second **get()** method as shown in Listing C-6.

Listing C-6. Extracting the contents from the **server** section of the YAML file

```
Config greeting = config.get("server");
```

Routing

The **Routing** interface represents composition of HTTP request-response handlers with rules for routing. This allows for request matching criteria to bind requests to a handler that will implement your custom business logic.

Signature

The **Routing** interface has the following signature as shown in Listing C-7.

Listing C-7. The **Routing** interface signature

```
public interface Routing extends ServerLifecycle
```

This interface extends the **ServerLifecycle** interface that defines basic server lifecycle operations and declares two methods: **beforeStart()** and **afterStart()**. Routing also has its own builder pattern and declares a method, **route(BareRequest bareRequest, BareResponse bareResponse)**, that processes a bare minimal request and response.

Builder Pattern

The **Routing.Builder** class builds an instance of the **Routing** interface. Here is a basic example as shown in Listing C-8.

Listing C-8. Building an instance of the **Routing** interface

```
Routing routing = Routing.builder()
    .get("/hello", (request, response) -> response.send("Hello World!"))
    .build();
```

The **builder()** method creates a fluent API builder of the **Routing** interface and returns a static instance of **Routing.Builder** from which the following methods are used in this example.

There are three overloaded versions of the **get()** method as shown in Listing C-9.

Listing C-9. The overloaded **get()** methods

- **get(Handler... requestHandlers)** routes all **GET** requests to provided handler(s).
- **get(PathMatcher pathMatcher, Handler... requestHandlers)** routes all **GET** requests with the corresponding path via the **PathMatcher** interface to the provided handler(s).
- **get(String pathPattern, Handler... requestHandlers)** routes all **GET** requests with the corresponding path via a **String** to the provided handler(s).

In the example in Listing C-8, the third **get()** method from Listing C-9 is used to define a **/hello** endpoint to print "Hello World!".

Then finally, the **build()** method builds an instance of the **Routing** interface.

Routing.Builder also provides corresponding overloaded methods, similar to the **get()** method, for handling other HTTP requests as shown in Table C-1.

Table C-1. *List of HTTP requests and corresponding methods*

HTTP Request	Corresponding Routing.Builder Method
GET	.get()
PUT	.put()
POST	.post()
HEAD	.head()
Any request	.any()

Putting It All Together

Now that you've learned how to create and start a web server, let's put it all together and build an application! You can find the full source code and relevant documentation at the **helidon-book** GitHub repository (*https://github.com/mpredli01/helidon-book*) under the **wsreactive** module. Inspiration for these examples was adapted from the Helidon examples GitHub repository (*https://github.com/helidon-io/helidon-xamples/*).

To demonstrate the Helidon WebServer component in action, let's examine the **startServer()** method defined in the **Application** class as shown in Listing C-12.

Dependencies

Let's start with Maven and Gradle dependencies that you would use in your application.

Note The examples associated with this book use Maven as a build tool. The Gradle dependency is listed here for completeness and for the possibility of adding Gradle as a build tool to complement Maven in the future.

Appendix C Microprofile Release History

If Maven is your build tool, use the dependency as shown in Listing C-10.

Listing C-10. The Maven dependency

```xml
<dependency>
    <groupId>io.helidon.webserver</groupId>
    <artifactId>helidon-webserver</artifactId>
    <version>3.2.9</version>
</dependency>
```

If Gradle is your build tool, use the dependency as shown in Listing C-11.

Listing C-11. The Gradle dependency

```
implementation group: 'io.helidon.webserver', name: 'helidon-webserver',
version: '3.2.9'
```

Listing C-12. The **startServer()** method defined in the **Application** class

```java
static Single<WebServer> startServer() {
    LogConfig.configureRuntime(); ❶
    Config config = Config.create(); ❷
    WebServer server = WebServer.builder(createRouting(config))
            .config(config.get("server"))
            .addMediaSupport(JsonpSupport.create()) ❸
            .build();
    Single<WebServer> webserver = server.start(); ❹
    webserver.thenAccept(ws -> { ❺
        System.out.println("WEB server is up! http://localhost:" +
        ws.port() + "/greet");
        ws.whenShutdown().thenRun(() -> System.out.println("WEB server is
        DOWN. Goodbye!"));
        })
    .exceptionallyAccept(t -> { ❻
            System.err.println("Startup failed: " + t.getMessage());
```

```
            t.printStackTrace(System.err);
    });
return webserver;
}
```

- ❶ The **configureRuntime()** method defined in the logging configuration utility class, **LogConfig**, reconfigures logging with runtime configuration if the application is converted to a native image via GraalVM. On application startup, methods are invoked by Helidon, so you do not need to explicitly configure logging as long as a file **logging.properties** is on the classpath or in the current directory. You can also configure logging explicitly using System properties such as **java.util.logging.config.class** and **java.util.logging.config.file**.

- ❷ As you learned earlier in this chapter, the **create()** method defined in the **Config** interface loads the default configuration file, **application.yaml**.

- ❸ The **addMediaSupport(MediaSupport mediaSupport)** method accepts an implementation of the **MediaSupport** interface to register readers and writers for your application. Implementing classes are as follows:

  - **DefaultMediaSupport** registers default readers and writers to the contexts.

  - **JacksonSupport** provides support for Jackson integration.

  - **JsonbSupport** provides support for JSON Binding (JSON-B) integration.

  - **JsonpSupport** provides support for JSON Processing (JSON-P) integration.

  - **MultiPartSupport** provides support for multimedia.

    Instances of **MediaSupport** may be used with both WebServer and WebClient components.

④ Since the WebServer component is a reactive web server, the **start()** method starts the server and returns an instance of the **Single<WebServer>** interface that represents a **Flow.Publisher** from Java Concurrent API that may signal one item and then complete without an item or signal an error.

⑤ The **thenAccept(Consumer<? super T> action)** method accepts an instance of **Consumer<T>**, which, similar to **Supplier<T>**, is another functional interface defined in Java SE that may be used as an assignment target for a lambda expression or method reference. This method is used when you don't want to return anything from a callback function and only want to run some code once a **Future** completes. As you can see, the lambda expression contains two statements that provide information for server startup and shutdown, respectively.

⑥ Similarly, the **exceptionallyAccept(Consumer<Throwable> consumer)** method also accepts an instance of **Consumer<T>** that initiates the error message and printable stack trace upon an exception.

Summary

In this appendix, you were introduced to the reactive WebServer component that includes the **WebServer**, **Routing**, and **Config** interfaces, how to establish routing and configuration, and an examination on how it all fits together in a Helidon application.

Details on the virtual WebServer component may be found in Chapter 5.

Index

A

ABAC, *see* Attribute-Based Access Control (ABAC) Authorization
addService() method, 88, 132
/admin endpoint, 149
Ahead-of-time (AOT), 5, 11, 41
AOT, *see* Ahead-of-time (AOT)
Apache Jakarta Project, 35
applicationUpTime() method, 189
applicationUpTime metric, 198
application.yaml file, 138, 142, 150
app.yml file, 53, 157
archetype:generate, 50, 155
asNodeList(), 145
asString() method, 145
@Asynchronous annotation, 205, 208
AtomicReference<String>, 158
Attribute-Based Access Control (ABAC) Authorization, 137

B

Base metrics, 176, 177
baseUri() method, 87
blocking() method, 211
builder() method, 87, 95, 132
@Bulkhead annotation, 205, 206

C

call() method, 220–222
CCR, *see* Compatibility Certification Request (CCR)
CDI, *see* Contexts and Dependency Injection (CDI)
@CircuitBreaker annotation, 203
classloader.loadedClasses.count, 178
classloader.loadedClasses.count measurement, 193
classloader.loadedClasses.total, 178
classloader.unloadedClasses.total, 178
CLI, *see* Command-Line Interface (CLI)
ClientApplication class, 92
Command-Line Interface (CLI), 9, 57, 162
Compatibility Certification Request (CCR), 18
config() method, 88
ConfigAuthenticationApplication class, 141, 142
config.get() method, 140
config.get(String), 145
ConfigMapper interface, 105
ConfigMapperProvider interface, 106
@ConfigProperty(name="app.greeting") annotation, 158
Configuration, 99
   addParser() method, 107
   anatomy, 100
   Application class, 112
   application.yaml file, 108, 109
   build and execute, 117
   characteristics, 101
   component, 99, 119
   create() method, 100, 108
   directory() method, 113

INDEX

Configuration (*cont.*)
    DirectorySources class, 112
    directory structure, 110
    execution, 118
    files, 106
    filters, 101
    filters and overrides, 107
    GitHub repository, 109
    Gradle dependency, 111
    interfaces, 99, 104
    load configuration, 108
    loading data, 104
    mappers, 105
    Maven dependency, 111
    MergeSources class, 114
    MultipleConfigSources class, 115
    OverrideSource, 102
    parsers, 101, 106
    signature, 100, 103, 107
    source, 104, 115, 116
    sources and formats, 102
    token, 102
ConfigValue<String>, 145
@ConstrainedTo annotation, 187
Consumer<T>, 86
ContainerResponseFilter, 187
Context Propagation, 31
Contexts and Dependency Injection (CDI), 5, 21
CORS, *see* Cross-Origin Resource Sharing (CORS)
@Counted annotation, 179, 180, 188
countedName(String) method, 180
cpu.availableProcessors, 178
cpu.processCpuLoad, 178
cpu.processCpuTime, 178
cpu.systemLoadAverage, 178
create() method, 91, 138
createNamedDelete() method, 130
Cross-Origin Resource Sharing (CORS), 5, 13
curl command, 54, 159–161

D

DB Client
    application, 122
    Caterpie, 135
    component, 121, 125, 136
    configuration, 124, 127
    dependencies, 125
    features, 121
    GitHub repository, 136
    interface, 121
    interface signature, 123
    JDBC database, 124
    Pokémons, 135
    Rattata, 134
    signature, 122
    supports, 122
    types of metrics, 123
DB Client
    create() method, 122
    curl command, 133
    DBBuilder interface, 122
    DbClientTracing interface, 123
    DbExecute interface, 129
DbClientHealthCheck interface, 123
-Dexec.mainClass=<fully-qualified-class-name> flag, 146
Docker 18.09, 154
Docker.jlink file, 157
Docker.native file, 157

E

Eclipse Working Groups, 17, 36
exec:java, 146
Exec Maven plugin, 146
Exec Maven Plugin, 81, 133

F

@Fallback annotation, 206, 207
fallbackMethod() method, 210
Fault Tolerance
    annotations, 199, 200
    @Asynchronous annotation, 208
    @CircuitBreaker, 203
    build and package, 212
    descriptions, 199
    endpoint, 213
    fallbackHandler(), 209
    Maven dependency, 209
    parameter, 200
    retryHandler(), 211
    terminate() method, 210
    @Timeout, 202
followRedirects() method, 95

G

@Gauge annotation, 179–181, 189
GaugeMetric class, 183, 188
gc.time, 177
gc.total, 177
get() method, 80
getDefaultMessageHandler() method, 80
getMessageHandler() method, 80
get() method, 145
getProperties() method, 218
getRegistry() method, 179
getResponseAsAnJsonObject() method, 96
Google Login Authentication, 137
GraalVM, 10, 13
Gradle dependency, 76, 90, 126, 127, 141, 142, 277
GraphQL, 31
/greet endpoint, 155, 158, 160
GreetingProvider class, 158
GreetResource class, 158

H

Header Assertion, 137
Health checks
    annotations, 216
    application, 223
    dependencies, 217, 218
    endpoints, 216, 226, 227
    interface, 217
    JAR file, 223
    JSON response, 225, 227
    SystemReadinessCheck class, 220
    SystemResource class, 218
    SystemStartupCheck class, 221
    types, 216
    web applications, 215
Helidon, 3, 14
    architecture, 7, 8
    CLI, 9
    flavors, 59
    GraalVM, 10
    Helidon 0.10.0, 12
    Helidon 1.0.0, 12, 13
    Helidon 2.0.0, 13
    Helidon 3.0.0, 13, 14
    Helidon 4.0.0, 14
    IntelliJ IDEA, 11

Helidon (cont.)
   Jakarta Persistence specification, 10
   Kotlin, 11
   Log4j2, 11
   methods, 9
   Micronaut Data, 11
   microservices frameworks, 8
   MicroStream, 11
   Quickstarts, 9
   starter projects, 10
   versions, 59
Helidon 2.0, 162, 164
   See also Helidon CLI tool
Helidon 3.0, 164, 168
   See also Project Starter
Helidon 4.0, 164
helidon-book GitHub repository, 141
Helidon CLI tool, 162
   install Helidon CLI
      available application types, 165
      available media types, 165
      available versions, 164
      curl command, 162
      custom options list, 165
      helidon command, 163
      org.development loop, 166
      org.redlich, 166
      PowerShell command, 163
      quickstart-mp directory, 167
      resulting directory structure, 166
      utility on macOS, 162
helidon command, 163
helidon init command, 166
Helidon Metrics, 175
   annotated methods, 175
   base metrics, 176, 177
   build and execute application, 190
   exercise application, 190–198
   histogram metric, 185–188
   Maven and Gradle dependencies, 183
   methods, 175
   metric registry, 179
   Prometheus format, 189
   scopes, use cases and corresponding endpoints, 176
   using a Gauge, 188, 189
   using @Counted and @Timed annotations, 184
Helidon Metrics annotations
   @Counted annotation, 180
   @Gauge annotation, 180, 181
   parameters, 182
   @Timed annotation, 181, 182
   and use cases, 179
Helidon MP, 5, 153
   annotations, 6
   applications, 10
   command-line utility, 153
   components, 5
   declarative style, 6
      vs. functional style, 6, 7
      web server, 6
   Helidon Project Starter, 153
   HelloWorld class, 6
   Jakarta EE specifications, 153
   Quickstarts, 153, 155 (*see also* Quickstarts for Helidon MP)
Helidon Níma, 4
helidon-quickstart-mp, 155, 158
helidon-quickstart-mp.jar, 159
Helidon SE, 3, 49, 68, 153, 164
   CLI
      application types, 60
      custom options, 60, 61
      development loop, 61
      directory structure, 61, 62

helidon command, 58
helidon build command, 62
helidon command, 59
init option, 59
installation, 57
Linux, 57
media types, 60
PowerShell command, 58
project name, 61
components, 3, 4
functional programming style, 4
interfaces, 5
prerequisites, 49, 50
Project Starter, 63
    application type section, 64
    customize project section, 66
    flavor section, 63
    initiate and execute application, 67, 68
    media support section, 65
    myproject.zip file, 66, 67
Quickstarts, 50
    browser, 56, 57
    build application, 53
    command linc, 55, 56
    curl command, 54, 55
    generate application, 51–53
    initiate application, 54
    server shut down, 57
histogram() method, 187
http-basic-auth, 140, 141
HTTP Basic Authentication, 137
HTTP Digest Authentication, 137
HTTP GET operation, 158
HTTP requests and corresponding methods, 75
HttpRouting interface signature, 73
HTTP Signatures, 137
HttpStatusMetricFilter, 183
Hystrix Fault Tolerance, 12

I

IDCS Role Mapping, 137
IllegalStateException, 180
@Initialized annotation, 188
@Inject annotation, 175
IntelliJ IDEA, 11

J

Jakarta Annotations, 29
Jakarta Batch, 259
Jakarta Concurrency, 260
Jakarta Config, 260
Jakarta Connectors, 260
Jakarta Dependency Injection, 261
Jakarta EE, 35, 36, 46
    compatible implementation, 37
    Eclipse Foundation, 35
    evolution, 36
    Jakarta EE 8, 40
    Jakarta EE 9, 41
    Jakarta EE 9.1, 41
    Jakarta EE 10, 41
    Jakarta EE 11, 42
    profiles, 38
        Core Profile, 39, 40
        Platform, 38
        Web Profile, 38, 39
    Working Group, 37
Jakarta EE Core Profile, 250
Jakarta EE profiles, 255
    Core Profile, 257
    implementation, 255, 258, 259, 262
    MVC, 264

INDEX

Jakarta EE profiles (*cont.*)
    Platform, 255, 261
    profiles, 255
    specifications, 256–259
    transactions, 267
    Web Profile, 256
Jakarta EE profiles
    authorization, 259
    concurrency, 260
    Config, 260
    Connectors, 260
    contexts and dependency, 260
    Debugging Support, 261
    deployment, 261
    enterprise Beans, 262
    expression language, 262
    interceptors, 263
    JSON Binding, 263
    JSON Processing, 263
    Mail, 263
    managed Beans, 264
    management, 264
    messaging, 264
    NoSQL, 265
    Pages, 265
    RESTful Web Services, 265
    RPC, 266
    security, 266
    Servlet, 266
    SOAP, 266
    Standard Tag Library, 267
    validation, 267
    Web Services Metadata, 268
    WebSocket, 268
    XML Binding, 268
    XML Registries, 268
    XML RPC, 269
    XML Web Services, 269

Jakarta EE specifications, 21, 42
    Jakarta annotations, 42
    Jakarta authentication, 42
    Jakarta authorization, 43
    Jakarta concurrency, 43
    Jakarta Contexts and Dependency Injection, 43
    Jakarta data, 43
    Jakarta expression language, 44
    Jakarta faces, 44
    Jakarta interceptors, 44
    Jakarta pages, 44
    Jakarta persistence, 45
    Jakarta RESTful Web Services, 45
    Jakarta Security, 45
    Jakarta Servlet, 45
    Jakarta validation, 46
    Jakarta WebSocket, 46
Jakarta Faces, 262
Jakarta JSON Binding, 263
Jakarta Persistence, 10
Jakarta RESTful Web Services (JAX-RS), 22, 23
Java command, 174, 190
Java community, 35
Java EE, 35, 36
Java for Cloud (J4C), 3
Java Naming and Directory Interface (JNDI), 43
Java Persistence API (JPA), 10
Java Persistence Architecture (JPA), 5
Java Users Groups, 36, 46
JDK 21, 154
jlink tool, 157
JSON Binding (JSON-B), 12, 29
json_pp command, 55, 160
JSON Processing (JSON-P), 22
JSON Web Token (JWT), 25

jvm.uptime, 177
JWT Provider, 137

K

Kotlin, 11
Kubernetes 1.16.5, 154

L

Log4j2, 11
Long-Running Actions (LRA), 31

M

Maven 3.8.0, 154
Maven and Gradle dependencies, 111
Maven build tool, 155
Maven dependency, 90, 126, 127, 141, 142, 218
MediaSupport interface, 278
memory.committedHeap, 177
memory.maxHeap, 177
memory.usedHeap, 177
Message class, 158, 183
MetadataBuilder class, 187
@Metric annotation, 187
MetricRegistry, 179
MetricRegistry API, 179, 183
/metrics/application endpoint, 193
/metrics/base endpoint, 190
/metrics endpoint, 158
Micronaut Data, 11
MicroProfile, 15, 33, 231
    compatible implementation, 18
    Eclipse Foundation, 16
    founding organizations, 17
    goals, 15, 16

    and Java EE Guardians, 15
    JSR-based APIs, 19
    MicroProfile 1.0, 231
    MicroProfile 1.1, 232
    Quarkus, 16
    Red Hat's DevNation conference, 15
    specifications, 19, 231
    Starter, 32
    WildFly Swarm, 16
    Working Group, 17, 18
MicroProfile 1.0
    CDI, 21, 22
    Context Propagation, 31
    GraphQL, 31
    implementations, 232
    JAX-RS, 22, 23
    JSON-P, 22
    LRA, 31
    Reactive Messaging, 30
    Reactive Streams Operators, 30
    specifications, 232
    Telemetry, 31
MicroProfile 1.1
    Config specification, 23
    implementations, 233
    specification, 232
MicroProfile 1.2, 233, 234
    Fault Tolerance, 24
    Health Check, 26
    JWT Propagation, 25, 26
    Metrics, 24
    Rest Client, 27–29
MicroProfile 1.3, 234, 235
    Open API, 26
    Open Tracing, 26
MicroProfile 1.4, 235, 236
MicroProfile 2.0, 236, 237
    JSON-B, 29

INDEX

MicroProfile 2.1, 238
MicroProfile 2.2, 239
MicroProfile 3.0, 240
MicroProfile 3.1, 240, 241
MicroProfile 3.2, 241, 242
MicroProfile 3.3, 242, 243
MicroProfile 4.0, 243–245
MicroProfile 4.1, 245, 246
    Jakarta Annotations, 29
MicroProfile 5.0, 247, 248
MicroProfile 6.0, 248–250
MicroProfile 6.1, 250, 251
MicroProfile 7.0, 19, 252, 253
    compatible implementation, 21
    core specifications, 19, 20
    Metrics specification, 20
    Open Tracing specification, 20
    stand-alone specifications, 20
MicroProfile-compliant application, 175
microprofile-config.properties file, 157, 158
MicroStream, 11
Model-View-Controller (MVC), 44, 264
MongoDbApplication class, 130
MongoDB database, 124
MVC, *see* Model-View-Controller (MVC)
myproject.zip file, 172

N

name() method, 220, 222
/noRoles endpoint, 149

O

@Observes annotation, 189
Open API, 26
OpenID Connect, 137

Open source solutions, 35
Open Tracing, 26
Oracle branding policies, 35
org.redlich.metrics.
    TemperatureHistogramFilter, 197

P

parseBoolean() method, 210
performGetMethod() method, 95
performPutMethod() method, 95
personalizedGetCounter metric, 195, 196
PokemonService class, 129, 130
pom.xml file, 155
@PostConstruct annotation, 187
Project Starter, 153, 168–172
Prometheus format, 189
@Provider annotation, 187
/public endpoint, 149
put() method, 80

Q

quickstart-mp directory, 167
Quickstarts, 165, 174
Quickstarts for Helidon MP
    archetype:generate, 155
    build application, 158, 159
    Client URL and JSON Pretty Printer utilities, 159, 160
    exercise application via browser, 161, 162
    exercise application via command line, 160, 161
    generate application, 155–158
    initiate application, 159
    server shutdown, 162
Quickstarts for Helidon SE, 155

R

reactive() method, 210
Reactive Messaging, 30
Reactive Streams Operators, 30
@Readiness annotation, 221
README.md file, 157
register() method, 132
Representational State Transfer (REST), 9, 22, 45
REST, *see* Representational State Transfer (REST)
Rest Client, 27, 29
REST.request metrics, 175
@Retry annotation, 200, 201, 213
retryHandler() method, 211, 212
Routing, 274
    building, 275
    dependencies, 276
    get() methods, 275
    signature, 275
routing() method, 91

S

saveResponseToFile() method, 96
Security.Builder class, 138
Security component, 141
    build and execute application, 146
    builder pattern, 138
    configuration, 138–140
    create method, 138
    exercise application, 147–150
    login dialog box, 148
    Maven and Gradle dependencies, 141
    security interface, 137
    signature, 138
SecurityContext interface, 137
security node, 140

Security providers, Helidon applications, 137
ServerLifecycle interface, 73
setup() method, 91, 145
/simple-greet endpoint, 155, 160
/simple-greet/Mike endpoint, 196
SimpleGreetResource class, 158, 183, 195
SouJava, 19
src/main/java/io/helidon/examples/quickstart.mp folder, 157
src/main/resources/META-INF folder, 157
startServer() method, 131
SystemLivenessCheck class, 219
SystemStartupCheck class, 221, 222

T

TCK, *see* Technology Compatibility Kit (TCK)
Technology Compatibility Kit (TCK), 18
Telemetry, 31
temperatureHistogram metric, 196
TemperatureHistogramFilter class, 183, 185, 187, 196, 198
thread.count, 177
thread.daemon.count, 177
thread.max.count, 177
threadpool.activeThreads, 177
threadpool.size, 178
@Timed annotation, 179, 181, 182, 188
@Timeout annotation, 202
type() method, 220, 222

U, V

updateGreetingHandler() method, 80
updateHistogram() method, 188
/user endpoint, 149, 150

INDEX

W, X, Y, Z

WebClient component, 85
    in action, 89
    application.yaml file, 88
    Config component, 87
    configuration, 87
    configuration file, 88
    configuration properties, 89
    create() methods, 86
    dependencies, 90
    features, 85
    get() methods, 86
    HTTP client, 85
    JAR file, 96
    java command, 96
    Prototype.Api interface, 86
    RuntimeType class, 86
    server, 97
    ServerApplication class, 90
    signature, 85
    source code, 89
    WebClient.Builder, 87
    YAML file, 89
WebServer.Builder, 87
WebServer component, 69, 271, 279
    Application class, 76
    build and execute the application, 80
    build() method, 72
    builder() method, 72
    Config, 71
    Config component, 273
    configuration file, 274
    configure, 273
    create() methods, 70, 272
    curl command, 81, 82
    default configuration file, 72
    dependencies, 75
    directly configure, 71
    get() method, 74
    GreetService class, 78
    interface, 70
    ListenerConfig interface, 71
    parameter, 82
    port(int port) method, 72, 273
    Routing and HttpRouting
        interfaces, 73
    routing() method, 72, 74
    Routing.Builder, 74
    signature, 69, 272
    start() method, 72
    WebServer.Builder, 272
    WebServerConfig.Builder class, 71
    wsvirtual module, 75
WebServerConfig interface, 71